ANTONINE LITERATURE

EDITED BY

D. A. RUSSELL

CLARENDON PRESS · OXFORD

1990

Oxford University Press, Walton Street, Oxford OX2 6DP
Oxford New York Toronto
Delhi Bombay Calcutta Madras Karachi
Petaling Jaya Singapore Hong Kong Tokyo
Nairobi Dar es Salaam Cape Town
Melbourne Auckland
and associated companies in
Berlin Ibadan

Oxford is a trade mark of Oxford University Press

Published in the United States
by Oxford University Press, New York

British Library Cataloguing in Publication Data
Antonine literature.
1. Classical literature—Critical studies
I. Russell, D.A.F.M.
880.09
ISBN 0-19-814057-6

Library of Congress Cataloging-in-Publication Data
Antonine literature/edited by D. A. Russell.
Includes bibliographical references
1. Greek literature—Rome—History and criticism.
2. Literature, Comparative—Greek and Latin.
3. Literature, Comparative—Latin and Greek.
4. Latin literature—History and criticism.
5. Rome—Civilization—Greek influences.
6. Rome—History—Antonines, 96–192. I. Russell, D. A. (Donald Andrew)
PA3086.A58 1989   880'.09—dc20   89–23104
ISBN 0-19-814057-6

Set by Eta Services (Typesetters) Ltd., Beccles, Suffolk
Printed in Great Britain by
Bookcraft Ltd., Midsomer Norton, Avon

PREFACE

It gave me a special pleasure, in the year in which I was due to retire, to arrange the seminar which gave rise to these papers, and which was held in Oxford in Hilary Term 1988. We all share an interest in the literature of the second century, and think it a not unworthy memorial of the time when 'the Empire of Rome comprehended the fairest part of the earth, and the most civilized portion of mankind'. We have followed Gibbon also in allowing into our purview the whole of the 'happy period of more than fourscore years' which he would call the Age of the Antonines. We have thus said something of Plutarch and Dio, who are important witnesses to the outlook of the whole century, and in particular to its view of the relationship between present and past. We have written on what we individually chose, and from various (and not always compatible) points of view. So this is far from a history of Antonine literature; but we hope that our contributions will be of some service to future historians of the period, which badly needs a comprehensive view, embracing both Greek and Latin. I should like to express my thanks to Richard Hawley for undertaking the work of the Index, and to all those concerned at the University Press for their help at every stage.

D.A.R.

CONTENTS

ABBREVIATIONS

We use standard abbreviations for many texts, periodicals, and works of reference. Note also the following:

ANRW   *Aufstieg und Niedergang der römischen Welt*, ed. H. Temporini and W. Haase (Berlin and New York, 1972–   ).

CHCL   *Cambridge History of Classical Literature*. i. *Greek Literature*, ed. P. E. Easterling and B. M. W. Knox (Cambridge, 1985); ii. *Latin Literature*, ed. E. J. Kenney and W. V. Clausen (Cambridge, 1982).

GDRK   Heitsch (1961) and Heitsch (1964).

GVI   W. Peek, *Griechische Vers-Inschriften* (Berlin, 1955).

Halm   *Rhetores Latini Minores*, ed. C. Halm (Leipzig, 1863, repr. Frankfurt, 1964).

HE   Gow and Page (1965).

MAMA   *Monumenta Asiae Minoris Antiqua*, ed. W. M. Calder *et al.* (Manchester, 1928–   ).

Spengel   *Rhetores Graeci*, ed. L. Spengel (3 vols.; Leipzig, 1852–6).

Walz   *Rhetores Graeci*, ed. C. Walz (9. vol.; Stuttgart, 1832–6, 1 repr. Osnabrück, 1968).

ANTONINE LITERATURE: SOME DATES

	Literary events	*Other events*
117	? Death of Dio. ? Birth of Aristides.	Accession of Hadrian.
118–21	Suetonius *ab epistulis*.	
119	Suicide of Euphrates. ? Herodes presented to Hadrian.	
*c.*125	Death of Plutarch. Birth of Lucian. Birth of A. Gellius.	
129	? Birth of Galen.	
130	Poems of Julia Balbilla.	Death of Antinoos.
130–8	? Composition of Dionysius' *Periegesis*.	
131–2	Arrian in Pontus: *Periplus*.	
138		Accession of Pius.
140	? Death of Polemon. Earliest possible date for Florus' *Epitome*.	
142	? Aristides' *Sarapis* (44 K). ? Lollianus holds first chair of rhetoric in Athens.	
143	Herodes Atticus consul; Fronto *cos. suff.*	
144	Aristides goes to Rome; his illnesses being.	
147	Aristides: *Apellas* (30 K), *Sons of Asclepius* (38 K), *Capito* (47 D). Ptolemy's *Almagest* now finished.	
148	Birth of Hermogenes.	
150	Justin, *First Apology*.	
153	Aristides, *Athena* (37 K).	

155	? Aristides, *Aegean Sea* (44 K), *Panathenaicus* (1 K), *Rome* (26 K).	
156		Martyrdom of Polycarp.
158	Trial of Apuleius: *Apologia*.	
160	Justin, *Second Apology*.	
161	Apuleius, *Florida* 9. Gaius, *Institutes*. Galen in Rome.	Accession of Marcus.
165	Death of Peregrinus. Lucian: ? *Hermotimus*, ? *Cataplus*, ?*Bis Accusatus*. ? Death of Appian. ? Martydom of Justin.	Parthian wars.
166	Lucian, *Quomodo historia conscribenda sit*.	
166–7	Aristides in Cyzicus (27 K, 40 K). ? Death of Fronto.	
170	Aristides begins *Hieroi logoi* (47–52 K).	
c. 170	? Birth of Aelian and Philostratus.	
173–5	Pausanias' *Periegesis* in progress (5. 1. 2); composition lies between *c.*160 and *c.*180.	
177	Aristides, *Monody for Smyrna* (18 K). Death of Herodes Atticus.	
*c.*175–80	Phrynichus' *Lexeis*.	
180		Death of Marcus.
? *c.*185	Death of Aristides.	

I

Introduction: Greek and Latin in Antonine Literature

D. A. RUSSELL

1

There is obviously no reason why deaths of emperors should also mark epochs in literary history. Hadrian was indeed an active patron of letters, his successor less so; but whatever changes there were were gradual, and the concept of a specifically 'Antonine' period of literature is bound to be artificial. But it is not therefore useless; for it is possible to discern a distinct stage, in the middle part of the century, in the development of what I like to regard as the bilingual literature of the Empire.

There had for a long time—since the age of Cicero—been three different audiences, three reading publics: one conversant in Greek, one in Latin, and one in both. These last, *docti sermones utriusque linguae*, were the most influential, since all educated and powerful Romans knew Greek, while few Greek magnates or possible patrons knew Latin. In the great age of Trajan and Hadrian, Latin and Greek were in some sort of balance. Dio and Plutarch, Tacitus and Pliny, all born around the middle of the first century, came into bloom in the *felicitas temporum* that began, as they thought, with Nerva; not long after them come Favorinus and Polemo, Suetonius and Juvenal. There is a contrast to be drawn with the situation towards the end of the century, which again seems to have a special flavour. Philostratus and Aelian, born around 170, look back to a sophistic age which they were already inclined to treat as classical. The rhetor Hermogenes (a young man under Marcus) is ready to include second-century rhetors among the models for imitation. Greek literature, both prose and verse, is now flourishing; Latin is not, for there are no Latin names of note, with the significant exception of the first great Christian writers, Tertullian and Cyprian.

So what lies in between? A period defined, if definable, by the careers of four major writers: Aristides, Lucian, Apuleius, and Fronto. This is of course to take literature in a rather narrow sense, and to say nothing of the main contributors to our civilization which this age produced: Galen, Ptolemy, the great jurists. But these four do seem to go together. Aristides, born in 117, the year of Dio's death, was active and productive in the 140s,[1] and survived Marcus only by a few years. Lucian, born about 125, was at his height in the 160s; *Hermotimus* and *Peregrinus* both date from about 165.[2] Apuleius, Lucian's near contemporary, faced his judge on the charge of magic in 158. Fronto was rather older, consul in 143, and so born around the beginning of the century, but his correspondence with Marcus does not begin till after the death of Hadrian, and he is an important witness to the tastes of Antonine literati. We shall have much to say in this book of all these four.

2

Many explanations have been given of the phenomenon that we have just noticed: the apparent shift, in the course of the second century, from a literary culture in which both Greek and Latin masterpieces stand out, to one in which the dominance is very definitely with the Greeks. It is reasonable to attach weight to the growing wealth and confidence of the Greek educated classes, and to the philhellenic attitudes of the courts of Hadrian and the Antonines and their successors. If the shift is real, it must be largely in these social and political facts that the cause is to be sought; but it is prudent to leave open the possibility that it is dearth of evidence, not real development, that confronts us. We can never be quite certain, after all, of the answer to the question that Henry Bardon so trenchantly put in the words 'absence ou néant?'[3] But if we take things to be as they seem, there are areas of enquiry which look profitable. I propose to discuss two of these. They may appear at first sight

---

[1] See below, p. 200, on the date of *Sarapis*, perhaps among his earliest works.
[2] The date for *Herm.* rests on assuming Lucian to have been born in 125; *Peregr.* must be very soon after the event it commemorates (165).
[3] Bardon (1956), 299 ff., with reference to a much later period.

marginal, but in fact they relate to the heart of the matter, because they are concerned with the education of the writer. One is the history and status of translation from Greek into Latin. The other is the use of the two languages as languages of instruction in the rhetorical schools. For the second point, the main witness is Fronto. For the first, we need to go back quite a long way.

3

It is a familiar idea that, right from the start, the genres, metres, and techniques of Latin literature were almost all modelled on the Greek. But it is also clear, though less often stated, that the mode by which this transference was made was adaptation rather than translation. The contrast with Renaissance Europe is striking. No Roman did for Herodotus what Amyot did for Plutarch; no one made Homer a Latin classic as Chapman and Pope made him an English one. There was no succession of poet-translators, responsive to the tastes of their age, as we have in Dryden, Pope, Cowper, Calverley, Day Lewis, and the rest. It is true that English tastes have changed radically and in ways that make new translations always needed; but then so did Roman tastes, since what pleased Cicero's contemporaries was very different from what pleased Pliny's. The role of actual translation seems surprisingly subsidiary. It is true that Livius Andronicus' *Odyssey* was among the earliest Latin classics, and this and Cn. Matius' *Iliad* were well-known school texts in later times. But even the scanty fragments we possess make it clear that these were very free renderings. They may indeed have been severely abridged versions of the voluminous epics. It is worth recalling that the verb *vortere*, commonly used of trans-lation, applies also to the kind of adaptation of New Comedy that Plautus and Terence practised.[4] There never was a Latin Aeschylus or Sophocles or Euripides; only adaptations, from Ennius right down to Seneca, on the one hand, and individual speeches and extracts, such as those made by Cicero for his philosophical works, on the other. Part of Cicero's process of

---

[4] Plautus, *Trinummus*, 19; Terence, *Eunuchus*, 5.

adapting Greek popular philosophy was the use of the poets as
authorities for moral attitudes; he uses Latin where he can, but
is sometimes driven to translate Greek.[5] Catullus' licence with
Sappho and Callimachus can still be assessed. So can Cicero's
with Aratus, and this is the more significant case: Aratus' versi-
fied astronomical treatise, more important for its information
than for its literary qualities, considerable as these are, was the
most often translated of any Greek poem. Varro of Atax, Germanicus, Avienus, and (so it is said) one of the Gordians followed in Cicero's footsteps. The reason is Aratus' educational
importance. Statius' father[6] included him in his school curriculum. Commentaries, often very philosophical, abound.[7] He
could be used to give a semblance of science in the grammarian's curriculum, a potent source of interesting *historia*. As to
translations of Attic prose classics, it is again Cicero who led the
way. His *Timaeus*, for example, was not emulated till the late
third or early fourth century, when Chalcidius' version and
commentary appeared.[8] There is nothing else recorded till the
Antonine period, when Apuleius' lost *Phaedo* and the extant
De mundo claim attention. But the authenticity and date of *De
mundo* are very much in doubt, and it is odd that it fails to
acknowledge that it is a close translation: the preface (137.
1 Thomas) merely asserts that it is based on 'Aristotle, most
prudent and most learned of philosophers, and Theophrastus'.
This is not an expression of doubt about the authorship of the
original (which is indeed not Aristotle's) but the translator's
misleading description of his own endeavours. Translation is
less honourable than adaptation; it is the thought of the authorities, not their words, that matters.

It is hard not to conclude that, for the two centuries after
Cicero, translation, in the sense in which it is characteristic of
modern European literatures, was little valued. There is an
obvious reason for this: educated men could experience the
originals. A wide knowledge of Greek poetry was possible in the
Latin world. Statius' father, according to his son's doubtless en-
comiastic account, taught, as *grammaticus*, not only Homer and

---

[5] *Tusc.* 2. 11. 26: 'sicubi illi defecerunt, verti etiam multa de graecis'.
[6] *Silvae*, 5. 3. 23.
[7] Hadot (1984), 304.
[8] Waszink (1962), pp. ix–xvii.

Hesiod but Epicharmus (*Siculus senex*), Pindar, Ibycus, Alcman, Sappho, Corinna, Sophron, Callimachus, Lycophron. Moreover, he was

> well used to bearing equal yoke with Homer,
> and matching the hexameter in prose
> with shorter steps, but never left behind.[9]

This is paraphrase, not translation—and not necessarily in Latin. To transfer the qualities of the Greek classics into Latin was to create something new, valid in its own right and not simply as a reproduction. It was also, naturally, to perform the patriotic service of putting Rome on a level with Greece even in the arts of the word. This idea — familiar in Ciceronian and Augustan practice — is well seen, in the early second century, in a quite trivial example from Pliny's letters (4. 3, 4. 18, 4. 27, 5. 15). Pliny admires the Greek epigrams of Arrius Antoninus, an elderly consular, grandfather of the future emperor Pius, at whose court Greek was to be greatly in favour. Arrius writes epigrams and mimiambi, rivalling Callimachus and Herodas. It is easy to guess what he could do in Latin, if he does so well 'hoc insiticio et inducto sermone'. It is a marvel to Pliny that a Roman can write Greek so well: 'hominemne Romanum tam graece loqui? non medius fidius ipsas Athenas tam Atticas dixerim' (4. 3. 5). The best proof of admiration (4. 18. 1) is 'quod quaedam Latine aemulari et exprimere temptaui', though this is naturally 'in deterius'. not only because of Pliny's incapacity but because of the traditional 'inopia ac potius, ut Lucretius ait, egestate patrii sermonis'. Translation here is not interpretation or reproduction, but a kind of emulation springing from high regard, like any other form of *imitatio*. It is no part of its function to make Arrius available to readers who could not understand his Greek.

Aulus Gellius, a generation later, is an important witness on all these things.[10] He is much interested in translation, as in

---

[9] *Silvae*, 5. 3. 146–62, with the notes by Frère in Frère and Isaac (1943–4), 199. The lines translated are 159–61:

> tu par assuetus Homero
> ferre iugum senosque pedes aequare solutis
> versibus et numquam passu breviore relinqui.

[10] Holford-Strevens (1988) is now the best source of information on all Gellian problems. Much that is relevant to the issues discussed here may be found, esp. in ch. 6 on Favorinus and in chs. 11–12.

many questions of verbal scholarship, both Latin and Greek. So far as I can see, he too fails to make any distinction between a reproductive rendering and a competitive imitation. Thus he frequently reports criticisms of Virgilian imitations of Homer and other Greek poets. This is of course one of the staple themes of ancient — as of modern — discussion of Virgil.[11] Gellius has various ways of expressing the relationship of Greek model to Latin copy, all of which would be just as appropriate to an acknowledged translation as to the imitative adaptation that Virgil's work actually is. So Virgil 'follows' his model (consectaretur, sequebatur: 12. 1. 20), 'emulates' him (aemulatus est, 13. 27, cf. 17. 10. 8), 'turns him' (vertisse, 9. 12), and there is no discernible difference between these terms. There seems to be nothing in Gellius to correspond with the contrast made by Pliny (7. 30. 5) when he says that he kept Demosthenes' Midias speech in his hands when he was writing a speech of his own, 'non ut aemularer . . . sed tamen imitarer et sequerer'. A particularly instructive example is Gellius' remark (19. 11) about the young friend who 'licentius liberiusque vertit' the famous couplet, supposed to be by Plato, about kissing Agathon. The simple original runs:

> τὴν ψυχὴν Ἀγάθωνα φιλῶν ἐπὶ χείλεσιν ἔσχον·
> ἦλθε γὰρ ἡ τλήμων ὡς διαβησομένη.

'As I was kissing Agathon, I had to hold back my soul on my lips, for the poor thing had come there in hopes of crossing over.'

The version runs to seventeen iambic dimeters, elegant and sensuous, but quite alien to the spirit of the epigram. It begins:

> Dum semihiulco savio
> meum puellum savior
> dulcemque florem spiritus
> duco ex aperto tramite . . .

> While with half-gaping kiss
> I kiss my darling boy
> and draw out from the opened path
> the sweet bloom of his breath . . .

and so on. It looks as though, at least so far as verse is con-

---

[11] 17. 10 (description of Etna in Pindar and *Aen.* 3. 571–2) and 12. 1 (*Aen.* 4. 637 and its Homeric analogue) are both from Favorinus.

cerned, the only type of 'translation' Gellius envisages is one which consciously tries to improve upon or rival the model. To appreciate it, the reader needs to know both languages. It is not very different with the prose translations. Here too Gellius gives the impression that he is aiming not so much to give information to the Greekless as to display a skill to readers who can appreciate both languages. When he translates a letter of Philip of Macedon (9. 3), he gives the Greek as well. When he puts a piece of Epictetus into Latin (19. 1. 15–20), he leaves the Stoic technical terms in Greek but explains them: συγκατάθεσις is first glossed as 'probatio', and later on used as though the reader has learned its meaning. His frequent quotations from Favorinus of Arles are sometimes in the original Greek, sometimes in Latin. When he puts the long extract 'Against Astrologers' (14. 1) into Latin,[12] he calls his own rendering 'sicca et incondita et propemodum ieiuna', altogether unworthy of the 'copia' and 'venustas' of Favorinus' Greek. Now Gellius is an enthusiast for Latin literature and antiquities, and for the study of the early Roman writers as classics in their own right. He did not think much of Favorinus' knowledge of things Roman (20. 1. 20, 2. 26. 8, 2. 18. 7)—and indeed the sophist from Arles was so completely Hellenized that he spoke in Greek at Rome and charmed audiences ignorant of the language by the elegance and emotional power of his delivery.[13] At the same time, it seems, Gellius is prepared to accept the conventional view of the *egestas* of Latin and its inferiority to Greek—not only to classical Greek but to the contemporary Atticizing style of a Favorinus. One is left with the impression that translation was seen as an educational exercise or a display of culture directed at the bilingual connoisseur, rather than as a literary achievement designed to widen the Latin speaker's cultural horizons.

The evidence of Quintilian confirms this. It is well known that he advises (1. 1. 12, 1. 4. 1) that children should learn to speak and write Greek a little before they learn Latin, so that their grasp of both languages is secure from the start. It is not till much later in the *Institutio*, when he is dealing with

[12] Fr. 3 Barigazzi (1966).
[13] Philostr., *VS* 491–2.

advanced students and talking about the ways of acquiring *hexis*, or right habits of writing, that he comes to discuss the value of translation (10. 5. 2–3). The context is a discussion of the mechanics of the business—the importance of revision and correction, writing materials (wax tablets are better because you are not always having to stop to fill your pen), leaving space for annotation, and so on. What then should the student write? The ancients (*veteres*) believed that putting Greek into Latin was the best exercise: witness Crassus, Cicero's versions of Plato and Xenophon,[14] or Messala the Atticist's successful reproduction of the *subtilitas* of Hyperides' delicate *Defence of Phryne*. Greek authors are rich in content, and brought much art into eloquence. The Latins are bound to stretch their resources in vocabulary in translating them, as well as having to develop different *figurae*, because those which are effective in Greek are not always right for Latin. The two languages have different idioms. This is surely a lukewarm recommendation, and indeed Quintilian goes on to say that rewriting Latin models or paraphrasing Latin poems is just as good a way of acquiring the desired facility.

Quintilian's pupil Pliny seems however a little more positive. At any rate, he recommends Fuscus (7. 9) to spend leisure in translating not only Greek into Latin but Latin into Greek; but once again there seems to be no special value in this compared with the alternative form of *aemulatio* which consists in putting in your own words the tenor of something you have read and then comparing your effort with the original.

Finally, there are two pieces of evidence that translation from Greek did in fact sometimes form part of the Roman rhetors' courses of progymnasmata. This is stated by Suetonius[15] in a generalized account of the practice of early teachers, before they came (as in his own day) to abandon the progymnasmata to the *grammatici* and concentrate on the more interesting and ambitious *controversia*. It is implied also by Fronto (*De eloquentia*, 4. 2 = 2. 82 Haines), perhaps repeating the views of his Greek teacher Dionysius 'Tenuior'. He finds fault with the philosophers for not demanding from their pupils regular work, such

---

[14] This perhaps refers to the *Oecon.* 'translation', but Cicero's rendering of this was in three books. Cf. also the long extract of *Cyropaedia* at the end of *De sen.*

[15] *De gram.* 25. 8; Fairweather (1981), 115–22.

as (presumably) the rhetor expected: reading aloud, memorizing, looking out words, gathering synonyms, and translating from Greek into Latin. Here the exercise of translation appears in a quite elementary curriculum, or so it would seem.

All this confirms one's impression that translation was not regarded, in general, as a means of introducing the Latin reader to Greek literature. The assumption is that he does not need the help. Educated people were expected to be at home in Greek. Such seems to be the assumption also in a late second-century Christian text: a speaker in Minucius Felix's *Octavius* (33. 4) advises reading Josephus if you want to learn about the Jews—'vel si Romanis magis gaudes', Antonius Julianus. It is represented as a matter of choice, though of course this could be mere politeness. Not to read Greek gives ground for reproach: Apuleius (*Apol.* 30) can make fun of Tannonius Pudens for not being able to read Pudentilla's Greek letter.

Yet things may have been changing. Apuleius' *Phaedo* is perhaps a sign of a new attitude; it was certainly used later to instruct Latin readers in Plato, and Sidonius (*Ep.* 2. 9. 5) commends it as an accurate rendering 'ad verbum sententiamque'. There is also another area where we have evidence of translation for practical purposes: the mythical history of the Trojan War. The Latin Dictys seems to have been a faithful rendering of a Greek original, a fragment of which survives in an early third-century papyrus.[16] This is a clear instance of a Greek book needed in Latin and rendered with care. The Latin Dares probably has a similar history. But it was of course Christianity that did most to raise the status of translation as a means of extending knowledge, because the translation of the Bible was a necessary stage in the conversion of the world. Much of the Old Testament was available in Latin by the middle of the second century, and there is clear evidence of Latin New Testament texts by 180. A little later, Origen and other theologians were translated, and in all this, naturally, accuracy mattered.[17] It was no longer a question of *aemulatio* but of faithful interpretation.

---

[16] *P.Teb.* vol. ii, p. 9 (Grenfell–Hunt); Dictys, ed. W. Eisenhut (1955), 134.

[17] Quasten (1968), i. 512 (Biblical translation), i. 360 (Origen).

4

We have already had to involve ourselves in the proceedings of
the rhetorical schools. Let us now look a little closer, and ask
what can be said about the language of instruction in which the
educated Roman learned his rhetoric.

There are many reasons for stressing the independence of the
Greek and Latin traditions. As we saw, the Latin rhetors had
abandoned the progymnasmata to the *grammatici* by the time of
Suetonius. Yet, in the Greek tradition, rhetorical treatises on
these exercises continue right down to late antiquity: Theon is
succeeded by 'Hermogenes', Nicolaus, Sopatros, and so on.
Further back, the elder Seneca provides clear evidence of the
separation. In his anthology of declamation tricks, the Greeks
are always treated by themselves, at the end of the chapter.
Moreover, the judgement passed on them is in general negative. They indulge in obscenity (*Controv.* 1. 2. 22), in points
which are frivolous or improper (1. 7. 12), and though their art
is undeniable (cf. Quint. 10. 5. 3) their *sententiae* lack vigour and
manliness (2. 6. 12). It is clearly unusual and perhaps absurd
(9. 3. 13–14) to practise in both languages. Argentarius and
Cestius, who were native Greek speakers, did not revert to their
native tongue once they had taken up Latin. Sex. Clodius, who
used both, is criticized for it (cf. Suet. *De rhet.* 29). Even to
imitate Greek *sententiae* in Latin is a procedure of doubtful
value; when Arellius Fuscus does it (9. 1. 13), he excuses himself
by saying that his motive is 'exercitatio' not 'commendatio' or
'furtum'—an exercise, not a recommendation of the Greek
speaker or a plagiarism. It looks as if Seneca's declaimers were
concerned to assert the independence of the Latin rhetorical
tradition.

How successful were they? We should note that the evidence
at our disposal provides no examples of didactic technical treatises between the time of Cicero's *De inventione* or the *Rhetorica
and Herennium* and the fourth and fifth centuries AD, whence
many such books survive. Once again, 'absence ou néant?'
'Néant' is almost inconceivable; but consider what we have.
Important as it is, it is not of the same nature as *De inventione*
and *Rhetorica ad Herennium*. Cicero's later works are directed to
the adult amateur in public life, and are largely a defence of his

own life's work. Quintilian's *Institutio* is a manual for teachers
and interested parents, not directly aimed at the pupils. What
we do possess from the early imperial schools is the activity of
the declaimers: Seneca, Calpurnius Flaccus, and the two Quin-
tilianic sets, both of which may well belong to the second century. Of these, Seneca and the *Declamationes maiores* are not
simple teaching material; the other two collections probably
are. All this, however, is relatively advanced work. There is
nothing in Latin to correspond to the Greek progymnasmata —
handed over, if we believe Suetonius, to the *grammatici*—or to
the technical treatises on στάσις (though the *Institutio* of course
handles this) or style (again, discussed in Quintilian, but not in
the manner of Hermogenes or pseudo-Aristides).

Not that there is no sign of the absent school-books. An important passage of Quintilian (3. 1. 19–21) gives some clues:

After Cicero, the most modest course would be to say nothing, had
not he said himself that his rhetorical books had escaped from him as
a young man, and his oratorical books deliberately left out the basic
details. Cornificius wrote extensively on the same subject, Stertinius
did something, and the elder Gallio made a contribution. Earlier than
Gallio, and more accurate, were Celsus and Laenas, while in our own
time there are Verginius, Pliny, and Tutilius. There are distinguished
writers in the same field today also ... the time will come for their
praise.[18]

The contrast made here between the *rhetorici* and *oratorii libri* of
Cicero is clearly important; Quintilian does not regard the *De
oratore*, *Orator*, and *Brutus* as books for students. By Cornificius,
it is generally agreed, he means the author of the *Rhetorica ad
Herennium*. Of Stertinius we know nothing. The elder Gallio is
presumably the elder Seneca's friend, who adopted the latter's
eldest son. Celsus, the encyclopaedist, wrote in Tiberius' time.
Popilius Laenas is quoted elsewhere (10. 7. 32, 11. 3. 183) for

---

[18] ... M. Tullius, post quem tacere modestissimum foret, nisi et rhetoricos suos ipse
adulescenti sibi elapsos diceret, et in oratoriis haec minora, quae plerumque desideran-
tur, sciens omisisset. Scripsit de eadem materia non pauca Cornificius, aliqua Stertinius, non nihil pater Gallio, accuratius uero priores Gallione Celsus et Laenas et aetatis
nostrae Verginius Plinius Tutilius. Sunt et hodie clari eiusdem operis auctores, qui si
omnia complexi forent, consuluissent labori meo: sed parco nominibus uiuentium;
ueniet eorum laudi suum tempus (with the last sentence, cf. 10. 1. 96, 10. 1. 122: Quintilian is always anxious to keep in with his contemporaries).

minor points about written *commentarii* and types of delivery. It sounds as if his *ars* was decidedly practical. The polymath Pliny called his book *Studiosi*, 'Students'; it seems to have been directed, like Quintilian's *Institutio*, at teachers and parents rather than at the pupils themselves. Gellius (9. 16) criticizes it for faulty judgement of declamatory *sententiae*. Tutilius is otherwise unknown, since the identification of him with Quintilian's father-in-law is unlikely (Plin. *Ep*. 6. 32, with the note by Sherwin-White). The most significant name is that of L. Verginius Flavus, presumably the same as the teacher of Persius (*Vita Persi*, p. 169 Rostagni = p. 31 Clausen). He alone of those mentioned here is quoted regularly in other parts of the *Institutio*, and on strictly technical issues: Quintilian questions his interpretation of Theodorus (4. 1. 23) and cites his views on a point of status theory (7. 4. 24, cf. 3. 6. 45). Like Quintilian himself, he was obviously interested in the practicalities of delivery and personal impression; he disapproved of walking about while speaking, and 'interrogavit de quodam suo antisophiste quot milia passuum declamasset'—'he asked of a rival sophist how many miles he had declaimed' (11. 3. 126); so he was a *sophistes* himself.

Some few names could be added to these; especially that of C. Valgius Rufus (3. 1. 18), the most accurate Latin representative of Apollodorus' teaching, as Atticus was the most accurate in Greek. Quintilian quotes him also (5. 10. 4) for the choice of *adgressio* as a rendering of ἐπιχείρημα.

Much must be hidden from us; but one does not get the impression of a very rich tradition of rhetorical *theory* in Latin, but rather one of a strong practical concern with declamation and delivery. So, if well-educated youths often attended both Greek and Latin *rhetores*—like the young man in Gellius (9. 15) who was 'practising with masters in both languages and exercising his Latin for pleading causes at Rome'—they would have got their theory mainly from the Greek, their practical advice from the Latin. Thus the younger Pliny was a pupil of Quintilian, but he also heard the great Greek rhetor, Nicetes of Smyrna. He must indeed have learned Greek thoroughly as a child, if he wrote a tragedy in that language at the age of fourteen (*Ep*. 7. 4); indeed, his Latin hendecasyllables, so he asserts, were so famous that Greeks learned Latin in order to understand them (ibid.). The most interesting evidence he affords of his Greek rhetorical training is in *Ep.* 9. 26. Here he is defending the audacity of some of his metaphors and phrases in the *Panegyricus*. Examples and arguments strongly recall *De sublinitate*: the term παράβολα for 'bold' or 'risky', the example of 'the heavens trumpeting' (Longin. 9. 6), and a particular passage of Demosthenes (*De corona*, 296; Longin. 32. 2) are common to Pliny and the unknown Greek critic. Perhaps Nicetes was Pliny's source. In any case we see him deep in the kind of learning that the better Greek rhetors provided. Like 'Longinus', too, he uses the trick of illustrating his point by the form of what he says (9. 26. 4 and 13). At the same time, Pliny is also involved with Latin rhetors. We note his recommendation of Julius Genitor (3. 3. 5, cf. 7. 20) as a teacher of unquestioned character, who will give instruction in *mores* first, and also in *eloquentia*; and (4. 13) the correspondence with Tacitus about finding a teacher for the school at Comum. All this seems to corroborate our general picture: Greek teaching is sought for theory and prestige, Latin for practical use and impact on a wider circle of the young. They did not presumably need a Greek rhetor down at Comum.

From Pliny to Fronto is a considerable leap. Fronto was over forty years younger, probably not born in the year of Pliny's consulship and the great *Panegyricus*. Moreover he has quite different literary tastes. He has no inclination for 'Longinian' sublimity. He was much more interested in earlier Latin. Pliny does indeed mention Ennius and Accius once (5. 3. 6), but that is for their *sanctitas morum*, not the quality of their poems; and, though Plautus and Terence are classics for him (6. 21. 4) and the purity of their language is a standard (1. 16. 6), all this is very far from Fronto's attitude. For Fronto is, to some extent at least, trying to do for Latin letters what the Atticists had long been doing, and with such success, for Greek—that is, to go behind recent corruptions to a purer and simpler past. His correspondence with his pupil Marcus, our main evidence for his tastes, extends over a period of some thirty years. It is difficult to catch the flavour of this friendship. One can hardly believe that the consular teacher and the heir to the principate were typical of ordinary people, or that their letters were not meant to be published. And to judge from Marcus' own autobiographical

account (*Meditations* 1. 11, cf. *Ad Verum* 2. 7 = 2. 155 Haines), it
was Fronto's character and understanding of human kindness,
not his rhetoric, that made the deepest impression upon him.
All the same, there is a lot of rhetorical technicality in the correspondence, and it throws some light on the relation between
the two languages in this field. Fronto (*Ad M. Caes.* 1. 8 = 1.
123 Haines) presents himself as something of a late learner. He
assures Marcus that, at his age (which was 22) he had no experience of the *veteres lectiones* which he now advocates. That is
to say, in the early years of Hadrian he had not yet formed his
archaistic taste, or the liking for Cato and Sallust, whom he
now recommends his pupil to imitate. It is high praise (*Ad M.
Caes.* 3. 11 = 1. 12 Haines) that Marcus has written *gnomai* (a
progymnasma, let us note) so perfectly 'ut poni in libro Sallustii
possit, nec discrepet aut quicquam decedat'. The sententious
Sallust is perhaps a natural model for this particular exercise.
This is the tone of a new movement, of which Fronto is a leader;
what had been a minority fashion in the previous century, and
had seemed ridiculous to the younger Seneca (*Ep.* 114. 13–19)
has now taken the centre of the stage. Traditionally, the
ὀψιμαθής does not know his new learning very well; but Fronto
is clearly proud of his achievement. About his Greek, he sounds
more modest (and perhaps is genuinely so) though he had
studied in Alexandria and had Greek literary men like Appian
as friends. Thus (*Ad M. Caes.* 1. 8 [2. 1] = 1. 125 Haines) he has
written to Marcus' mother, Domitia Lucilla, who had a circle
of Greek literati about her, in Greek; but he is afraid it may be a
bit barbaric. So he asks Marcus to look the letter over before
handing it on, on the grounds that he is 'a Graecis litteris recen-
tior'. Even if this is mere politeness, or is meant to make Marcus
think his tutor will not write to his mother behind his back, the
excuse is interesting. It implies that Greek, prominent in early
education and essential for technical rhetoric and of course for
philosophy, is here taken to be something which the grown
man might let grow rusty.

The actual rhetorical instruction which the letters convey
contains at least two very unusual features. One (*Ad amicos* 1.
11 = 2. 86 Haines) is the assertion that tropes are subsumed
under figures. This undermines the whole discussion of σχήματα
and τρόποι as we know it from the Greek theorists, but it is not a

unique view. Quintilian (9. 1. 2) reports that it was held by a
Roman rhetor called C. Artorius Proculus. Another (*Ad M.
Caes.* 3. 16 = 1. 105 Haines) is the connection made between
epideictic and the grand style. According to Fronto, the
'middle' style is only occasionally useful in this branch of oratory. Yet the traditional Greek view is that Isocrates, the
master of the middle style, is the epideictic model *par excellence.*
We should perhaps recall Pliny's *Panegyricus*, and the defence he
makes of its audacity. On the whole, however, Fronto follows
reasonably conventional lines, though with some special
emphases. He makes Marcus do some elementary exercises (*Ad
M. Caes.* 3. 11 = 1. 12 Haines), as we saw, and sets him also
regular declamations. For these (*Ad M. Caes.* 5. 22 [37] = 1.
210 Haines; *Ad M. Caes.* 5. 27 [42] = 1. 214 Haines) he recommends two themes out of Roman history. One is that of the
consul who fights wild beasts in the arena, kills a lion and is
subject to a censorial *nota.* Marcus says this is ἀπίθανος. That is
to say, he puts it under the same head of 'implausible subjects'
that Hermogenes illustrates by the theme of 'Socrates the
brothel-keeper' (33. 7 Rabe). The other is the case of a *tribunus
plebis* who improperly put a citizen in prison. Marcus is to plead
this cause on both sides, but he finds he has no time to do so,
because of his philosophy lessons. But the subject which turns
up most often in the correspondence is that of εἰκόνες—
'images', whether in simile-form or not.[19] Fronto tells us (*Ad M.
Caes.* 4. 12 = 1. 204 Haines) that on this subject he follows the
guidance of his own teacher Athenodotus, whom he classes
with Dio and Euphrates among the pupils of Musonius, and so
at least half a philsopher.[20] No doubt Athenodotus' background
gives his name authority with Marcus, given the young man's
strong inclination to the philosophical camp. No doubt also the
use of εἰκόνες is a topic which a would-be philosopher would
find congenial: Marcus' own *Meditations* abound in them, and
Plutarch is a constant, even obsessive, 'image-maker', in
Fronto's sense. It is, however, Fronto's aim to present this topic
as part of technical rhetoric, and so of practical use. He does so
by making a link with the doctrine of ἐπιχειρήματα, 'arguments'. We hear (1. 38 Haines) that he has read with his pupil a

[19] McCall (1969), 243–51.
[20] Hense (1905), p. xxvi: cf. Marcus, *Medit.* 1. 13.

treatise of Theodorus of Gadara on this subject. He extracts from it a list of headings which he says can also be used in classifying and developing εἰκόνες. Though this list does not correspond very closely with any extant discussion, there is nothing particularly strange about it; Hermogenes (140–50 Rabe), Minucianus (9. 601 Walz), and Julius Victor (399–400 Halm) give material which is broadly of the same kind. What is interesting is that Fronto tries to stiffen the marginal subject of εἰκόνες by introducing this rigid structure of acceptable 'headings', appropriate in a general discussion of invention. Luckily, we can see him working an example (*Ad M. Caes.* 3. 7–8 = 1. 32–9 Haines). Marcus, it appears, has been given a list of εἰκόνες to work up. This suggests that, like the *gnome*, this is a progymnasma, though the usual curriculum does not include any such item. An εἰκών involves elements of *ekphrasis*, but also some argumentation. The exercise seems to be to find an application for the image, and this means drawing out all the implications of the object suggested for description. Marcus is puzzled about one of the ten topics on which he has been working. It is that of the lake on the island of Aenaria, which has an island itself in it. Fronto explains how this could be used in Marcus' address of thanks to his father, probably for the title of 'Caesar' bestowed on him in 139 (so Haines, but not Champlin,[21] who dates the letter later). Antoninus is like the main island, Aenaria, because he protects his young successor, who corresponds to the sheltered island in the inland lake. The point of analogy is an accident (συμβεβηκός) of the subject, the similarity between the safety and pleasure of the inner island and that of the cherished young prince.

McCall,[22] following Haines, believed that Fronto was educated first in Greek rhetoric, came later to Latin studies, and represents a stage in the history of rhetoric in which the Greek and Roman traditions are united. Yet Fronto came from Cirta, from a thoroughly Romanized Numidian family.[23] It is unlikely that he should have been brought up otherwise than in Latin, with Greek as a prestige addition. The rhetorical teaching of the Letters in fact consists of two distinct elements:

---

[21] Champlin (1980), 132; Haines (1955), i. 32.
[22] McCall (1969), 243–4; Haines (1955), vol. i, p. xxiii.
[23] Champlin (1980), 4 ff.

Greek-based theory, like the elaborate doctrine of εἰκόνες, and Latin stylistic doctrine, archaizing in taste and directly largely at epideictic. The archaism, on Fronto's own admission, was a late acquisition; but it does not follow that his basic practical training was anything but Latin.

The shifting and often puzzling relationship between the Hellenic and Roman elements in Antonine literary culture is necessarily a main theme of any treatment of this period. Not only Fronto, but the other great writers—Aristides, Lucian, Apuleius—all raise this issue. The balance was surely shifting, and not to the advantage of Rome. *Graecia victa* was establishing her victory more and more securely, unconscious of pending changes, and of the new vigour that Christianity was to impart to later Latin literary masters, and that the more scholastic traditions of the East gave more sparingly to their Greek counterparts.

II

Truth and Fiction in Plutarch's *Lives*

C. B. R. PELLING

> As for Solon's meeting with Croesus, some scholars fancy
> that they have disproved this on chronological grounds.
> Yet, when a story is so famous and well-attested, when
> (more important) it fits Solon's character so well, and is so
> worthy of his wisdom and largeness of spirit, I am not pre-
> pared to reject it because of the so-called rules of chrono-
> logy. So many scholars are continually revising these
> rules, and still there is no agreement on how the inconsis-
> tencies are to be reconciled.
>
> (Plutarch, *Solon*, 27.1)

It would be equally inappropriate to exclude Plutarch from a
volume on Antonine Literature on the ground of so-called
chronology, just because he died under Hadrian. So many
aspects of his style and thought mark an intellectual affinity
with Antonine authors, both Greek and Latin.

As it happens, that *Solon* passage affords a useful text for
this discussion. Such an approach to chronology is not perhaps
ridiculous: in this particular case the chronological experts
doubtless had it right and Plutarch was wrong—but there
was a wider sense in which he was right to be sceptical of the

This paper, and especially its annotation, could easily have got out of hand. Perhaps
indeed they have. Some of the issues have recently been the subject of extensive theoretical discussion, though without specific reference to Plutarch: the ground is imposingly
mapped by Cameron in an as-yet unpublished paper, 'Between True and False'. Many
of the detailed examples are also mildly controversial. And comparison with historiography is essential to my purpose; but there is a lot of historiography, and I am conscious of eliding distinctions between Greek and Roman, among different authors, and
indeed (as I fleetingly suggest in the closing pages) among different parts of the same
author's work. My generalizations should be taken as indicating an approach which
may *often* be helpful, no more. Earlier versions were given as talks in Oxford, Boston,
Chapel Hill, Athens, and Lexington, Virginia. I am grateful to all audiences for helpful
and stimulating discussion; to Professor Woodman for his urbane and perceptive comments on a penultimate draft; and to the editor for (among other things) his enlightened interpretation of the bounds of Antonine Literature.

chronologists, even if this made him credulous of the story. The chronologies of early Greek, Persian, and Lydian history were hardly secure, and the different systems were not easy to harmonize: Plutarch knew the problems very well.[1] It would have been rash for him to build large consequences on such speculative grounds, particularly as the meeting of Solon and Croesus afforded one of the more firmly attested synchronizations for the experts to build their systems around; and, even on their own terms, the case against the story was scarcely clear-cut.[2] Plutarch was not indifferent to chronology,[3] but he liked it to rest on firmer grounds. Still, his cavalier attitude here certainly gives one pause. He makes no attempt to grapple with the chronological problem himself, he simply discards it; his placing of the story implies that he accepted the traditional dating shortly after Solon's reforms, a context which made the chronological problem more acute;[4] and, after he has made the reasonable point that the story is suported by a wealth of evidence, we are surprised that he goes on to put more weight on the way it fits Solon's character—precisely the reason, of course, why it was

---

[1] Cf. in particular *Numa* 1–2, *Cam.* 22. 2, *Them.* 27. 2 (where I am inclined to read οὐδ' αὐτοῖς ἀτρέμα συντεταραγμένοις with Cobet, Flacelière, and Ziegler[3]: Plutarch's usage of ἀτρέμα does not allow us to extract the required sense from συντεταγμένοις or συντεταγμένοις, *pace* LSJ[9], Frost, and Ziegler[4]).

[2] Heracleides Ponticus allowed Solon to live on well into Peisistratus' reign (*Sol.* 32. 3): admittedly, Heracleides himself may have been influenced by the desire to accommodate the Croesus-story, but this will not have been clear to Plutarch. Even the more moderate estimate of Phanias of Ephesus placed Solon's death in 560/59 (ibid.). Croesus succeeded to the Lydian throne fourteen years before the fall of Sardis, i.e. *c.*561/60 (Weissbach, *RE* Suppl. 5 (1931), 457), and Plutarch will at least have known the synchronization with Peisistratus (Hdt. 1. 59. 1). If he thought about it, he could reasonably wonder if the error might lie in associating the meeting with Solon's ten-year travels after his lawgiving (Hdt. 1. 29. 2–30. 1, etc): why could Solon not have made the trip in his notoriously sprightly old age (*Sol.* 31. 7), as Diog. Laert. 1. 50 seems to have inferred? After all, on one view he was in Cyprus when he died (Diog. Laert. 1. 62, Val. Max. 5. 3. ext. 3, Suda s.v. Σόλων, cf. *Sol.* 32. 4), and some talked of voluntary exile under Peisistratus (Diog. Laert. 1. 51–4, Suda, [Dio Prus.] 37. 4, Gell. 17. 21, cf. *POxy.* 4. 664. 9–10): he was not immobile—or so Plutarch might infer. We of course approach such questions rather differently, and regard all such data as totally unreliable, 'representative' rather than authentic: cf. esp. Lefkowitz (1981), 45. Such an approach is as dismissive as Plutarch's attitude to the chronologists, and both have much good sense to commend them.

[3] *Them.* 27. 2 is itself enough to show that (n. 1): cf. e.g. *Arist.* 5. 9–10, *Them.* 2. 5, *Per.* 27. 4, with Hamilton (1969), pp. xlvi–xlvii and Gomme (1945), 58 and n. 3 (less misleading than Hamilton's criticism suggests).

[4] Cf. n. 2.

doubtless made up. Momigliano has argued that 'the border-
line between fiction and reality was thinner in biography than
in ordinary historiography',[5] and that 'the biographers felt in
principle much freer than the historians in their use of evidence':[6] this, perhaps, is one instance where Plutarch shows less
concern to investigate historical truth than we should like.

Still, Momigliano's thesis is a large one, and deserves more
critical discussion than it has received; and the enquiry will
now be more complex because of recent, well-argued attempts
to demonstrate that 'ordinary historiography' itself showed less
regard for the truth than Momigliano implies, and perhaps
assumed a different concept of 'truth' from our own.[7] Yet the
comparison of biography and historiography can still be a rewarding one, and Plutarch is the only Greek political biographer who allows serious analysis—really, indeed, the only
substantial figure of whom we even know.[8] He clearly thought
hard not only about biography, but about how history should
be written too: the *De malignitate Herodoti* is sufficient demonstration of that, and the Lamprias catalogue attests a work on
How We Are to Judge True History (Lampr. cat. 124). Our
enquiry should be profitable.

It will be in three parts, though they overlap. The first will
discuss Plutarch's historical criticism, the criteria he uses for
accepting or rejecting material as plausible or implausible. The
second will turn to his narrative manipulation, what he does
with a story once he has decided to include it: how far he can
add circumstantial detail, how far he can change small details
of it, how far he can shift around its chronology, how far he can
strain its interpretation to suit his thesis, and so on. The third
will revert to Momigliano's formulations, and explore the relation between Plutarch and historiography.

---

[5] Momigliano (1971), 56.

[6] Momigliano (1985), 87.

[7] See now particularly Woodman (1988), esp. the Epilogue (197–215). His book
begins with criticism of Momigliano's assumptions about historiography (as expressed
elsewhere, Momigliano (1978)); cf. also his p. 213 n. 17. Of other recent literature,
Wiseman (1979) and (1981) and, very differently, Brunt (1979) are especially thought-
provoking.

[8] On the unlikely possibility of extensive Hellenistic political biography see now
Geiger (1985).

1. PLUTARCH'S CRITICAL ABILITY

Even by modern standards, many of Plutarch's historical arguments are quite impressive. Take the discussion of Aristides' wealth at *Arist.* 1.[9] He discusses the various arguments used by Demetrius of Phalerum to suggest that Aristides was quite well off—his tenure of the eponymous archonship, his ostracism, and the suggestion that he set up a choregic monument. He counters the last point by suggesting that friends might have subsidized him, as they did with Plato and Epaminondas in similar cases; then he adds the epigraphic argument which he draws from Panaetius—that the letter-forms show that this inscription is the wrong date, and must have been dedicated by a different Aristides. We would of course think the second point decisive, and wonder why he spent time on the first; still, both the points are reasonable, and he need not have been wholly confident that Panaetius had his letter-forms correctly dated. Against the other points—the archonship and the ostracism—he shows fairly easily that others were ostracized without being rich or noble (Damon), and cites Idomeneus to demonstrate that Aristides was elected archon, not drawn by lot from the *pentakosiomedimnoi*. Once again, he might have done a little better (e.g. by quoting Aristotle's *Constitution of Athens*),[10] but not much: he is using his wide reading and general knowledge very effectively. And, most important, he cared: this is worth two pages of fairly hard argument, and in the first chapter of a pair, where he usually prefers a more gripping and less learned opening—indeed, something more like the reflections on Justice in ch. 6, which could easily have been made into a prologue.

Of course, there is a sense in which the scholarship suits Plutarch's rhetorical concerns as well. Aristides' poverty will be important to his literary presentation of the pair, both confirming the famous incorruptibility and making it more remarkable; the elder Cato's justice, austerity, and domestic management will be rather more qualified and problematic.[11]

---

[9] Well discussed by Hamilton (1969), p. xlviii.

[10] A point fairly made by Gomme (1945), 76, and Hamilton.

[11] Cf. esp. the thoughtful reflections in the *Synkrisis* (*C. mai.* 30(3)–31(4)). As often, the first *Life* of a pair is the more straightforward, while the second presents a morally interesting variation.

The point will be important enough for Plutarch to return to it at the close of the *Life*, with another, balancing display of intelligent learning: Craterus cannot have good authority for his claim that the elderly Aristides was condemned for corruption, for, if he had, it would have been in his manner to quote it, and the item would anyway have featured in the canon of stories of the ungrateful *demos* (*Arist.* 26. 2–5). And Aristides' poverty is also confirmed by the fate of his children and grandchildren after his death: again an impressive parade of learning confirms the point (27). But, strictly in rhetorical terms, the scholarly technique is not ideal: Craterus' obloquy was for instance obscure enough to be ignored rather than countered, and the initial points would have been more forceful if they had been briefer; and, more important, nothing suggests that the rhetorical point of the argumentation was here in conflict with what Plutarch believed to be *true*. We often, and fairly, concentrate on the ways in which rhetoric could distract writers from historical truth, but there were other ways in which it positively helped: in fostering a powerful memory, for instance,[12] and encouraging wide and cultured reading; in providing the techniques to impose a clear, ordered structure on chaotic source-material; in affording a sensitivity to bias; in encouraging discrimination among more or less reliable witnesses; in providing arguments from *eikos* which could stimulate a sceptical approach to unlikely stories. The *Aristides* affords a good instance of this, with Plutarch's rhetorical expertise helping his critical alertness to the truth. Some modern theorists have stressed the analogy between historical research and forensic technique, with historians asking questions of 'witnesses' and elaborating techniques to check their testimony:[13] in this case, at least, one sees what they mean.

There are plenty of other examples of good argument: the remark at *Crass.* 13 that one cannot trust Cicero when he

---

[12] Hamilton (1969), pp. xxi–xxii, is again good on this.

[13] See esp. Fogel and Elton (1983), 13–15, 21–2, 49–50, 90–5. There is of course a blunter sense in which all historical *writing* is necessarily rhetorical: a point especially associated with Hayden White, e.g. (1973) and (1978). Cf. n. 70, below. White gives disquietingly little attention to this gathering and criticism of evidence, as Momigliano (1981) fairly observes; but when Momigliano retorts that 'rhetoric has long been for the historian an effective (never essential) device to be used with caution', that too is surely a misunderstanding of rhetoric. Cf. Woodman (1988), pp. 88 and 108 n. 72.

incriminates Caesar and Crassus in a work he published after both were dead; the discussion of Phocion's social standing at *Phoc.* 4. 1–2, including the sensible remark that, if Phocion had been of low birth, he would not have attended the Academy or indulged in other privileged pursuits in his youth; the use of more reliable chronology to demonstrate that Stesimbrotus had got his dates wrong in making Themistocles the pupil of Melissus and Anaxagoras (*Them.* 2. 5). He is alert to bias as well, as befits one who is familiar with the rhetorical arts of misrepresentation: Oppius cannot be trusted when he writes about Caesar's friends or enemies, so one cannot believe his story of an atrocity of Pompey during the Sullan period (*Pomp.* 10. 9); Antiphon's slanderous stories about Alcibiades should be discounted, given the conventions of invective (*Alc.* 3. 2); Andocides' anti-democratic bias and Phylarchus' sensational style discredit their stories about Themistocles' death (*Them.* 32. 4); Duris of Samos can always be relied upon to magnify his country's sufferings (*Per.* 28. 3); a story of Phylarchus would not be worth accepting but for the fact that it is supported by Polybius, for Phylarchus would always bend the truth in Cleomenes' favour (*Arat.* 38. 12);[14] and Theopompus is more reliable when praising people than when blaming them, so his version of Lysander's financial integrity deserves some respect (*Lys.* 30. 2). And he certainly knows when truth is particularly hard to attain, whether because of the remoteness of the period or because it was so heavily overlaid by propaganda (*Per.* 13. 16, *Thes.* 1. 2–5, *Lyc.* 1. 1, *Mor.* 326 A).

---

[14] On a literal interpretation, this principle would seem to be equivalent to discarding Phylarchus completely and simply following Polybius. But by looking at Plutarch's practice one can see what he meant. For instance, at *Phil.* 5 and *Ag.–Cl.* 44–6 he describes the fall of Megalopolis in 223, and clearly draws on Phylarchus: that seems established by comparison of the tenor of his versions with Polybius' criticisms at 2. 61–2. Thus Plutarch's generous attitude to Cleomenes and his stress on Megalopolis' wealth both seem distinctively Phylarchan. But Plutarch knows Polybius' account too (cf. e.g. *Ag.–Cl.* 46. 5), and carefully avoids committing himself to the details which Polybius criticized. Thus Polybius (2. 62) trenchantly attacked Phylarchus' figure of 6000 talents for Cleomenes' booty; Plutarch simply has a cautious χρημάτων εὐπορήσαντι (*Phil.* 5. 5, cf. *Ag.–Cl.* 46. 1). He apparently feels he can retain other details which Polybius did not criticize (or criticized so obliquely that the point could easily be missed: contrast *Ag.–Cl.* 45 and Plb. 2. 55. 8 (with Walbank's note), the embassy of Lysandridas and Thearidas). When Polybius is being so captious, he could reasonably be regarded as 'confirming' Phylarchus' other details if he did not explicitly attack them.

He knows the value of contemporary and eyewitness sources, too—that often emerges.[15] Of course, some contemporary sources could be rather embarrassing to have:

It is time for me to appeal to the reader for indulgence, as I treat the events which Thucydides has already handled incomparably: in this part of his narrative he was indeed at his most emotional, vivid, and varied. But do not assume that I am as vain as Timaeus, who thought he would outdo Thucydides in brilliance and show Philistus to be totally vulgar and amateurish ... Of course, it is not possible to omit the events treated by Thucydides and Philistus, for they include material which gives an especially clear notion of the man's character and disposition, so often hidden by his many calamities. But I have summarized them briefly and kept to the essentials, just to avoid the charge of total negligence. I have tried instead to collect material which is not well known, but scattered among other authors, or found on ancient dedications and decrees. Nor is this an accumulation of useless erudition: I am conveying material which is helpful for grasping the man's nature and character. (*Nic.* 1. 1, 5.)

It is Thucydides' artistic qualities, we notice, that make him inimitable: he is so emotional, vivid, varied, brilliant. But Plutarch will compensate, not by literary virtuosity (the area where we might have thought he *could* compete), and not just by altering to a biographical focus: he will find out new facts. All this study of 'other authors' and 'ancient dedications and decrees' sounds like serious historical enquiry committed to the truth; and indeed *Nicias* is quite full of such out-of-the-way evidence, including epigraphic material, and he prefers to pursue this approach rather than strain every last ounce from Thucydides.[16] He quite often uses inscriptions elsewhere, too.[17] One

---

[15] Cf. e.g. *Pomp.* 72. 4, *Cim.* 4. 5, *Gracch.* 4. 6, *Mar.* 25. 6, *Ant.* 77. 3, *Aem.* 15. 5 with 16. 3; cf. the extensive reading in contemporary, often non-chronological material before writing *Cicero* (Pelling (1979), 88–9). Further instances in Hamilton (1969), p. xlvii, who here seems to me right against Gomme (1945), 58–9.

[16] Cf. then 3. 3, 3. 7–8 (inscriptions); 4. 5–8. 8. 3–4, 11. 7 (comic poets, not very shrewdly exploited); 4. 2 (dialogue of Pasiphon); 10. 1, 11. 10 (Theophrastus); 17. 4 (Euripides); 23. 8 (Philochorus); 28. 5 (Timaeus). For other, unattributed non-Thucydidean material, cf. Gomme (1945), 71–2. Not straining every ounce from Thucydides: cf. esp. 6. 4, where he might have said more about both Mende (for instance mentioning Nicias' wound, Thuc. 4. 129. 4) and Cythera (where the fifth column might interestingly have presaged events at Syracuse, Thuc. 4. 53–4).

[17] e.g. *Ages.* 19. 10 ('I discovered in the Λακωνικαὶ ἀναγραφαί ...'), *Arist.* 5. 10, 10. 9–10, 19. 7, *Cim.* 13. 5, *Sol.* 11. 1–2: Theander (1951), 78–83, Hamilton (1969), p. xlix.

need not overdo it: there are of course spectacular weaknesses as well, especially when he argues from silence;[18] his attempts to reconstruct the political climate of a different age can be disquietingly crude and simple;[19] and he does not always seem to us to give weight to the right evidence or arguments—in different ways, *Arist.* 1 and *Solon* 27 were both examples of that. Even in *Nicias* Gomme is probably right, and we should not really think of 'research': the collection of material was doubtless too unsystematic.[20] But it is not unfair to speak of 'scholarship', the thoughtful application of extensive learning in the interest of getting facts right; and, without overdoing it, we can at least say that he is as critical, as intelligent, and as committed to the truth as most ancient writers about the past[21]—*when he wants to be.*

There is evidently a sting in that tail, but we have already seen enough of Plutarch's commitment to the truth to justify two additional points. First, a good deal of this political biography is very committed to getting it right. Now that evidently contrasts with literary biography, which is so often 'representative' and fictional;[22] it also probably contrasts with any other models of Greek biography that Plutarch knew. As

[18] Cf. esp. *Caes.* 8. 4, *Alc.* 32. 2, *Alex.* 46. 3, *Cic.* 49. 4.

[19] On Greek history, cf. Gomme (1945), 59 ff., 73–4; on Roman, Pelling (1986).

[20] Gomme (1945), 76. But elsewhere 'research' is not an unfair description: we can detect that he undertook a quite extensive and systematic course of reading when preparing some Roman *Lives.* Cf. Pelling (1979).

[21] Cf. Wiseman's generalizations about historians' critical research, in his chapter titled 'Unhistorical thinking': 'The historians of Greece and Rome [except for Thucydides] did *not* "put their authorities to the question". They did not have the questions to put, because they were incapable of the "historical imagination" needed for the historian to relive for himself, as Collingwood puts it, the states of mind into which he inquires . . . "Evidence" as the main preoccupation of the historian is a modern concept . . . for people brought up on the techniques of rhetoric, the first plausible story was good enough . . . [Livy and Dionysius] could assess the accuracy of what their sources told them only by the rhetorician's criterion of inherent probability' (Wiseman (1979), 42, 47, 48, 50). All these are arguably overstatements (cf. e.g. Rawson (1985), p. 217 n. 16); but scarcely extreme ones. In this company Plutarch can hold his head high.

[22] See above all Lefkowitz (1981); Fairweather (1973). This distinction between literary and political biography is a rough one, and is clearly unsatisfactory in the formal terms in which it was articulated by Leo (1901): for a succinct statement of the reasons, cf. Momigliano (1971), 87–8. But, however rough, the distinction remains indispensable in illuminating such central points of difference as length, style of presentation, and focus of interest, as well as this issue of truthfulness. So, rightly, Geiger (1985), 18–29.

Momigliano brought out,[23] in formal terms the *genera proxima* to biography were, first, encomium, and secondly the biographical novel on the model of Xenophon's *Cyropaedia*. Both, evidently, were quite popular genres in the Hellenistic period, and both certainly indulged in fictional elaboration, particularly of matters such as their subjects' childhood.[24] Momigliano was quite right to observe that the fictional quality of such works could well topple over into biography itself. In the case of literary biography, that indeed happened; but Plutarch's political biography was generally different—even though it was usually public figures, not intellectuals, that those mendacious *genera proxima* treated, and we might consequently expect political biography to be the more susceptible variety. Perhaps Plutarch had Hellenistic forerunners in the political genre who were equally historically committed, but I doubt it;[25] more likely, he was largely creating his own genre, and creating it in a mould which was unexpectedly truthful, a closer cousin to historiography than to the formally more similar encomium or biographical novel.[26] Consider, for instance, his use of Onesicritus' *How Alexander Was Brought up*, apparently a charming, romantic, and extravagant work written on the model of the *Cyropaedia*.[27] Plutarch seems to draw on this a little in the first few chapters of *Alexander*,[28] but the remarkable thing is that he does not draw on it more. As Hamilton brings out clearly, he is much more restrained in the *Life* than in his essays (or speeches) 'On Alexander's Fortune': in the *Life*, for instance, he does not develop the motif of the 'philosopher in arms' civilizing the barbarous world, though we know this featured in the work of Onesicritus (*FGrH* 134 F 17), and we might expect it to be to Plutarch's taste: it was certainly fundamental to the essays, particularly the first.[29] Yet he had sufficient knowledge of the historical

---

[23] Momigliano (1971), ch. 4.

[24] Pelling (1990), 217–18; more on childhood below, pp. 36–8.

[25] On the possibility of Hellenistic political biography see now Geiger (1985), 30–65, with whose sceptical approach I sympathize.

[26] Cf. Geiger (1985), 9–29, 114–15.

[27] At least, Diog. Laert. 6. 84 specifically links the two, and what we know of the content supports the connexion. Cf. esp. Strasburger, *RE* xviii/1 (1939), 464–5; Brown (1949); Hamilton (1969), pp. lvi–lvii; Momigliano (1971), 82–3; Geiger (1985), pp. 48–9 n. 43, though he is perhaps too cautious.

[28] Hamilton (1969), pp. liii, lvi–lvii.

[29] Cf. Hamilton (1969), pp. xxiii–xxxiii, lvi–lvii.

tradition to be sceptical. He felt that this sort of material was inappropriate for the sort of biography he was writing, however suitable it might be for a rhetorical essay: and it is pretty remarkable that he did, and that he prevented his biography from drifting into the fictional conventions of its formal *genera proxima*. In this as in other ways, Plutarch's closest precursor was perhaps Nepos, as Geiger has suggested:[30] for Nepos was not, it seems, mendacious, and certainly not sensational. Still, in that case our respect for Plutarch's massive originality will be all the greater, for the gulf between the two is so immense; and it is still remarkable that Plutarch should have turned to that model rather than any other. For instance, he clearly knew hagiographic literature such as Thrasea Paetus' *Life of Cato*,[31] but that was not to be his style. There were so many forces which were driving Plutarch, if he wrote biography, into writing in the manner of the *Scriptores Historiae Augustae*, fictional and extravagant: it is striking that he, like his contemporary Suetonius, chose to write something much more historically faithful.

The second point here is the range of information he adduces—inscriptions, speeches, letters, oral traditions, comic poets, as well as mainstream historians. We are so used to this that we almost take it for granted, and are indeed accustomed to complain about the way he takes the comic poets too seriously;[32] but more striking is the fact that he uses them at all. This sort of range does not regularly appear in historiography: some historians would use out-of-the-way material some of the time, of course, but this is still much more the sort of polymathy that we associate with antiquarianism. For instance, Millar commented on Cassius Dio's strange use of Cicero's speeches: 'This illustrates a curious, but important, feature of ancient historiography—while it was possible to use Cicero's speeches for putting together a speech "by Cicero", it was not possible to use them to provide evidence for the main narrative; that was supplied by the narrative sources alone.'[33] That is surely right

---

[30] Geiger (1985), esp. 117–20.

[31] Geiger (1979), and (1985), 60–1, 120.

[32] In itself, of course, a very fair point: cf. especially Gomme (1945), 60, 69–70.

[33] Millar (1964), 54–5. Professor Woodman observes that historians, notably Velleius, regularly echo the phraseology of Cicero's speeches in their narratives, both when

about Dio, and probably about Appian too. But Plutarch does use Cicero quite extensively as a historical source, especially the *Second Philippic* in *Antony* (we shall come back to that).[34] In this respect Plutarch is closer to our modern idea of respectable historical activity than most of the historians were, and there is indeed an essential historical seriousness about what he does. Once again, the parallel with his contemporary Suetonius is suggestive. For all the difference in literary form, there is still a similar use of antiquarian material and method, and similar commitment to getting things right.[35]

To go back to that earlier sting in the tail: Plutarch is quite good at historical argumentation when he wants to be. Sometimes—not necessarily very often or extensively—he does not. His biography is a most flexible genre. Sometimes he is very interested in history, in isolating the historical forces that carried Caesar to power, for instance, or Themistocles, or that made and then broke the Gracchi; sometimes his interest in history is much slighter.[36] This can be seen most easily in his reluctance to give historical background: there is far more on the historical setting, for instance, in the *Caesar* than in the *Antony*, to take two figures who dominated their respective decades. It can be seen in the seriousness of the political analyses he gives, with much more trivial versions emerging in some *Lives* than in others; and it can also be seen in the depth or shallowness of his critical discussions. When his mind is not fundamentally concentrated on the history, his standards of criticism tend to relax. For instance, he knows perfectly well that invective cannot be trusted: as we have seen, he is quite capable of rejecting Andocides' attack on Alcibiades on those grounds (*Alc.* 3). At times, he is therefore critical of Cicero's invective against Antony— but, if it suits him to stress Antony's luxury, he will use Cicero.[37] If the propaganda which reviles Cleopatra fits his

---

describing the same events as Cicero and elsewhere. That is rather different from using Cicero as a historical 'source' in Plutarch's manner; but it is a valuable reminder of the problems of definition involved in categorizing what is and what is not a 'source'.

[34] Pelling (1979), 88–90, and (1988), 26–7.

[35] Nepos too made some use of such material: Geiger (1985), 109–10.

[36] I have elaborated this point elsewhere, especially in Pelling (1980) and (1986).

[37] The *Second Philippic* is explicitly criticized at *Ant.* 6. 1, and similar material is rejected at *Ant.* 2. 2–3; but other passages, especially in *Ant.* 9–13 and 21, are largely based on the *Philippic* (Pelling (1988), 26–7, and nn. ad locc.).

general picture of the queen, he will use it—then briefly confess
it may be false (*Ant.* 58. 4–59. 1). When he comes to discuss less
'historical' areas or people—not necessarily those living in
mythical times, incidentally, but rather those who had become
enveloped in the sort of tradition which made it difficult to
write a more 'historical' biography—he can be much less critical of his material and perpetrate much sillier arguments. Sertorius yearns for the Isles of the Blessed; Antony comes to hate
Octavian more fiercely because he always loses at dice; the
young Cassius bloodied the nose of the young Faustus Sulla,
hence the usual view of Cassius' motive for tyrannicide must be
wrong. We should believe the miraculous stories of Rome's
foundation, despite the criticism of sceptics, for the Roman
state would hardly have advanced to such might if it did not
have a wondrous and divine origin.[38] Indeed, that argument
(or rather lack of it) about Solon and Croesus also belongs in
this list. All this does strike a very different tone from the acute,
sceptical argumentation discussed earlier; but, for one reason
or another, he thought that the sort of material he was treating
in these less historically committed passages did not lend itself
to argumentation of such rigour. In Aristotelian terms, one
should only seek the ἀκρίβεια appropriate to the ὕλη, the material the writer was describing. And even here Plutarch is not so
far removed from the historians. Livy, for example, knew that
people added venerability to antique stories by including the
supernatural, and proclaimed his indifference to such material;
but, he goes on to say, the Romans went on to win such martial
glory that they of all people might naturally be permitted to
trace their descent from Mars (*praef.* 6–7). That is almost
exactly the same point as Plutarch makes in *Romulus*, though
Livy puts it a little more sardonically; and it is hardly the style
of argument which recurs in his later books. And even Thucydides concludes his *Archaeologia* with the claim that he has
relayed the facts with sufficient accuracy, given their antiquity
(ὡς παλαιὰ εἶναι, 1. 21. 1):[39] it would be unreasonable, clearly,
to expect the same rigour or precision as with more recent and
verifiable events. Thus in the *Archaeologia* he has strained to

---

[38] Sertorious and the Isles of the Blessed, *Sert.* 8. 2–9. 2; Antony, Octavian, and dice,
Ant. 33; Cassius and Faustus Sulla, *Brut.* 9. 1–4; gods and Rome's foundation, *Rom.* 8. 9.
[39] I am grateful to Prof. D. M. Lewis for reminding me of this.

extract conclusions from Homer, with a surprising lack of scepticism;[40] 'a funny kind of history',[41] indeed, and one which is not going to be prominent in the rest of his work. It is unthinkable, for instance, that he would use Euripides as evidence for Athenian war-weariness, or exploit Aristophanes on Cleon; with harder history, that was not his way.

There were various reasons why Plutarch might favour a different style of argument and degree of rigour. It might be the period, as with Romulus; it might be the type of figure—Sertorius really did belong in a different world from Sulla, Pompey, or Caesar, even if he lived in the same period; or it might be the style of *Life*—*Antony* or *Brutus* do have rather different, less 'historical', styles than many of the others. It is certainly very hard to find arguments as unrigorous or material as implausible as this in *Lives* like *Caesar*, or *Gracchi*, or *Themistocles*. This also helps to explain a feature which disturbed Momigliano, Plutarch's readiness to write confidently about figures like Romulus, instead of confessing his inability to judge deficient evidence.[42] That is true—though it is also true that Plutarch begins *Thes.–Rom.* by giving a general caveat and asking for indulgence; but in any case that does not mean that he was as uncritical when he wrote of the later, more solid figures. His genre was flexible enough to accommodate both sorts of figure, but he knew he could not ask the same questions with the same rigour about them all. The use of evidence may 'lack consistency', as Momigliano protests;[43] but not irrationally so. And even when we do find those less rigorous elements, his approach is usually not wholly indifferent to the truth, not simply ahistorical. He may be accepting material too credulously, but in each case it is to support a view that he genuinely holds, and often for good reason: the rest of the *Life* usually makes that plain. He really believes that Antony and Cleopatra were infatuated and extravagant, that Sertorius was a dreamer, Solon a courageous sage, and Cassius a fierce hater of tyrants: he just

---

[40] Cf. Gomme on 1. 9. 4. It is piquant to find Thucydides hailed as the grandfather of cliometrics on the basis of 1. 10 (Fogel, in Fogel and Elton (1983), 69): not in fact the style of evidence or argument where Thucydides is at his surest.

[41] Finley (1985), 12, of attempts to extract history from unlikely poetic sources.

[42] Momigliano (1985), 87.

[43] Momigliano (1985), 88.

allows himself to make the points a little too easily. He is not presenting a false picture, just helping his truth along a little.

So far we have been applying our own standards of what a historian ought to be about. Plutarch's canons were rather different, and he conveniently sets them out at the beginning of *De malignitate Herodoti*.[44] For instance, the historian should not use severe words if milder ones should suffice; he should not drag in irrelevant material which is discreditable to a character, but should not suppress anything that puts him in a good light; when two versions of an incident are current, he should select the more creditable one; when the motivation of an action is disputed, he should give a character the benefit of the doubt; he should not include stray abuse and then admit it to be false, for such innuendo can only detract from a character's moral stature; and so on. How far did Plutarch the biographer practise what he preached for historians?[45]

The answer is at first sight surprising. The *De malignitate* principles certainly strike us as 'moralistic': a character must be given the benefit of any ethical doubt, and his moral stature must not be gratuitously impugned. And yet it is (to put it crudely) the most 'historical' *Lives* which are most scrupulous in observing those canons: those *Lives* such as *Caesaer* or *Themistocles*, where the moralism is typically subtle and muted, and the interest in exploring historical background is unusually intense. The moralism of other *Lives* is more open, for instance in *Cato minor* or *Antony*: yet it is those *Lives* which more often flout the *De malignitate* principles.

In *Caesar* Plutarch thus makes little of discreditable facts, for instance Caesar's sexual habits; indeed, he avoids malicious comment even when it would have been justified, for example in his treatment of Caesar's vulgar demagogy, or his extrava-

---

[44] 855 A–856 D: cf. esp. Homeyer (1967), Wardman (1974), 189–96.

[45] The question was usefully asked by Theander (1951), 32–7: he found that Plutarch *did* largely practise what he preached, at least in his own narrative of those controversial events discussed in the body of *De malignitate*. Many of those are of course treated in *Themistocles*, one of the more historically alert *Lives* ('had we only the *Themistokles* . . . we should have a good opinion of Plutarch's learning and not a bad one of his judgement', Gomme (1945), 61): thus Theander's conclusion cannot be extended to other *Lives* without qualification, as we shall see. Wardman (1974), 191–6, also overstates the absence of 'malice' (i.e. the κακοήθεια of *De malignitate*) in the *Lives*.

gance, or his debts.[46] Caesar's ambition was for tyrannical power (*Caes.* 57. 1, 69, 1), and the theme is important to the *Life*:[47] Plutarch of course strongly disapproved,[48] but in *Caesar* he kept his disapproval to himself. If there is ever a word of criticism, it tends to be a mild one: for instance, the description of the *Anticato* is much more temperate in *Caesar* (54. 3–6) than in *Cato minor* (11. 7–8, 36. 5, 54. 2). The *De malignitate* principles can sometimes be seen working on a smaller scale. When Caesar refuses to give evidence against Clodius but insists on divorcing his wife, Plutarch's explanation is very proper: some say that Caesar was sincere, others that he was courting the goodwill of the masses (9. 10). His historical thesis would really welcome the second interpretation, for he is stressing Caesar's scheme of rising to power as the people's champion;[49] but he includes the more favourable explanation as well. Again, at *Them.* 31. 5 he strains plausibility in his attempt to find a creditable motive for Themistocles' suicide; *Gracchi* 22. 6–7 takes the most generous view possible of Gaius' reasons for entering popular politics.

So far the principles of *De malignitate* really do seem to obtain; but other *Lives* are different. *Antony* retails that long catalogue of abuse which Calvisius cast at Cleopatra—then adds that 'Calvisius was doubtless lying' (58. 7–59. 1). Precisely the sort of innuendo which the *De malignitate* had outlawed. The principles can always be ignored when Plutarch is painting a villain, a Cleon or a Sulla or (in his decline) a Marius. Cleon opposed the peace-proposals in 425 because of his personal enmity with Nicias (*Nic.* 7. 2): not what Thucydides had said (4. 21), for all his stress on that enmity (4. 27. 5) and his distaste for Cleon. Sulla had claimed that he indulged the captured Athens because of the world's debt to Athens' past: Plutarch dismisses this, for his Sulla is simply 'sated with vengeance' (*Sulla* 14. 9). Hardly 'giving Sulla the benefit of the ethical doubt'. In other *Lives* Plutarch praises Sulla's constitutional

---

[46] e.g. *Caes.* 4. 4–9, 5. 8–9, 11. 1: contrast Plutarch's disapproval of vulgar demagogy at e.g. *C. min.* 46. 8, 49. 6, *Aem.* 2. 6, *Brut.* 10. 6, *Prae. rei p. ger.* 802 D *al.*; of extravagance and debt at *Praecepta* 802 D, 821 F, 822 C–3 E, and *De uitando aere alieno*.

[47] Pelling (1980), 136–7.

[48] Cf. esp. *Otho* 17. 11, *Pyrrh.* 14; Wardman (1974), 53–5, 109–10, 217.

[49] 4. 8, 5. 8–9, 6. 9, etc: Pelling (1980), 137.

settlement,[50] but not in *Sulla* itself: scarcely 'including everything to Sulla's credit'. The second half of Marius is similar in
texture: Plutarch regularly assumes the worst about Marius'
motives, often rejecting the man's own explanations as dis-
ingenuous or silly;[51] and the close of this *Life* wallows in the
slaughter, wilfully exonerating Cinna to emphasize Marius'
own role.[52]

But it is not just ethical outcasts who are denied the benefit of
any ethical doubt. When the moralism is crude, even the most
favourable *Lives* can show little respect for the *De malignitate*
precepts. *Cato minor* is favourable enough, and Plutarch indignantly rejects the story that Cato was once drunk as praetor
(44. 2). Yet he still includes that story; it adds nothing, the
innuendo can only detract from the subject's character, and the
De malignitate principles should have led him to suppress it completely: the historian, we recall, should not include stray abuse
which he then admits to be false. *Pericles* similarly includes various slanders about the genesis of the war (esp. 31), just as
earlier it has mentioned and dismissed Idomeneus' allegation
that Pericles murdered Ephialtes (10. 7) and Duris' charge of
Athenian atrocities at Samos (28); and Plutarch has also
assumed the worst motivation for appointing Lacedaemonius
to the Corcyrean expedition (29. 1–2). At *Cic.* 29. 1–2 he allows
that Cicero's allegations against Clodius were fair and true, but
that is not (says Plutarch) why he made them: he was simply
trying to put himself right with Terentia. Much of *Pompey*, too,
is sympathetic; but Plutarch rejects out of hand the excuses
made by his friends for his conduct in 59 (*Pomp.* 47. 7–8). He includes the attacks made on Pompey for marrying Cornelia, and
indeed affords them quite an expansive treatment (55. 1–5): a
more sympathetic approach would have been possible, and
just—and indeed would in some ways have suited the *Life*, with
its engaging stress on Pompey's uxoriousness. Plutarch then
concentrates on the bad aspects of the administration in 52, the
favouritism towards Scipio and Plancus and the arrogant treatment of Hypsaeus: then he curtly adds that in other respects he
did well, τὰ δ' ἄλλα καλῶς ἅπαντα κατέστησεν εἰς τάξιν. The

---

50 *Lucull.* 5. 5, *Cic.* 3. 3, 10. 2, *Pomp.* 5. 4–5, 81 (1). 2.
51 *Mar.* 29. 4, 30. 5–6, 31. 2–5, 32. 2, 33. 2, 34. 7, 41. 6.
52 *Mar.* 43. 7, 44. 9–10.

balance of the whole treatment could well have been more generous. None of all this is untruthful, of course: Plutarch really did believe that Cleon was petty, Sulla and Marius murderous, Cato drunken, Cicero henpecked, and Pompey impolitic. But there is surely a certain lack of charity.

And perhaps these variations among the *Lives* are not so surprising after all. The *Lives* are sometimes a little removed from historiography, sometimes closer; and the *De malignitate* was giving precepts for historians. Plutarch is alert and sensitive to the possibilities of his genre, and when he was writing a 'historical' *Life* he himself became far more of a historian, keeping more closely to the norms he thought appropriate to that genre. Those norms included both truthfulness and ethical generosity: when he felt it appropriate, he would pursue the truth thoughtfully and rigorously, but also with a proper readiness to err on the side of charity. At other times, he could be more relaxed.

2. PLUTARCH'S MANIPULATION OF HIS NARRATIVE

Quite evidently, Plutarch does not take over his historical material blindly: he does interesting things with it. Sometimes he criticizes it explicitly, as we have seen, making it clear why he is favouring one version or rejecting another; more often, he simply tacitly rewrites it, elaborating, reordering, giving different emphases, often revising the detail. What did Plutarch think he was doing when he recast material in this way?

If we could tackle Licinius Macer or Valerius Antias, I think they would each indignantly deny that their detailed and circumstantial narratives were all made up. I think they would argue that it *must* have been like that; their justification would be 'it stands to reason', with *a priori* probability—or what seemed to them to be probability—totally outweighing the lack of actual evidence.

Thus Peter Wiseman.[53] Whatever the case with Licinius or Valerius, what would Plutarch have said? When we can detect him adapting or improving his material, would he have given that explanation, 'it must have been like that'? Or would it have been a more pungent and robust 'don't be a pedantic old bore: I'm just making it into a better story'? Perhaps it is a bit of

⁵³ Wiseman (1981), 389, followed by Woodman (1988), 93.

both—so much a bit of both that it is hard to think that Plutarch would have drawn a hard-and-fast line between cases where he was sacrificing the truth and cases where he was reconstructing it. In that case, Wiseman's analysis may not be quite the right way to look at it, and we may instead have to develop a concept along the lines of 'true *enough*', more true than false. Still, his remark gives a helpfully sharp question, and we shall ask it.

First, though, we should notice what Plutarch does not do. His source-material sometimes left vast gaps, for instance the hole in *Themistocles* from 493 to 483. Some *Lives* indeed were veritable string vests, more hole than substance—*Phocion, Aristides, Philopoemen, Poplicola, Artaxerxes*, even *Crassus*. But Plutarch does not fill them with fabrication. Normally, we can see, he likes to pair two *Lives* of roughly similar length, but there are times when he cannot. He simply does not have enough material on Cimon, Phocion, Fabius, Marcellus, or Agesilaus to make them weighty enough matches for their pairs; he does not make it up. And this reluctance to fabricate is particularly plain in his treatment of boyhood and youth.[54] So many *Lives* have virtually nothing before adulthood: *Antony, Nicias, Phocion, Camillus, Flamininus, Marcellus, Fabius, Timoleon*, and more. We could all make up a few good stories about a schoolboy Antony or Nicias; Plutarch does not, Similarly with death: Plutarch would dearly like to know more about how Camillus or Flamininus met their ends, but he lets the gaps stand. These are precisely the sort of holes which literary biography would strain to fill; nor would encomium or the biographical novel have been silent. Plutarch is different. When he adds circumstantial detail, it is in much more limited ways: the circumstances of a conversation, perhaps, with a cautious plotter, a boisterous lover, a playful maid, a sneering innkeeper, or an officious servant. He can add a man to hold out his toga for Antony's vomit; or a new river or hill to make sense of a campaign; or new circumstances for Coriolanus' friend, once rich, now in penury.[55] But the big invention is not in his style.

---

[54] I have expanded this point, together with other questions concerning childhood, in Pelling (1990).

[55] *Ant.* 13, 10. 8–9, *Caes.* 9. 2–10. 11, *Mar.* 44, *Ant.* 9. 6, 48. 6, 49. 2, 76. 1–3, *Caes.*

He does do something to fill childhood gaps, though: the most usual sort of item we find is what one could call 'the routine generalization'.[56]

Romulus seemed to be more intelligent and politically shrewd than Remus; in his encounters with his neighbours in the countryside he showed that he was more a leader than a follower. (*Rom.* 6. 3)

Timoleon was patriotic and unusually gentle—except that he nourished a peculiarly intense hatred for tyranny and for evil people. In his military campaigns he showed such a finely balanced character that he displayed great understanding as a young man and great bravery in his old age. (*Tim.* 3. 4–5)

Cleomenes was ambitious, large-spirited, and no less well-endowed than Agis for living a disciplined and simple life. But he lacked Agis' extraordinary caution and mildness: by nature his spirit was easily goaded, and he was inspired to pursue his ideals with peculiar ferocity. He thought it best to dominate people if they were willing, but honourable even if they were not, and even if he had to force them in the proper direction. (*Ag.–Cl.* 22. 4–5)

This sort of thing is not limited to Plutarch, incidentally—the beginning of Suetonius' *Titus* is very similar; and again one notices the lack of the anecdotal register, the reluctance to make up stories. Such generalizations are so routine in Plutarch that they must be his own work, and he is simply retrojecting important aspects of the men's later careers. And sometimes the reconstruction is fairly circumstantial, even though it is not anecdotal. Marcellus admired Greek *paideia*, but his military training meant he had no time to study cultural subjects as much as he wished (*Marc.* 1. 3); in adolescence Agis abandoned the foppery which typified his degenerate Sparta, and turned to the old ways of austerity (*Ag.–Cl.* 4. 1–2); Coriolanus' youthful rivals 'excused their inferiority by attributing it all to his physical strength' (*Cor.* 2. 2).[57] In each case it is unlikely that such material stood in his sources; but in each case Plutarch could very reasonably infer it from later events. Indeed, Wiseman's 'must have been like that' principle so far works perfectly

---

19. 10, *Cor.* 10. 5. On the *Mar.* case cf. Carney (1960), 28–9; on *Cor.*, Russell (1963), 25; on *Ant.* and *Caes.*, Pelling (1980), 127–8, and (1988), 33–6, together with notes ad locc.

   [56] Other examples, and more extended discussion, in Pelling (1990), 226.

   [57] Further discussion in Pelling (1990), 226–7, and (on the *Cor.* passage) Russell (1963), 23.

well. Plutarch is not fabricating. He is simply inferring what sort of youth it must have been who grew up into the man he knew; just as in our earlier examples he was inferring how a slave or innkeeper must have behaved, how a battle must have been fought, and what must have happened to Antony's vomit. This is not fiction or invention, but creative reconstruction.

This type of inference can be more far-reaching. Consider the beginning of the *Antony*, where Plutarch does not know much about Antony's youth. What he does know, he seems to draw from Cicero's hostile portrait in the *Second Philippic*. Cicero there described Antony's early involvement with the young nobleman Curio; Plutarch reshapes it.[58] Cicero had stressed the erotic aspects of the relationship, likening Antony to a male prostitute; Plutarch omits that. Perhaps that is restraint, perhaps scepticism: as we have seen, he knew what invective could get up to. Cicero had given no hint that Curio was the leading partner, and of course had represented Antony as just as depraved as Curio. Plutarch prefers to make Curio a corrupting influence, subtly tempting Antony into submissiveness. Now, in these early chapters of *Antony* we should not be too ready to assume that Plutarch is simply giving Antony the benefit of the doubt: he is not usually so generous, at least in this part of the *Life*. But he is concerned to develop the notion of the man as brilliant but passive, the susceptible victim of others' wiles: first his wife Fulvia will render him submissive (χειροήθης, 10. 6, the same word as here), then of course Cleopatra and her flatterers. Plutarch is preparing the way here. That is both a literary and a historical point. Told this way, the story better prepares for the later developments; but it is also more plausible that Antony should have been behaving like this. His whole later life shows his passivity and susceptibility; so even in his youth he was very likely similar: 'it must have been true'.

Still, a few chapters later we find Plutarch suppressing any mention of Antony campaigning with Caesar in Gaul, something he must surely have known: that allows him to pretend that it was Curio, once again, who brought Antony over to Caesar in 50 (5. 2). Later in the same chapter he gives Antony a

[58] *Ant.* 2. 4–8, reshaping Cic. *Phil.* 2. 44–8.

speech which his source (it seems) ascribed to Caesar himself
(5. 10).[59] In these cases one's nose twitches a little more. Did
Plutarch really believe 'it must have been' like that, so clearly
'must have been' that Antony could not have been at Caesar's
side in Gaul, whatever his sources said, or that Caesar could not
have delivered his speech? Hardly; but it again suited the characterization to make Antony the passive one, and he was prepared to bend the truth in a small way. Similarly at the
beginning of *Caesar*: there Plutarch seems to have rearranged
Caesar's early adventures in order to place his period of study
in Rhodes just before his first rhetorical successes in Rome
(*Caes.* 3–4).[60] It is an elegant arrangement, allowing Plutarch
to group together all the foreign adventures before his narrative
focus returns decisively to Rome; it would have been far more
disruptive to have Caesar's first steps in Rome, then move off to
Greece, then back to Rome again. It is pleasing logically as
well. Caesar learns his rhetoric, then comes back and applies it.
But did Plutarch really think 'it must have been true', just
because it is all so neat? Surely not. Here he was adapting the
truth for literary purposes, and he knew it. And this is particularly clear when he gives strictly contradictory accounts of the
same events in different *Lives*. The debates of December 50 and
early January 49 are described inconsistently in *Pompey*, *Caesar*,
and *Antony*; the Lupercalia incident of 44 is interpreted differently in *Antony* and in *Caesar*; Antony's behaviour at Philippi
comes out differently in his own *Life* and in *Brutus*. *Crassus* (7. 7)
presents a summary of Roman politics over thirty years which
represents Pompey as the steady representative of the established order and Caesar as head of the *populares*; compared with
Pompey and *Caesar*, a ludicrous oversimplification. Clodius is in
one *Life* an independent figure, in another a subservient follower of the triumvirs' will. Plutarch's view of the origins of the
Roman civil war is subtly different in different *Lives*.[61] Yet all
these *Lives* seem to have been prepared at the same time, and

---

[59] Cf. Pelling (1988) on both passages. Plutarch probably also transfers certain
actions from Curio to Antony (5. 6, with my note), but that is too controversial to serve
as evidence here. Even if he did, he could reasonably infer that Antony and Curio
would have followed a similar line (as many modern scholars have been happy to
accept): 'it must have been true'.

[60] Pelling (1980), 128–9.

[61] Pelling (1980), 131–5, 139–40; (1986), 161–3; (1988), 126–30, 144–5, and 171–3.

with the same material: he simply cannot have thought them all true.

Coriolanus is interesting here. As we have already seen, there seems an unusually large degree of retrojection here—the envy of his youthful rivals, and the way they made excuses to themselves. There is also considerable tidying of detail: it looks as if Coriolanus' first military service has been transferred to the completely wrong battle, Lake Regillus, simply because the Dioscuri appeared at the battle of Regillus—all an appropriately miraculous and charged setting.[62] One suspects that such tidying was deliberate, though one cannot be certain: if it was, Plutarch might even have pretended that 'it must have been true', though possibly he would have found that a little strained. But what is perhaps most interesting is the treatment of Coriolanus' relationship with his mother.

Marcius set himself to surpass his own record in courage. And since he was always eager to attempt fresh exploits, he added one deed of valour to another and heaped spoils upon spoils ... But while other men displayed their courage to win glory for themselves, Marcius' motive was always to please his mother. The delight that she experienced when she saw him crowned, the tears of joy she wept as she embraced him—these things were for him the supreme joy and felicity that life could offer. (Epaminondas was very similar ...) It was his mother's will and choice which dictated his marriage, and he continued to live in the same house with her, even after his wife had borne his children. (*Cor.* 4. 5–8, trans. Scott-Kilvert)

This is one case where we can be sure what Plutarch was doing to his sources, for it is clear that he is dependent on Dionysius of Halicarnassus here;[63] and it is interesting how little Dionysius offers to support Plutarch's recasting. From Dionysius he knew the famous scene where his wife and mother, together in the same house, were persuaded to set off to urge Coriolanus to give up his campaign against Rome (*AR* 8. 40. 1, etc.): thus Plutarch knew that 'they continued to live in the same house even after marriage'. But the psychological recasting, 'it was his mother's will and choice that dictated the marriage', seems to be his own inference. Coriolanus was that sort of man, his wife and mother were evidently close—of course the mother must have

[62] Russell (1963), 23–4.
[63] Russell (1963).

approved, and of course her approval must have been the decisive factor. From a speech of Dionysius Plutarch also knew that Coriolanus was an orphan. But that speech reads very differently (8. 51. 4): 'when have I ever been free of grief or fear from you, from the moment you reached manhood? When have I ever been able to rejoice, seeing you fighting war upon war, battle upon battle, gaining wound upon wound?' That really is very limp, and it is hardly Plutarch's (or Shakespeare's) Volumnia: Plutarch's Volumnia weeps with joy at Coriolanus' martial successes, and would indeed be deeply ashamed and outraged if he did *not* fight war upon war, and battle upon battle. Once again, Plutarch is thoroughly reinterpreting: he has his own view of Coriolanus' personality, especially his dependence on his mother. That itself seems to be largely read back from the final scene, where Coriolanus collapses before her pressure: what sort of man must he have been to react like this, what sort of relationship must widowed mother and orphaned son have had? What sort of person must Volumnia have been? And Plutarch comes up with this, a psychologically deep and not unconvincing portrait. And could he have answered, 'it must have been like that'? I think he could: it was his way of getting at the truth, to apply later actions and events to reach a portrait which made psychological sense.[64]

So what do we conclude about Plutarch's attitude to the truth? He does not always behave as we would, certainly; he tidies and improves, and in some cases he must have known he was being historically inaccurate. But the process has limits, and the untruthful tidying and improving is never very extensive. The big changes, the substantial improvements tend to come where he could genuinely claim—'yes, it must have been like that'. Nor is this one of the features which vary significantly among the *Lives*: the examples both of reconstruction and of

---

[64] Just as Erikson explicitly started from later events to reconstruct the childhood of Martin Luther, in his case stressing an abnormal relationship with his *father*. 'A clinician's training permits, and in fact forces, him to recognize major trends even when the facts are not all available; at any point in a treatment he can and must be able to make meaningful predictions as to what will prove to have happened; and he must be able to sift even questionable sources in such a way that a coherent predictive hypothesis emerges'; the reconstruction of Luther's youth should proceed similarly. (Erikson (1958), 50, cf. esp. 37.)

untruthful improvement can be drawn as readily from *Caesar* as from *Antony*, from *Themistocles* as from *Theseus*. Even when he was at his most historically interested and alert, there was nothing in such rewriting to make him ashamed.

Yet it is not wholly satisfactory simply to conclude that Plutarch is usually reconstructing the truth, but sometimes consciously sacrificing it. It is so hard to believe that he thought he was doing anything totally different in the two cases: the techniques he employs in making Curio lead Antony into licentiousness (reconstructing truth), and then over to Caesar (sacrificing it), are simply too similar, and Plutarch surely did not regard them as belonging in different categories. It is better to start from the basic point that the process has limits: he will not bend the truth too far, and the big changes are indeed classifiable as 'creative reconstruction'. At some times—when, for instance, he simplifies his whole political interpretation in *Crassus*, or when he transfers a speech in *Antony*—he seems to us to be going a long way; but he is never there falsifying things that are central to the particular *Life*, even if they were central to others. He is perhaps giving his subject a bigger role, but a role which helps to support his characterization of the man as a whole, Crassus as an oscillator between political extremes, Antony as submissive and passive: once again, he is only helping the truth along a little, allowing himself some licence to support a picture generally true. It is not, I think, that the concept of truth was itself different;[65] if it had been, such disquisi-

---

[65] This is one point on which I disagree with Woodman (1988), though in practice the difference is largely semantic. Woodman argues for a different concept of truth, one more closely connected with impartiality (esp. 73–4, 82–3) and plausibility (87, 92–3); I prefer to think of a similar concept of truth, but one which was pursued and presented with different narrative conventions and licences. Woodman's position is neater, but I prefer mine for reasons analogous to those given above. Like Plutarch (above, p. 24), historians discuss the difficulties of recovering the truth; bias certainly figures among these to a greater degree than we might expect (Woodman, 73–4), but historians knew that there were other problems too, especially those concerned with the nature of documentary evidence. It is hard to see why, for instance, the loss of records in the Gallic sack (Livy 6. 1, cf. *Mor.* 326 A) or the confusion of the early *fasti* (Livy 2. 21. 4) or the secrecy of imperial records (Dio 53. 19) should be a hindrance to recovering truth, if truth be interpreted in terms of impartiality and plausibility. Such passages defy interpretation unless truth meant something close to what we mean today, events as they really happened, history *wie es eigentlich gewesen ist*. It does not follow, of course, that truth was pursued in the same way and with the same rigour in detail: though we too have our unrigorous licences, as I shall argue below.

tions as that in *Aristides* 1 would be hard to fathom. It is simply that the boundary between truth and falsehood was less important than that between acceptable and unacceptable fabrication, between things which were 'true enough' and things which were not. Acceptable rewriting will not mislead the reader seriously, indeed he will grasp more of the important reality if he accepts what Plutarch writes than if he does not. Truth matters; but it can sometimes be bent a little.

3. PLUTARCH AND HISTORIOGRAPHY

When defended in such theoretical terms, Plutarch's habits admittedly seem to invite Dover's disdain for 'a pretentious kind of falsehood' which, he thinks, 'the Greeks had more sense than to call . . . "ideal truth" ';[66] just as Plutarch's variations in critical rigour seem to imply an approach which a modern biographer would find bizarre. But perhaps Plutarch's mode of thought is less alien to us than we readily admit. On a cool estimate historians and biographers still regard different sorts of rigour as appropriate for different sorts of material. Take childhood anecdotes, for instance: can we really believe that the infant Gaitskell startled a strange lady by singing from his pram, 'Soon shall you and I be lying / each within our narrow tomb'? Yet that is what the standard biography claims, without reserve. Or that young Florence Nightingale took a morbid pleasure in sewing back together the dolls which her healthy elder sister had torn apart? A family friend was most indignant at that suggestion! Or that Franklin Roosevelt had such demonic authority and confidence that he *knew* a bird would wait on a tree while he walked several hundred yards for a gun?[67] The three biographies in question have different styles; but in each case this is not the sort of material which would have crept into the adult chapters. 'Helping the truth along', indeed.

And a whole new aspect of this discourse has now crept in. Modern writers have big ideas, grand interpretative themes,

---

[66] Dover (1981), p. n. 2, interestingly criticized by Woodman (1988), 197–215: it will be clear that I am in sympathy with most but not all of Woodman's points.

[67] For the first two instances (from Williams (1979) and Strachey (1918)), cf. Pelling (1990), 224, 240–1; for the last, Davis (1973), 83–4.

which they wish to present: so of course did the ancients. But
the ancients presented these through careful and supple narrative technique, while moderns prefer to set out their ideas and
arguments more directly, in passages of analysis rather than
narrative.[68] In such passages the *licensed overstatement* is extremely familiar—the sort of remark which emerges in exam-
ination papers with 'discuss' after it. Consider, for instance, the
following passage of A. J. P. Taylor:[69]

In his lazy fashion, Baldwin truly represented the decade. The ordinary Englishman, never attending church or chapel, probably without
a Bible in his house, expecting his children to swallow unquestion-
ingly a Christian education, was an exact parallel to the statesman
who made speeches supporting the League of Nations and never
thought of asking the chiefs of staff how the League could be supported. Façade became reality for a generation trained in cinema
palaces. Churchill really thought that there was a glorious Indian empire still to be lost; Baldwin really imagined that he was defending
democratic virtues; Left-wing socialists really anticipated a Fascist
dictatorship in England. So the watchers in the cinemas really felt
that life was going on among the shadows of the screen. Of course no
one supposed that the tinny words would take on substance or that
even the most menacing figures among the shadows could reach out
and hit the audience on the head. That is what happened before the
decade ended. The pretence turned out to be no pretence. Or perhaps
it merely eclipsed the real life underneath.

It is very familiar in style, especially in first and last paragraphs
of chapters (and that is a last paragraph). Nor is it bad writing,
even if we feel there are too many 'trulies', 'exacts', and 'real-
lies'. But some of those sentences are not true, at least not literally, really, or exactly true. *Never* attending church or chapel?
An *exact* parallel? *Never* thought? And so on. Some, of course,
we would unambiguously class as metaphors, such as the cine-

---

[68] True, narrative history is drifting back into fashion, or rather respectability: it can
never be out of fashion as long as people like stories, and care whether they are true. Cf.
esp. Stone (1985). But a feature of the new narrative historians is that 'analysis remains
as essential to their methodology as description, so that their books tend to switch, a
little awkwardly, from one mode to the other' (Stone (1985), 91, cf. 75). Witness Stone
himself: his next ch. begins 'one of the more striking features of Christianity has been its
perennial tendency to fission . . . There are two ways of looking at this crisis of European civilization . . .', and so on. Very different from the ancient style.

[69] Taylor (1965), 319–20.

matic analogy; but the whole passage in fact has a metaphorical quality.[70] It is a different sort of 'licence' from that which a Plutarch, a Livy, or a Tacitus would employ, but it could well be categorized in the same terms. The author helps the truth along, the sentences are true enough, it would be obtuse to draw a boundary between those sentences which are just about true ('Churchill really . . .') and those which are just about not ('The ordinary Englishman . . .'); the reader will understand more by accepting them all than by disbelief. 'A pretentious kind of falsehood', perhaps, but one we instinctively understand and applaud. This is good, stimulating, provocative history.

We are already comparing Plutarch with modern historians; what, finally, about the relationship with ancient historiography? It has not been possible here to carry through anything but a fitful comparison: but only a little has been found to support Momigliano's contention. True, in the first section we found that some *Lives* were closer to historiography than others, and in those others the truth is pursued in a less rigorous way: some slightly less censored material can slip in. But even there Plutarch's commitment to the truth was seen to be generally insistent, intelligent, and impressive. And when we consider the rewriting of material, it is clear that the same approach can be extended to the historians. Not, of course, that every historian would exercise his licence in the same way and with the same limits: doubtless Timaeus assumed different limits from Polybius, Antias from Sisenna, perhaps even Herodotus from Thucydides. On the whole Plutarch seems to belong with the more scrupulous group; and we can certainly see him operating in a similar way to the great historians who survive. With Livy or Tacitus, for instance, one will again find many examples which fit Wiseman's 'must have been true' rubric—but some, usually less important, cases which do not. Almost at random, let us take a few instances from the first pages of Livy.

---

[70] One is again reminded of Hayden White's emphasis on 'metaphor' as one of his four modes of discourse, the others being metonymy, synecdoche, and irony: cf. White (1973) and (1978), esp. 72–4, 252–3. But White, as usual with his borrowings of figures of speech, means something rather different, and indeed rather peculiar: for instance, he strangely associates 'metaphor' with the sixteenth and seventeenth centuries. Others evidently find this schematism more illuminating than I do.

It is not hard to detect that Livy has rewritten the vulgate version of the Aeneas legend, exaggerating the speed of Rome's early growth and suppressing the story of bad feeling between Lavinia and Ascanius.[71] 'Must have been true'? Perhaps: Livy might indeed have assumed that Rome's origins must have been in keeping with her later glories—though the concern for a rapid, nervous, and appropriately elevating introduction will also have played a part. But then a few chapters later one can detect further rewriting of the detail of Romulus' campaigns, carefully allocating one domestic event to follow each invasion: Caenina invades, and a temple is founded to Jupiter Feretrius; Antemna invades, and the offer of citizenship is made; Crustumerium invades, and colonies are sent (1. 10. 1–11. 4). Livy's source-material was much more messy, it seems: two invasions, then all the domestic decisions, then a last invasion.[72] Did Livy really think his smoother sequence 'must have been true', because events in life are always smooth, never messy? Surely not: this was sacrificing the truth,[73] because in this case sequence hardly mattered: it was a 'relatively harmless literary device',[74] no more. A little later he seems to have rewritten the first steps of Tullus Hostilius' reign to make him more *ferox* than his sources claimed: it is he, not Cluilius, who now stirs up the

[71] Cf. esp. 1. 3. 4; the battle between Ascanius and Mezentius after Aeneas' death was famous (Cato, *Origines*, frs. 9–11 P), and Livy's claim that Mezentius and the Etruscans were acquiescent on Aeneas' death is especially startling. 1. 3. 1 is similarly very bland, in view of Cato's story of Lavinia's flight from Ascanius to the woods (fr. 11 P, cf. Dion. Hal. *AR* 1. 70. 2–3).

[72] The fuller version of Dion. Hal. *AR* 2. 32–7 probably gives a fair idea of what Livy found in the source or sources they (surely) share. All such speculations are admittedly suspect; but at least one can here understand why Livy should have smoothed and abbreviated a version similar to that of Dionysius, but not why Dionysius should have confused and roughened a version with Livy's articulation but more detail. Cf. Burck (1934), 143, and (on the methodological principle) 5–6.

[73] Presuming, of course, that Livy thought his source's version true. But Professor Woodman may well be right when he suggests to me that Livy accepted his source's version on the same terms as he expected readers to accept his own: that is, he assumed that predecessors had smoothed events so thoroughly that their sequence or detail did not deserve any particular respect. That interpretation does not fundamentally affect the point I am making here. Livy would still be showing the same respect or disrespect for accurate sequence: on Woodman's view, he would simply be taking for granted the same assumptions in others.

[74] Cornell (1986), 73, who uses the phrase of small-scale fictitious inventions, acceptable enough (he thinks) provided they did not do violence to the traditional facts. In this case, they did not do *much* violence, and that was enough.

war with Alba.[75] 'Must have been true'? Yes, in this case it must: Livy had a clear idea of Tullus' character from later events, and could naturally assume that he must have been *ferox* here too.[76] But would Livy really have thought his techniques in the second case were different in kind from those in the first and third? Again, surely not. In small ways, his licence ran to improving the truth; but in general, the same techniques produced reconstruction rather than sacrifice.

More substantial and contentious instances may be drawn from Tacitus. Let us assume (though it cannot be quite demonstrated) that, in recounting the death of Augustus and accession of Tiberius, Tacitus borrows some details from events forty years later, when Claudius died and Nero succeeded: in particular, the detail of the barricades in the streets (*Ann.* 1. 5. 4) may well be imported from those later events (cf. *Ann.* 12. 68. 3). Tacitus certainly wishes us to notice the parallel between the two sequences, pointing it by by a series of verbal repetitions.[77] Possibly he 'may intend to suggest that Tiberius' accession was as questionable, disreputable, and indeed criminal as Nero's',[78] but that is unlikely to be the most helpful approach: this is not simply a blackening device. It is surely clear that Tacitus is interested in the character of the principate itself, not just the *principes*, and is concerned to analyse it, not simply denigrate. He is vitally involved in pointing the patterns of behaviour which are imposed on every new *princeps* alike: that is one reason why so many of the specific traits of Tiberius' principate are foreshadowed in the retrospect of Augustus—the ruthless elimination of rivals, the personal grudges, the bloodiness, the *luxus*, the choice of a successor who is even worse (1. 9–10). And

---

[75] Dion. Hal. *AR* 3. 2–5 again seems to come from the same origin. Note especially the contrast between Dion. Hal. 3. 5. 1 and Livy 1. 23. 4 on Cluilius' death: for Dionysius it is *genuinely* a divine visitation, 'because he stirred up a war between mother-city and colony that was neither just nor necessary'; for Livy Tullus *claims* that this was divine intervention, but that is simply piece of his fierce bluster. Livy's portrayal fits his individual portrayal of Tullus so closely that we are again surely dealing with his own rewriting.

[76] On Tullus' *ferocia*, Ogilvie (1965), 105–6, though this seems less traditional a characteristic than Ogilvie implies. Indeed, it is hard to trace much colour at all in his characterization before Livy: there is little in Dion. Hal., and Cic. *De rep.* 2. 31–2 does not suggest *ferocia*; not much can be extracted from Piso frs. 10, 13 P.

[77] On all this cf. Goodyear (1972), 125–9 and bibliography there cited.

[78] Goodyear (1972), 126; cf. e.g. Woodman (1979), 154.

now each accession necessarily proceeds on the same pattern. That is a point worth making for its own sake, and as important to Nero's principate as to Tiberius'. (It is sad that we lack the opening of Gaius' reign, and of Claudius': very likely some aspects of this pattern would have been even more insistent.) If the narrative here is given extra details to make the parallels closer, could Tacitus have felt 'it must have been true'? Yes, he could: if he concluded that events genuinely repeated them-selves in the same pattern, that in itself was grounds for infer-ring what must have happened, whether or not his source chanced to mention it. They must have wheeled out the barri-cades, because that is what they always do. He was probably right. It is not quite the modern historian's way, at least not with factual detail;[79] but it is not an absurd way.

Yet, again, we find the same paradox as with Plutarch: Taci-tus' techniques here are so similar to those he employs else-where, in cases where the 'must have been' analysis seems inadequate. Let us take another instance which Woodman has brilliantly illuminated,[80] the description of Germanicus' visit to the remains of Varus' camp (*Ann.* 1. 61–2), immediately fol-lowed by the German attack on Caecina (1. 63–7). Woodman has shown that the accounts are very close to two passages in the earlier *Histories*, 2. 70 and 5. 14–15: much too close for co-incidence. The events can hardly have been so similar to each other in fact, and probably not in Tacitus' sources for the two periods. It is then highly unlikely that much of the material in *Ann.* 1 is drawn from his sources for AD 15: whether or not Woodman's term of 'self-imitation' is the best way to describe it,[81] there must certainly be a high degree of imaginative free composition in the *Annals* passage; and very likely in the *Histor-ies* passages too.[82] In this case Tacitus can hardly be intending

[79] With mental detail, our conventions are of course different: what 'Livia' (or Tiberius, or Caesar, or Pericles) *'must have* intended' is often inferred on similarly slen-der grounds, and ones which postulate no better and no worse a model of continuity in human experience.

[80] Woodman (1979) and (1988), 168–79. Much of Woodman's analysis is rightly fol-lowed by Goodyear (1981).

[81] West and Woodman (1979) themselves suggest an alternative, and I think prefer-able, explanation in their Epilogue (195–6).

[82] 'Much of what we are told at 64–5 may have happened not in A.D. 15, but in A.D. 70' (Goodyear (1981), 108): an over-sanguine view. It is more likely that it did not happen at all: if Tacitus could 'invent' the one, he could invent the other as well.

to emphasize the parallels between AD 15 and events sixty years later: Woodman is surely right, and this would be pointless. It is rather that Tacitus finds all these sequences independently worth dramatic elaboration, and in each case sets about it in a similarly enthusiastic way.

We can also understand why Tacitus thinks this scene worth elaborating. It is not just a question of rhetorical effect and entertainment, though those interests doubtless played a part: this is a most critical moment, with Caecina himself in danger of re-enacting Varus' disaster. Well indeed may Caecina dream of Varus' ghost beckoning him to follow, or Arminius cry out that this is a second Varus delivered into his hands; and the description of Varus' camp even seems to be finessed to make the parallel closer.[83] Indeed, it is not extravagant to think of the sequence as recreating a picture of Varus' disaster itself, much as the early books of the *Iliad* subtly re-enact the earlier events of the war.[84] The effect is worth gaining, for Varus' defeat is so important in the background to Germanicus' campaign : this is the very lowly base from which his glorious successes of the next book will rise; and, just as suggestively, it conveys the dangers of the old-fashioned type of war which is Germanicus' speciality, and so alien to Tiberius. But 'must' all Tacitus' detail have been true, in his eyes? Surely not: once we have to postulate a third category, not quite 'true', not 'false', but 'true *enough*', that surely is where this case belongs. If pressed, Tacitus would have had to admit that this was imagination, not fact: but he would have been surprised to be pressed. It was a reasonable exercise of his licence to convey points of serious historical interest and insight. And it is again hard to believe that he would have thought he was doing anything very different here and in the case of Tiberius' accession. There too he is manipulating and creating detail, in that case to bring two events into clearer connexion with one another, here simply to make the moment

---

[83] 1. 61. 2 seems to suggest *two* camps for Varus (cf. Koestermann (1956), p. 443 n. 32 and Goodyear (1972) ad loc.): not quite what we would have inferred from the description of Varus' march at Cassius Dio 56. 19–21, but suggestively close to Caecina's efforts at 1. 63. 4–64. 3 and 1. 65. 7. Hence read *prima* with MSS at 1. 61. 2, not Koehler's *primo* (approved by Woodman (1979), p. 232 n. 2).

[84] Virgilian influence is of course important too: 'with this identification of Caecina with Varus, the present and past merge into one, as they do so often in the *Aeneid* . . .', Woodman (1988), 174, cf. 169.

more arresting and thought-provoking. As it happens, we would say that one was reconstructing, one was sacrificing, truth: our boundary falls between the two. The ancients' limit fell a little further on, and in some cases quite a long way further on; but it does not mean that it was ahistorical. Tacitus had a historical point to make, and employed his licence to make it more clearly.

Two last points, both suggesting ways in which this analysis of Plutarch suggests morals for historiography. First, we have seen that Plutarch's critical alertness is a variable rather than a constant: in less historical and more fluid areas he could be distinctly less rigorous than when writing of a Themistocles or a Caesar. Yet all these *Lives* belong in the same series. Herodotus' *logoi* and Livy's pentads and decades are also fused into a single work; doubtless with, in some senses at least, a greater unity than Plutarch thought appropriate for his series—but there too it is dangerous to assume that their principles or practice were always on the same lines. In describing Egypt, doubtless, Herodotus goes a long way to tidy his material. When he writes of Helen, he surely does claim that Egyptian sources have told him a story which in fact owes more to his own creative art (2. 112–20):[85] it is a Greek story, clearly owed to the *Odyssey* and to Stesichorus (and just possibly Hesiod, though fr. 358 MW is poor evidence). Certainly, Greek travellers or immigrants could have taken the story with them generations before, and Herodotus could have heard it out there[86] (though it is more difficult to believe that it was told him by his notorious priests)[87]—assuming, of course, that he went there at all. But he could not have heard it *like this*—it is too close to the Greek literary forebears, too clean, too ungarbled and uncon-

---

[85] Fehling (1971), 46–50, to which this whole paragraph is heavily indebted; but I take a less sceptical view of Herodotus' commitment to the truth, even if his 'licences' sometimes startle us.

[86] Cf. Henige (1982), 81 ff.: a particular danger for modern oral historians is that 'a great deal of testimony obtained from informants is really feedback; that is, it originated as information that entered the society and was absorbed into its traditions because it proved useful or entertaining'. Armayor (1978), 65, here seems to me too sceptical. Lienhardt (1985), 147, reports a case in the 1870s of simplified Christian eschatological doctrine being fed back to a missionary-traveller, who was less surprised than he ought to have been: a suggestive parallel.

[87] On these problematic priests cf. Fehling (1971), 54 ff.; Armayor (1978); West (1985), 298 and n. 97. On the other side, Lloyd (1975), 89–114.

taminated by disparate elements. The only real Egyptian feature is the bias: the hostility to Paris and Menelaus, who both abuse the laws of hospitality, and the contrast with the upright Egyptian king Proteus. But whatever Herodotus has done here and in similar cases, we should not necessarily infer that he proceeded similarly in later books, when he was dealing with more solid material. The difference between Helen and Xerxes was as great for him as the difference between Theseus and Caesar for Plutarch, or between Romulus and Pompey for Livy. Nor should we assume that Tacitus would naturally place his inventive limits in the same place with a romantic figure like Germanicus, in a remote and eerie forest, and with the grinding detail of senatorial business in Rome. There is more than a little of Plutarch's Sertorius about Tacitus' Germanicus, living in the same period but a different world from his harder-headed peers, and one which demanded description in a different style.[88] Even with Helen, too, we should not assume that Herodotus' procedure was simply fictional and ahistorical. If he *did* hear a garbled, contaminated Egyptian version, would he necessarily think it improper to compare it with his Greek literary authorities, and 'correct' the Egyptian version in their light? The aspects of the Egyptian version confirmed by Greek sources would seem more credible, and more worth retaining. If he sensed a garbling, it would be tactful to remove it: 'this is what they must have meant . . .'. Again, not a wholly absurd procedure,[89] but one which could easily leave a version more Greek than Egyptian—except, of course, for that irreducible bias.

Finally, a more general reflection. It is correct and important to observe the frequency of free composition in the ancient historians: Woodman is absolutely right to stress the central nature of *inventio* in theory and practice. That should now be

[88] On Sertorius, above, pp. 30–1.

[89] Nor very different, for instance, from the procedure followed by a biographer of a living person today, if he found after an interview that his subject's own reminiscences were contradicted in unimportant detail by a documentary record. In such cases, a certain amount of discreet tidying and cleaning up is part of the job. Cf. Henige (1982), 66–73, on the dangers of imposing one's own acculturated interpretations on material gathered in the field, and in particular the difficulties of integrating oral and written material. West (1985), 304–5, has some very valuable remarks on the relevance of such contemporary experience for our view of Herodotus.

taken as read. But it need not follow that the procedure has no limits. Plutarch, as we have seen, would fabricate more than we would, but there remains a stern divide between his creations and those of literary biography; there are still so many things which he would *not* invent. Reality can be bent, but not too far. We naturally place our limits and distinctions in a slightly different place; we too have our licences to improve, but exercise them rather differently. What is important is to try to discriminate exactly where the ancient limits were drawn, where historians would fabricate and where they would stop. There is still a gulf between Thucydides and pseudo-Callisthenes, between history and fiction. And that distinction, it seems to me, may be drawn because history will only invent and improve (*a*) within certain limits, however startling we may sometimes find them; (*b*) sometimes to overrule and reject certain well-attested 'hard-core' facts,[90] but more usually to supplement them and give them added clarity and vitality; and (*c*) ultimately with a historical purpose: that is, historians would hope to delight and divert their audience, but to do so by deepening their insight, helping them to understand events as they really happened and people as they really behaved. In this, Plutarch and the historians are at one.

[90] I draw the phrase 'hard-core facts' from Woodman (1988) (esp. 88–94), with whom I here wholly agree. I am less certain that we are at one on the first criterion, where he would assume different and more generous limits (I cannot for instance follow him in his treatment of Thucydides' plague, 32–40); or on the third, where his emphasis suggests a different balance between diversion and historical analysis. But his Preface (pp. xi–xii) does enter a caveat, and he readily accepts that diversion and 'deepening insight' often go hand in hand.

III

Greek Poetry in the Antonine Age

E. L. BOWIE

Although the Antonine Age produced much less Greek poetry
than prose, there is still far more than can be assessed ad-
equately in a single paper, and to help me in my task I focus on
a shorter period, the reigns of Hadrian, Pius, and Marcus. Even
here I must be selective, but I make no apology for including
the reign of Hadrian, since so many of the poets of the period
AD 117–80 flourished under him, some indeed as a direct result
of his interest.

I. EPIGRAMS

I discuss the poets of this period by genre (although some operate in more than one) and begin with epigram, a form that
retained its popularity century after century while that of
others waxed and waned. It remained popular for a number of
reasons: any well-read person (*pepaideumenos*) knew hexameter
and elegiac models that could suggest words and ideas, and did
not need to be a professional poet to write metrically for a few
lines. Moreover epigrams were short enough to risk on a
readership of friends, or on a convivial gathering, and continued to have a function in public life—particularly epitaphs,
but also dedicatory, honorific, and commemorative inscriptions. Thousands of such functional epigrams composed in this
period all over the Greek-speaking world survive on stone,
betraying various levels of skill and education, while a few,
mostly by established writers of prose or poetry, were gathered
into ancient anthologies. Although many of the former are
doubtless by local professional poets, very few are signed or precisely dated, and much more preliminary work needs to be
done before a history of Roman imperial epigram could be

written.[1] Later I shall pick out a few examples. But first I wish
to look at the poems that survive in a manuscript tradition,
since they are sometimes numerous enough to guide us to the
characteristic features of an individual or generation.

To judge from what survives in the *Palatine Anthology*, the
most favoured type of literary epigram in the latter part of the
first century AD had been the satirical, developed in Greek by
Lucillius and Nicarchus and carried to its limits in Latin by
Martial.[2] The only poem attributed to Trajan in the anthology
is in this genre, and we know of at least one by Hadrian.[3] It
continued to flourish in his reign in the hands of two Greeks
whose connections are with the province Asia, Ammianus and
Pollianus. One of Pollianus' most interesting poems disparages
derivative, Homerizing narrative epic and enrols its author in
the freer and less imitative tradition of elegy:

> Τοὺς κυκλίους τούτους, τοὺς αὐτὰρ ἔπειτα λέγοντας,
> μισῶ, λωποδύτας ἀλλοτρίων ἐπέων.
> καὶ διὰ τοῦτ᾽ ἐλέγοις προσέχω πλέον· οὐδὲν ἔχω γὰρ
> Παρθενίου κλέπτειν ἢ πάλι Καλλιμάχου.
> θηρὶ μὲν οὐατόεντι γενοίμην, εἴ ποτε γράψω,
> εἴκελος, ἐκ ποταμῶν χλωρὰ χελιδόνια.
> οἱ δ᾽ οὕτως τὸν Ὅμηρον ἀναιδῶς λωποδυτοῦσιν,
> ὥστε γράφειν ἤδη μῆνιν ἄειδε, θεά. (*AP* 11. 130)

These cyclic poets, those poets who say 'But then',
I hate them, plunderers of others' lines.
And so I am more attached to elegies: for I have nothing
To steal from Parthenius, or yet Callimachus.

---

[1] Kaibel's *Epigrammata Graeca* of 1878 (henceforth cited simply as Kaibel) and Peek's *Griechische Vers-Inschriften* of 1955 (henceforth *GVI*) remain basic, but the former is desperately obsolete, and of the latter only the first volume—epitaphs—has appeared. Many of the hundreds of epigrams to be published, or republished, since 1878 were worked on by Louis Robert, and his views, scattered through his voluminous writings, must always be taken seriously. Only a few poems either epigraphically transmitted or from the *Palatine Anthology* figure in Page (1981), and the notes in Beckby's and in the Budé edition (still lacking Books 10 and 12) are very selective. Robert (1968) is invaluable on Lucillius; Page (1978) is our only modern commentary on a *corpus* of an anthology poet of the imperial period. For a brief account of the popularity of epigram and other genres with particular reference to the provinces of Asia and Achaea, see Bowie in *BICS* 55 (forthcoming).

[2] Cf. Laurens (1965), Robert (1968).

[3] Trajan: *AP* 11. 418, cf. Page (1981), 560–1. Hadrian: *AP* 9. 137, Page, 564–5.

Like 'the long-eared beast' may I become, if ever
I write 'from the rivers, green celandine'.
But they plunder Homer so shamelessly
As even to write 'Sing, goddess, of the wrath'.

We shall see when we turn to hexameter poetry that Pollianus was swimming with the tide: indeed he could have expected the approval of Hadrian, who wrote a sepulchral
epigram for Parthenius' tomb.[4] By contrast Ammianus' readiness to attack not simply the rhetorical pretensions of sophists
(e.g. *AP* 11. 147, 150, 152) but the judicial integrity of Hadrian's friend M. Antonius Polemo (*AP* 11. 180, 181) was not
calculated to elicit imperial favour.

Both these poets, of whom Ammianus is demonstrably from
the province Asia, are well represented in the eleventh book of
the *Anthology* and offer interesting sidelights on Antonine culture. There are, however, few individual traits in their poems,
since the stance of the scoptic epigrammatist imposes a uni-
formity of tone and theme. This too impedes any attempt to
determine which epigrams in Book 11 are by Lucian: we can be
confident that several of the 63 that have at various times been
given to him are indeed his, but the ascription of each poem is
precarious, and in this context it is sufficient to note that his en-
gagement with the genre takes its popularity at least into the
150s.[5]

Another pointer to the popularity of satirical epigram is the
anthology of Diogenianus, arguably the first stage in the transmission of all these scoptic poets (and a few others less well
represented) to the *Palatine Anthology* where we find them. Sakolowski argued for its composition around AD 150, though if
Lucian's epigrams did indeed pass through this intermediary a
slightly later date is more likely. The Diogenianus who com-
piled it is most probably a learned doctor from Heracleia Sal-
bace in Caria, though the Suda also alleges a homonym from
Heracleia Pontica: both, according to the Suda, flourished
under Hadrian, but this dating may stem merely from a

[4] *IG* xiv. 1089 = *GVI* 2050 = Page (1981), Hadrian 7. For another Callimachean
démarche by Pollianus cf. *AP* 11. 127.

[5] For a discussion, both general and particular, of the attribution of Lucian's epigrams see Baldwin (1975) and for a probable candidate (and scoptic epigrams by his
contemporary Antiochus of Aegae) see my article in *ANRW* 11. xxxiii/1 (Berlin/N.Y.,
1989), 250–3.

reference to events of his reign which should be treated as no more than a *terminus post quem*.[6] Whatever the exact date of compilation and identity of the compiler, the anthology seems to have been of scoptic and sympotic epigrams. It can thus be used to show that their vogue persisted from the reign of Nero right through to that of Pius, perhaps even Marcus. Whether it then declined we cannot say, since the absence of a comparable third-century anthology may have robbed us of a further wave of poets.

The second century also saw one gifted composer of erotic epigrams, Strato of Sardis. These had been popular in the first century BC, and some of their writers can be allocated to the first half of the first century AD. But they probably received a boost from Rufinus, who seems to have published a collection of his amatory epigrams not later than *c.* AD 80, and perhaps as early as AD 40. The *terminus ante quem* follows from his influence on Martial, persuasively argued for by Cameron, who rebutted Page's case for putting Rufinus as late as AD 400. The earlier limit is given by Rufinus' absence from the *Garland of Philip*, usually thought to have been collected about AD 40, though Cameron sets it under Nero.[7]

Rufinus seems to have influenced Strato, and both (like Ammianus and Pollianus) were from the province Asia. Rufinus hailed from within a day's journey of Ephesus, which he knows well, and both Ephesus and Smyrna are within Strato's geographical horizons.[8] But whereas Rufinus' poems are all of

---

[6] Cf. Sakolowski (1893), 1–93. Sakolowski and others put Diogenianus' anthology as late as 150 or even the reign of Marcus. We have a *terminus post quem* in the notice in the *Et. Magn.* 34. 5 that Hadrian's name Aelius was mentioned in Diogenianus' *Chronika* (perhaps also Aelia Capitolina, but that part of the entry may not be from Diogenianus): and this may indeed be the source of the Suda's dating.

[7] Cameron (1982) and Robert (1982) simultaneously argued against Rufinus' dating by Page (1978). For the date of the *Garland of Philip* see Cameron (1982), Gow and Page (1968), pp. xlv–xlix, and Bowersock (1985).

[8] One of the Rufinus' poems, 1 Page = *AP* 5. 9, shows a good knowledge of Ephesus, but makes clear that his home was not there but somewhere no more than a day's journey away. A number of cities might be considered, but Smyrna is not unlikely for a man well versed in earlier poetry writing sensitively himself. It is accordingly tempting to conjecture that he was an ancestor of the later sophist Claudius Rufinus, *strategos* at Smyrna at the end of the second century, teacher of Hermocrates of Phocaea and perhaps the dedicatee of bk 9 of Phrynichus' *praeparatio sophistica* (Philostratus *VS* 2. 25, 608; *PIR*² C 998). For Strato's home Sardis, *AP* 12. *praef.*, and horizons, ibid. 193, 202, 226.

heterosexual love, Strato writes exclusively about boys. The reasons could be literary: Rufinus had come near to exhausting the available moves in poetry about girls, so Strato turns his pen to the obvious alternative. But another factor surely operates too. Cameron's chronology led him to put Strato's collection, the *Musa puerilis*, a little earlier than 117. This is because he accepted Buchheit's suggestion that Strato's two introductory poems influenced those set at the opening of the *corpus Priapeorum*, dated by Buchheit shortly after Martial.[9] But we have no precise *terminus ante quem* for the *corpus Priapeorum*: *c.* AD 120 or 130 would be just as likely as *c.* AD 110; and one of Strato's satirical epigrams seems to belong in or close to Hadrian's reign, since it is arguably aimed at Artemidorus Capito, a doctor whose edition of Hippocrates we know from Galen to have earned approval by Hadrian.[10] It is probable, then, that Strato's collection was published when Hadrian was already emperor, and some chance that it falls in the period of his two tours of the province Asia, 123–4 and 129, by the latter of which, if not earlier, Hadrian's relationship with the Bithynian Antinoos must have been widely known. It can hardly be a coincidence that Strato's decision to cultivate the pederastic Muse was made under a philhellenic emperor whose homosexual tastes were on public display. It is unfortunate that his subject has alienated so many generations of critics, for he is not simply a prolific poet (about 458 lines in Book 12 are his) but a good one, ready with both wit and passion, and as deserving of a modern edition as Rufinus.[11]

One or two amatory epigrams by other second-century figures may lurk in the *Palatine Anthology*,[12] and it is interesting to find the Platonic philosopher and sophist Apuleius composing some in Latin Africa (*Apol.* 9). The survivals in the

---

[9] Cameron (1982), 171; Buchheit (1962), 109 ff. Clarke (1984) argues that Strato must antedate the domination of Roman coinage in Asia on the grounds that the equivalence of 20 drachmae to a stater is implied by *AP* 12. 239. I doubt if the implication is necessary: the progression 5–10–20 may be the only point, with a *further* escalation in the second line's introduction of χρυσοῦς.

[10] *AP* 11. 117, cf. Galen 15. 21 Kühn, Cameron (1982), 168–71. Clarke (1984), 215–16, is over-sceptical about this identification.

[11] Among the recent work on Strato cf. Clarke (1976) and (1984), Maxwell-Stuart (1972).

[12] Dionysius the sophist, 5. 81 and 82, cf. Page (1981), 44; Fronto 12. 174, 233, cf. Page (1981), 115.

anthology may only be the tip of an iceberg, and as with satirical epigram the absence of a collection later in the second or in the third century may have been crucial.

With dedicatory epigrams and poems commemorating the dead or (less often) the living we move to poetry whose surviving examples on stone greatly outnumber those anthologized in antiquity. It is hard to discern major exponents, and only broad changes in practice stand out (such as the growing preference for hexameters over elegiacs).[13] As I have already said, much more work needs to be done before a synthetic study of this material could be attempted, and my few examples are necessarily unrepresentative.

Few epitaphs on stone can be securely and precisely dated, and even fewer are signed. We know that an elegiac couplet on the sarcophagus of Iulius Hermes at Thessalonice (*GVI* 385) belongs to AD 119, and another from Saitta in Lydia (*GVI* 516) to AD 175, but the poems themselves are unremarkable. More interesting is a signed eighteen-line elegiac epitaph, probably of the second century, commemorating a young woman, Socratea of Paros, who died from haemorrhage during the birth of her third child at the age of 26.[14] The poem blends these details with sonorous poetic language and is a fine piece of work: unusually, it is signed, by an otherwise unknown Dionysius of Magnesia, who may even be the person who carefully checked and emended the stonecutter's text.

It is frustrating that we have no idea what other verses Dionysius composed that encouraged him to sign himself as *poietes*. His work compares well with two epitaphs by Antiphon of Athens on whom we do happen to have further information.

---

[13] Cf. Wifstrand (1933), 155–77. For a concise but full account of the fortunes of various metres in the imperial period see West (1982), 162–85.

[14] *GVI* 1871 = Kaibel 218 = *IG* xii. 5. 310. I note some other datable epitaphs: *IG* vii. 118 = Kaibel 858, 6 elegiac lines for a dead Diogenes at Megara, probably post 126/7 (cf. *IG* ii² 3734); *IG* ii.² 3743 = Kaibel 963, 6 elegiac lines for the statue base of a dead Athenian ephebe Philotimus, dated by the archonship of T. Aur. Philemon to 158/9; *MAMA* ix. 79 = Kaibel 375 = *GVI* 607, from Çavdarhisar in the Aezanitis, an elegiac couplet for the tomb of a horseman Menogenes who died in a plague, so probably AD 165 or shortoy after; *GVI* 1613, 6 elegiac lines by Herodes Atticus on one of his τρόφιμοι or children, probably of the 160s; *IG* xii. 9. 1179, 6 elegiac lines for Amphicles of Chalcis by his homonymous father, probably of the 170s. I discuss these last two, and the poems of Flavius Glaucus of Marathon, some of them epitaphs, and all probably later than AD 180, in *ANRW* II. xxxiii/1 (Berlin/N.Y., 1989), 232–43.

The epitaphs are for brothers from Acharnae, Ti. Flavius Diophantus and Glaucias, whose deaths fell close together soon
after AD 131/2. The poet who signed their epitaphs, Antiphon,
himself an Athenian, also appears in the records of a competition at Thespiae: he was victor in the *prosodion* (as poet) and in
New Comedy (both as poet and as actor): he is, therefore, a
professional.[15] The epitaphs are rather mechanical, although
judgement of the first is impeded by the loss of more than half of
each line. The second runs:

καὶ τόνδ' Ἠλύσιός τε δόμος καὶ χ[ῶρος ἀμείνων]
  Γλαυκίου υἷα μιῆς δεύτερον [ἐκ γενεῆς]
Ζηνὸς ἐνὶ προύχοντα χοροστασί[ηισιν ἔδεκτο],
  αὐτοκασιγνήτωι ξύνδρομ[ον ἀρτιθανεῖ].
ἀλλ' ἐπὶ καὶ τῷ στῆσε πόλις τόδ[ε πὰρ μακάρεσσι]
  λάινον ἀτμήτου σᾶμα θε[οῖσι κόμης].

This man too the Elysian mansion and a [better place] received,
  a son of Glaucias, the second from a single family,
as he showed his prowess in the choral dances for Zeus,
  speeding to join his own brother [who had lately died.]
But for him too the city raised this memorial [before the blessed gods]
  in stone to mark his unshorn [hair.]

Dedicatory poems that can be dated are more numerous,[16]
but many of them are dull and flat: unlike epitaphs, they rarely
have a place for pathos, and usually add little ornament to their
catalogue of the basic facts attending a dedication or the erec-
tion of an honorific statue. Thus there is little rewarding in the
series of short poems (an elegiac couplet, or two or three trimeters) on herms honouring Athenian *kosmetai*, many of them
dated.[17] The longer the poem, the greater the scope, even if it is
not always exploited: the sophist Hadrianus of Tyre's 8 elegiac
lines for a statue at Ephesus honouring Cn. Claudius Severus
(between AD 163 and 169) are no more inspiring than the 4 for
a statue of the sophist Hordeonius Lollianus in Athens of the

---

[15] *IG* ii.² 3963–4 = *GVI* 2025–6. The victories are attested by *IG* vii. 1773 (Thespiae).
[16] For a dedication whose date is unusually secure cf. the 6-line elegiac dedication of
a statue of Hadrian at Syros, *IG* xii. suppl. 239, dated by the accompanying prose text
to 134/5 (*trib. pot.* XIX).
[17] e.g. *IG* ii.² 3744 = Kaibell 964, under Hadrian or Pius; *IG* ii.² 3740 = Kaibel 959
of 142/3 and 2055 = Kaibel 960 of 145/6.

140s.[18] But once there is a story to tell the poetry acquires more life. Thus a group of three poems associated with Eleusis, honouring the hierophant Iulius (?) Heraclides, escapes banality by highlighting his successful preservation of the secret cult-objects (*arrheta*) from the Costoboci in their invasion of AD 171. I cite one which should precede 176, since it makes no mention of the hierophant's initiation of Marcus in that year.[19]

> Μνῆ]μα τόδ' ὑψιφανὲς Δη[οῦ]ς [ζ]α[κόρ]οιο δέδορκας,
> μυρίον ἐν σοφίῃ κῦδος ἐνεγκαμένου,
> ὃς τελέτας ἀνέφηνε καὶ ὄργια πάννυχα μύσταις,
> Εὐμόλπου προχέων ἱμερόεσσαν ὄπα.
> ὃς καὶ δυσμενέων μόθον οὐ τρέσεν, ἀλλ' ἐσάωσεν
> ἄχραντα ἀρρήτων θέσμια Κεκροπίδαις.
> ἁ μάκαρ, ὃν καὶ δῆμος ἐπεστεφάνωσε γεραίρων

· · · · · ·

You behold here the lofty memorial of an attendant of
    Demeter,
  the winner of measureless renown in wisdom,
who displayed the mysteries and night-long rituals to
    initiates,
  pouring forth the lovely voice of Eumolpus:
who also feared not the enemies' battle-din, but saved
  untainted the secret ritual objects for the sons of Cecrops.
Ah! blessed is he, whom the People also crowned in honour

· · · · · ·

This poem neatly sets off conventional praise of hierophants against Iulius' special achievement. Another Eleusinian poem went too far: of the 12 elegiacs for a statue of the *hierophantis* who initiated Hadrian (so probably about AD 130), 8 focus on that initiation, and 4 of these list great figures whom she did not initiate! Excessive too, in a number of ways, are the 38 elegiacs from Marathon (there were once more) commemorating the return of Herodes Atticus, probably in 174/5. But they may serve to remind us that epigram could be developed in the

---

[18] Hadrianus, Kaibel 888*a* = I. Ephesus 1539 = Page (1981), 566–8 (wrongly ascribing to the emperor Hadrian); Lollianus *IG* ii.² 4211 = Kaibel 877. See *ANRW* II. xxxiii/1 (Berlin/N.Y., 1989), 248.

[19] *IG* ii.² 3639 = Kaibel 97*a* (p. 518), on the road from Eleusis to Athens; cf. from Eleusis the 4 elegiacs in *Annuario*, 22–3 (1959–60), 421–7, and *IG* ii.² 3411, 8 or 10 elegiacs mentioning both the rescue of the *arrheta* and Marcus' initiation, hence after AD 176.

direction of other genres—here the hymn[20]—and that some poems we find on stone were intended—perhaps primarily—for recitation.

The standard elegiac, hexameter, or trimeter epigram can also be made more interesting by the choice of a recherché metre. Thus Hadrian used hendecasyllables in his dedication of a bear's *akrothinia* to the god Eros at Thespiae in AD 124, and his civil servant L. Iulius Vestinus combined several metres to construct his *bomos*—a poem composed in lines of varying length in the shape of an altar—to Hadrian himself, perhaps in AD 131/2.[21] His polymetric virtuosity also reflects contemporary taste in recitations, a medium which will have bulked large in an Antonine Greek's perception of poetry. Our best understanding of live poetic performance is actually furnished by a poet with a Greek background who wrote in Latin, Statius, though there are some traces in Book 11 of the *Palatine Anthology*.[22] But a text from Athens, perhaps as early as the first century AD but possibly of the second, honours a poet from Pergamon (who had been given Athenian citizenship), Q. Pompeius Capito, for his virtuosity in extemporizing 'in every rhythm and metre' as well as for his moral dignity.[23]

Before leaving epigram I shall cite some examples from a series of commemorative poems (of the sort parodied by Lucian in *Verae historiae*, 2. 28), many of which have the advantage of being both signed and dated, although only a few can be commended as poetry, viz. the bizarre collection inscribed on the legs of one of the Memnon colossi by Roman tourists. Not surprisingly the most ambitious are by an associate of Hadrian, Julia Balbilla. Her four poems of between 7 and 18 lines clothe elegiac couplets in a superficially Aeolic dialect and are

---

[20] The *hierophantis*, *IG* ii.² 3575; Herodes, *IG* ii.² 3606, cf. Ameling (1983), 2, 205–11, no. 190, and an English translation in Oliver (1970), 34. For dedicatory epigrams that have also acquired hymnic features, cf. below (p. 67) on Marcellus and the inscribed poem of Aristides, Habicht (1969), 144–5, no. 145.

[21] Hadrian's dedication, *IG* vii. 1828 = Kaibel 811 = Page (1981), 5. Vestinus' *bomos*, *AP* 15. 25. I discuss these in forthcoming work on Hadrian.

[22] See Hardie (1983), Coleman (1988). Note also C. Iulius Longianus of Aphrodisias who was honoured at Halicarnassus by 20 statues, one 'next to old Herodotus', for varied displays of poetry of every sort (ποιημάτων παντοδαπῶν ἐπιδείξεις ποικίλας), although he seems chiefly to have been a tragedian, *MAMA* viii. 418.

[23] *IG* ii.² 3800, discussed by Hardie (1983), 22, 83–4.

precisely dated to the visit of the imperial party on 19–21 November of the year 130.[24]

Julia Babilla was granddaughter of the last king of Commagene, C. Iulius Antiochus Epiphanes, and, it seems, of Ti. Claudius Balbillus, prefect of Egypt in AD 55. Her brother, C. Iulius Antiochus Philopappus, was the addressee of Plutarch's essay *De adulatore et amico* and builder (about 114–16 AD) of the impressive mausoleum which still crowns the hill of the Muses in Athens.[25] From this and from his archonship in 87/8 it seems that Athens was Philopappus' principal residence, and Balbilla may well have lived in Athens too, but apart from the poems on Memnon's thigh we have no trace of her existence. We may guess—but it is only a guess—that she had accompanied Hadrian since he left Athens in 129, though her visit to Memnon with Sabina hints that she was chiefly the empress's companion, perhaps her answer to Hadrian's Antinous.

None of Balbilla's verse is great poetry, and some is atrocious. The two best epigrams commemorate Memnon singing for Sabina on 20 November at the first hour and again for Hadrian at the second:

Αὔως καὶ γεράρω, Μέμνον, πάι Τιθώνοιο,
    Θηβάας θάσσων ἄντα Διός πόλιος,
ἢ 'Αμένωθ, βασίλευ Αἰγύπτιε, τὼς ἐνέποισιν
    ἴρηες μύθων τῶν παλάων ἴδριες,
χαῖρε, καὶ αὐδάσαις πρόφρων ἀσπάσδε[ο κ]αὖτ[αν]
    τὰν σέμναν ἄλοχον κοιράνω 'Αδριάνω.
Γλῶσσαν μέν τοι τμᾶξε [κ]αὶ ὤατα βάρβαρος ἄνηρ,
    Καμβύσαις ἄθεος· τῶ ῥα λύγρῳ θανάτῳ
δῶκέν τοι ποίναν τῶτῳ ἀκ[ρῳ] ἄορι πλάγεις
    τῷ νήλας Ἄπιν κάκτανε τὸν θεῖον.
'Αλλ' ἔγω οὐ δοκίμωμι σέθεν τόδ' ὄλεσθ' ἂν ἄγαλμα,
    ψύχαν δ' ἀθανάταν λοῖπον ἔσωθα νόω.
Εὐσέβεες γὰρ ἔμοι γένεται πάπποι τ' ἐγένοντο,
    Βάλβιλλός τ' ὁ σόφος κ' 'Αντίοχος βασίλευς,
Βάλβιλλος γενέταις μάτρος βασιλήιδος ἄμμας,
    τῶ πάτερος δὲ πάτηρ 'Αντίοχος βασίλευς·
κήνων ἐκ γενέας κἄγω λόχον αἷμα τὸ κᾶλον,
    Βαλβίλλας δ' ἔμεθεν γρόπτα τάδ' εὐσέβε[ος]. (Bernand 29)

---

[24] For the date, and the best text of the poems, Bernand (1960), 80–98, nos. 28–31. See also an interesting dicussion of Balbilla by West (1978).

[25] On Philopappus and his ancestry cf. *PIR*[2] I. 161. On the monument Kleiner (1983).

Memnon, son of Dawn and of revered Tithonus, sitting before the
Theban city of Zeus, or Amenoth, Egyptian king, as the priests who
know the ancient tales relate, hail! and may you be keen to welcome
by your cry the august wife too of the lord Hadrian. Your tongue and
ears were cut by a barbarian, the godless Cambyses; hence by his
wretched death he paid the penalty, smitten by the same sword with
which in his heedlessness he slew the divine Apis. But I do not judge
that this statue of yours could perish, and I perceive within me that
your soul shall be immortal.[26] For pious were my parents and grand-
parents, Balbillus the wise and Antiochus the king, Balbillus the
parent of my royal mother, and Antiochus the king, father of my
father. From their line do I too draw my noble blood, and these are
the writings of Balbilla the pious.

The poem for Hadrian has an identifying rubric—'By Julia
Balbilla: when Hadrian Augustus heard Memnon':

> Μέμνονα πυνθανόμαν Αἰγύπτιον ἀλίω αὐγᾳ
> αἰθόμενον φώνην Θηβαΐ⟨κ⟩ω 'πυ λίθω.
> 'Αδρίανον δ' ἐσίδων τὸν παμβασίληα πρὶν αὔγας
> ἀελίω χαίρην εἶπέ ⟨F⟩οι ὡς δύνατον.
> Τίταν δ' ὄττ' ἐλάων λεύκοισι δι' αἴθερος ἵπποις
> ἐν σκίᾳ ὡράων δεύτερον ἦχε μέτρον,
> ὡς χάλκοιο τύπεντος ἴη Μέμνων πάλιν αὔδαν
> ὀξύτονον· χαίρων καὶ τρίτον ἆχον ἰή.
> κοίρανος 'Αδρίανος τοτ' ἄλις δ' ἀσπάσσατο καὖτος
> Μέμνονα κἂν στάλᾳ κάλλιπεν ὀψιγόνοις
> γρόππατα σαμαίνοντά τ' ὄσ' εὔϊδε κὦσσ' ἐσάκουσε·
> δῆλον παῖσι δ' ἔγεντ' ὥς ⟨F⟩ε φίλισι θέοι. (Bernand 28)

I had been told that Memnon the Egyptian, warmed by the ray of the
sun, spoke from his Theban stone. And when he saw Hadrian, king of
all, before the rays of the sun, he greeted him as best he could. But
when Titan, driving through the sky with his white horses, held the
second measure of the hours in shadow, Memnon again uttered a
sharp-toned cry as of bronze being struck: in greeting he also uttered
a third call. Then the lord Hadrian himself also offered ample greetings to Memnon and on the monument left for posterity verses mark-
ing all that he had seen and all he had heard. And it was made clear
to all that the gods loved him.

Of the other verses on Memnon some are clearly the work of

[26] For the improvement to Barnand's text at l. 12, giving 'I perceive within me'
(ἔσωθα νόω) instead of 'I have saved with my mind' (ἔσωσα νόω), see West (1977), 120.

amateurs who would have been better to restrain their Muse, others are by men who call themselves poets, and can sometimes do better. Thus Gallus Marianus, a Hadrianic *epistrategos* of the Thebaid, attempted his own hexameters:

Θήβης ἐν πεδίοισι [παρα]ὶ βα[θ]υδινήεντ[α]
Νεῖλον ἀναπλώσας [σῆς ἔ]κλυ[ε], Μέμνον, ἀϋτῆς
[Γάλ]λος ἐπιτροπ[έω]ν Θηβηΐδος ἡμαθ[οέσσ]ης
[θεινο]μ[έ]νων χαλκῷ ἰκέλη[s ......]ΑΔΕΙΑ.. μῦθος.
Πηλεΐων ἐδάμ[ασσε τ]ὸν Ἡὼ(s) τίκτε ποτ' υἷα.
Ὁπποῖον γὰρ ἐνὶ Τ[ροίῃ Σιμ]όεντος ἔ[π' ὄχ]θαις
ἔβραχε τεύχ[εα κείν]ου, ὅτ' ἐν [κονίη]σι τάνυστο,
τοῖο[ν] νῦν [κ]τυ[πέ]ει λίθος ἄσπετος ἐγγ[ύθι] Ν[εῖλο]υ. (Bernand 36)

In the plain of Thebes by the deep-swirling Nile Gallus, custodian of the sandy Thebaid, sailed up and heard your voice, Memnon, like the bronze of men being struck ... the tale. The scion of Peleus overpowered the son whom Dawn bore; for even as the armour of Memnon clanged at Troy on the banks of the Simoïs, when he sprawled in the dust, so too does the marvellous stone ring out near the Nile.

This is not bad for an amateur. We also have traces of professional poets. A poem in trimeters (but including at least one scazon!) was composed by a companion to a *strategos* of two *nomes* who visited Memnon with his wife on 5 September 122 (as he noted in a prose graffito):

Φουνεισουλανὸς ἐνθαδεὶ [Χα]ρείσιος
στρατηγὸς Ἑρμωνθιός τε [καὶ] Λάτων πάτρης
ἅγιον δάμαρτα Φουλβίαν ἀκήκοεν
σοῦ, Μέμνον, ἠχήσαντος, ἥν[ίχ' ἡ] μήτηρ
ἡ σὴ χυθεῖσα σὸν δέμας ἀπ ...... φει
θύσας δὲ καὶ σπείσας τε ΚΑΡΤ ...
τοῦτ' αὐτὸς ἤϋτησεν εἰς σεῖ[ο κλέος·
    λάλον μὲν Ἀργὼ παῖς ἔ[ὼν .....]
    λάλον δὲ φηγὸν τὴν Διὸ[s ...]
    σὲ δ' αὐτὸν ὅσσοις μοῦνον ἐδ[ράκην ἐμοῖς]
    ὡς αὐτὸς ἠχεῖς καὶ βοήν τιν ...
τοῦτον δέ σοι χάραξε τὸν στίχο[ν] ...
ὃς εἶπε ταὐτῷ φίλτατος τ .... (Bernand 19)

Here Funisulanus Charisius, *strategos* of Hermonthis and the land of Lato, together with his wife Fulvia heard you calling, Memnon, when your mother spread herself [over ?] your body. After offering sacrifice and libation he uttered this himself to your glory: 'That the Argo talked I was told as a child, and that the oak of Zeus [at Dodona] talked: but you alone have I seen with my own eyes, how you yourself called out and uttered a cry.' This verse was inscribed for you by the dearest friend who was in his company, T[——]

Funisulanus seems to have felt less competent to compose a poen than his friend, but that does not prove that the latter was a professional poet. Such, however, was the writer of 4 lines (probably Hadrianic) signed 'By Areios the Homeric poet from the Museum when he heard': the lines are appropriately made up of Homeric phrases:

'Ὦ πόποι, ἦ μέγα θαῦμα τόδ' ὀφ[θαλμοῖσιν ὁρῶμαι]·
ἦ μάλα τις θεὸς ἔνδον, οἳ οὐρανὸν εὐρὺν ἔχουσιν,
ἤϋσεν φωνήν· κατὰ δ'ἔσχεθε λαὸν ἅπαντα.
Οὐ γάρ πως ἂν θνητὸς ἀνὴρ τάδε μηχανόῳτο.
'Αρείου 'Ομηρικοῦ ποιητοῦ ἐκ Μουσείου ἀκούσαντος. (Bernand 37)

Ah me! this is indeed a great wonder that I see with my eyes! Indeed some god within, of those who inhabit the broad heavens, has uttered his cry, and has hushed the whole people. For in no way could a mortal man have devised this.

Two other epigrams by a professional poet may be associated with Hadrian's visit to Memnon in 130. They are by Paion of Side, and in one he writes on behalf of himself:

Αὐδήεντα σε, Μέμνον, ἐγὼ Παιὼν ὁ Σιδήτης
τὸ πρὶν ἐπυνθανόμην, νῦν δὲ παρὼν ἔμαθον. (Bernand 12)

Your talking, Memnon, was before known to me, Paion of Side, by repute, but now I have been here to learn for myself.

The other he writes for a Mettius:[27]

Εἰ καὶ λωβητῆρες ἐλυμήναντο δέμας σόν,
ἀλλὰ σύ γ' αὐδήεις, ὡς κλύον αὐτὸς ἐγώ,
Μέττιος, ὦ Μέμνον· Παιὼν τάδ' ἔγραψε Σιδήτης. (Bernand 11)

Even if vandals have defaced your body, yet you still have your voice, Memnon, as I, Mettius, heard for myself. This was written by Paion of Side.

The contrast between learning by proxy and in person was clearly one that was traditional in Memnon-poems (cf.

[27] *PIR*² M 568 rather than M 572, cf. Robert (1980), 17–21.

Bernand 19 and 28)—did Roman tourists bring Herodotus Book 2 as bedtime reading?—and is here handled somewhat crudely. The 3 lines composed for Mettius (2 hexameters sandwiching a pentameter) are rather better, reworking the *topos* of the contrast between a perishable mortal body and imperishable words, used for example by Callimachus in his epitaph on Heraclitus:[28] applied to Memnon's stone body and non-mortal voice it gives a pleasing conceit.

We can fill out some details of Paion's career as a professional poet. As L. Robert saw, he is surely that P. Aelius Pompeianus Paion of Side whom we already know from a decree of the World Guild of Dionysiac Artists' meeting in Ephesus about AD 142. Paion was both the proposer of this decree to honour T. Aelius Alcibiades of Nysa and (as often) one of the envoys commissioned to carry copies of the decree to Alcibiades and to his city Nysa. He is there described as a citizen of Tarsus and Rhodes as well as of Side, and as [ποιη]τοῦ πλειστονίκου, μελοποιοῦ καὶ ῥαψ[ῳδοῦ θε]οῦ Ἀδριανοῦ θεολόγου ναῶν τῶν ἐν Π[εργαμῳ].[29] His involvement with the Dionysiac Guild and the epithet πλειστονίκης show him to be a professional rather than a dabbling member of the upper classes. As *melopoios* he will have composed hymns, as *rhapsodos* hexameter poetry. That he wrote some hexameter poetry seems also to follow from his honour at Side as 'the new Homer'.[30]

2. HEXAMETER POETRY

I now turn to other hexameter poets, beginning with one of the best of the period, Marcellus, who was also from Side. His work is comparatively well preserved: 101 didactic hexameters, and perhaps an epigram, survive in manuscript tradition, and 2 hexameter poems, of 59 and 39 lines respectively, on stone. But they are a small fraction of a voluminous production. The Suda knows an *Iatrika* in 42 books which included a section on lycanthropy. This must be the same as the epigram's *Chironides*, here given 40 books (presumably a rounding-off of 42). The

---

[28] Callimachus 34 (*HE*).
[29] *I Ephesus* 22a = *SEG* iv. 418, cf. Robert (1938), 45 ff, Robert (1980).
[30] Bean (1965), no. 107.

epigram, conceivably by Marcellus himself, also tells us that both Hadrian and Pius had the books 'dedicated' in Rome, i.e. acquired by the imperial libraries:

Μαρκέλλου τόδε σῆμα περικλυτοῦ ἰητῆρος,
φωτὸς κυδίστοιο τετιμένου ἀθανάτοισιν,
οὗ βίβλους ἀνέθηκεν ἐϋκτιμένῃ ἐνὶ Ῥώμῃ
Ἀδριανὸς προτέρων προφερέστερος ἡγεμονήων,
καὶ πάϊς Ἀδριανοῖο μέγ᾽ ἔξοχος Ἀντωνῖνος,
ὄφρα καὶ ἐσσομένοισι μετ᾽ ἀνδράσι κῦδος ἄροιτο
εἵνεκεν εὐεπίης, τήν οἱ πόρε Φοῖβος Ἀπόλλων,
ἡρώῳ μέλψαντι μέτρῳ θεραπήϊα νούσων
βίβλοις ἐν πινυταῖς Χειρωνίσι τεσσαράκοντα. (*AP* 7. 158)

This is the tomb of the renowned doctor Marcellus, a most glorious mortal honoured by the gods, whose books were dedicated in well-built Rome by Hadrian, foremost of our leaders of yore, and Hadrian's son the outstanding Antoninus; so that he might win glory among future men too for the eloquence which Phoebus Apollo gave him, when he sang the remedies of diseases in heroic verse, in 40 sage books called *Chironides*.

Hadrian's discovery of Marcellus could be independent of his patronage of Paion—we saw that his eye was somehow caught by Artemidorus Capito's edition of Hippocrates—but probably the favour acquired by the one led to the introduction of the other. Which first, we cannot say: but that it was in Hadrian's later years that he arranged for Marcellus' books to be lodged in Rome's libraries follows from Pius' involvement—presumably the work was still being written when Hadrian gave it his imprimatur.

Marcellus' other surviving work supports the attribution of his *Chironides* to the 130s. Two signed poems on stone, commissioned by Herodes Atticus after the death of his wife Regilla late in the 150s, have been found on her estate off the Via Appia near the third milestone, an estate which she had brought to Herodes in her dowry and where—conjecturally in his consulate of AD 143—he had consecrated a temple to the recently dead and deified Faustina.

The first is an elegant and allusive dedication of a statue of Regilla to which the women of Rome are urged to offer cult, giving Marcellus the opportunity to open his extended dedicatory epigram with a formula that suggests a hymn:[31]

> Δεῦρ' ἴτε Θυμβριάδες νηὸν ποτὶ τόνδε γυναῖκες
> 'Ρηγίλλης ἕδος ἀμφὶ θυοσκόα ἱρὰ φέρουσαι.

Come hither to this temple, ladies of Tiber, bearing sacred objects of sacrifice about Regilla's seat.

He goes on to describe the heroizing of Regilla, a reward from Zeus, and her son's elevation to the patriciate, a consolation from Pius to Herodes. Their ancestry (30–40) brings him back to cult:

> σὺ δ', εἰ φίλον, ἱερὰ ῥέξαι
> καὶ θῦσαι· θυέων ἀτὰρ οὐκ ἀέκοντος ἀνάγκη,
> εὖ δέ τοι εὐσεβέεσσι καὶ ἡρώων ἀλεγίζειν.
> οὐ μέγ γὰρ θνητή, ἀτὰρ οὐδὲ θέαινα τέτυκται·
> τοὔνεκεν οὔτε νεὼν ἱερὸν λάχεν οὔτε τι τύμβον,
> οὐδὲ γέρα θνητοῖς, ἀτὰρ οὐδὲ θεοῖσιν ὅμοια.
> σῆμα μέν οἱ νηῷ ἴκελον δήμῳ ἐν 'Αθήνης,
> ψυχὴ δὲ σκῆπτρον 'Ραδαμάνθυος ἀμφιπολεύει.
> τοῦτο δὲ Φαυστείνῃ κεχαρισμένον ἧσται ἄγαλμα
> δήμῳ ἐνὶ Τριόπεω, ἵνα οἱ πάρος εὐρέες ἀγροί
> καὶ χορὸς ἡμερίδων καὶ ἐλαιήεντες ἄρουραι. (40–50)

but do you, if you will, perform ritual
and sacrifice: yet of sacrifice there is no need from the
    unwilling
but it is well for the reverent to heed heroes too.
For she is not mortal, yet neither is she a goddess:
hence she has been given neither temple nor any tomb,
nor honours like those of mortals, yet not like those of gods.
There is a memorial to her in the shape of a temple in the
    country of Athena
but her soul attends the sceptre of Rhadamanthys.
But this statue, pleasing to Faustina, has been set up
in the country of Triopas, where before were her broad
    fields
and a chorus of tended vines, and olive groves.

The second poem is a prayer to Athena and to the Nemesis of Rhamnous to punish any encroachment on Herodes' estate

---

[31] The basic and still best discussion is that of Wilamowitz (1928), though he overstresses Homeric / Hesiodic and misses Hellenistic features. See also Peek (1979), Ameling (1983). For epigrams with hymnic features cf. above n. 20.

whether for cultivation or burial: its stern curses contrast sharply with the first poem's emollient tone. Although both have many Homerisms, the influence of Hellenistic poetry is also apparent, and these examples of Marcellus' mature work are a pleasure to read.

Less so the fragment of the *Chironides*. In dealing with the medicine that can be manufactured from fish, Marcellus catalogues the finny tribe with tedious monotony:

Εὖ δὲ καὶ εἰναλίων ἐδάην φύσιν ἰήτειραν
⟨σχ⟩ήμασι παντοίοισιν ἐμὸν νόον ἐξερεείνων,
ὡς αὐτός τ᾽ ἐνόησα καὶ ἄλλων μῦθον ἄκουσα·
ὧν τοι ἐγὼ πληθὺν ἠδ᾽ οὔνομα πᾶν ἀγορεύσω.
Βένθεα χητώεντα πολυσκοπέλοιο θαλάσσης
ἰχθύες ἀμφινέμονται ἀπείριτοι ἀργινόεντες
παμμέλανες περκνοί τε καὶ αἰόλον εἶδος ἔχοντες (Heitsch 63. 1–7).

And well too have I learned the healing properties of the creatures of the sea, searching out my mind in manifold ways, both as I have observed myself and have heard told by others: of these shall I tell you the whole multitude and every name. The monstrous depths of the crag-strewn sea are the abode of countless fish, all-black, dusky, or glittering.[32]

33 lines follow in which names of fish are ingeniously accommodated to the hexameter.

Marcellus' medical poem was not unique. At some time in the second century Rhodiapolis honoured its son Heraclitus as the 'Homer of medical poetry' and 'first in all history to be a doctor, a historian, and a poet of medical and philosophical works'. His statue was erected in the theatre to commemorate his *paideia*, and he was also honoured by Alexandria, Rhodes, and Athens (where his backers included the Areopagus and the Garden of Epicurus), and by the World Guild of Dionysiac Artists.[33] Unlike Marcellus, Heraclitus' horizons are those of

[32] Cf. Heitsch *GDRK* ii. no. lxiii with bibliography (p. 16), to which add Effe (1977), 196 ff. Effe considers the fragment to be from a different work from the *Iatrika*, surely unnecessarily. It is long enough to show that Marcellus' work is in some way related to the popular medical/paradoxographical *Koiranides* of disputed date. Keydell (1941) showed that Marcellus did not directly use the *Koiranides*, and Heitsch (1963) that they did not use Marcellus, so a common source is likely, contrary to the view of Wellmann (1934) that Marcellus was versifying the *Koiranides*.

[33] *TAM* ii. 910 = *IGR* iii. 733, cf. Robert (1980), 14. A temple of Asclepius and Hygieia dedicated by Heraclitus (who was their priest) is mentioned in the honorific inscription, and fragments remain of its dedication (*TAM* ii. 906 = *IGR* iii. 732).

the Eastern Mediterranean: he gave copies of his prose- and verse-works to his own city and to Alexandria, Rhodes, and Athens, but not, it seems, to Rome.

Marcellus and Heraclitus are but two of a number of poets who show that Greek didactic poetry flourished in the Antonine age.[34] We also have the incomplete remains (totalling over 2000 lines) of an astrological poem attributed by tradition to Manetho and indeed professing to be addressed to a king Ptolemy. Three of the six surviving books seem to belong together (1, 3, and 6) and the horoscope given in one of them places the writer's birth in AD 80.[35] It is likely, then, that the writer was active in our period.

More interesting than these, however, and transmitted complete, is Dionysius of Alexandria's *Guide to the Inhabited World*.[36] It stands in the hellenistic didactic tradition which aimed both to instruct and to please, and to do so within a small compass. To reduce a description of the whole world to 1187 hexameters inevitably involves vast omission and extreme brevity in describing what is admitted: but for mere catalogues with only occasional descriptive epithets there were precedents in the *Iliad*'s Catalogue of Ships and in the *Theogony*, and by careful signposting of new sections and by cross-references Dionysius succeeds in setting out a description that gives the reader an intelligible picture of the world, even if it would not allow him to construct an accurate map. Dionysius takes his didactic purpose seriously, notwithstanding his reliance on outdated geographical models, and to achieve it he exploits a variety of traditional poetic techniques.

For example, he first uses the invocation of the Muses as a source of knowledge to make the transition from his treat-

---

[34] It had been lively too in the first century: witness a didactic elegiac poem in 174 lines dedicated to Nero by his court physician Andromachus (Heitsch, *GDRK* ii. no. lxii) and the long astronomical work of Dorotheus of Sidon, of the 80s AD, which survives only in Arabic translation (ed. D. Pingree, Leipzig, 1976).

[35] The *apotelesmatika* were edited by E. Koechly in 1858. He thought the earlier sections Severan, the later fourth-century or later, and was followed by Schmid–Stahlin[2] ii. 2. 974 and E. Berneker in *Kleine Pauly* iii. 953 (despite Garnett (1895)), cf. Neugebauer and van Hoesen (1959), 92, no. L 80, demonstrating a birthdate of 28 (or 27) May, AD 80, for the writer of iii. 738–50.

[36] The most recent edition of Dionysius remains that of C. Müller in *Geog. Gr. min.* ii. (Paris 1861), 103–76: for a note of 56 MSS not used by Müller see Livadaras (1964). For dicussion see works cited below and Jacob and Christian (both 1984).

ment of the encircling Ocean (1–57) to the Mediterranean (58–168):

> Ὑμεῖς δ', ὦ Μοῦσαι, σκολιὰς ἐνέποιτε κελεύθους,
> ἀρξάμεναι στοιχηδὸν ἀφ' ἑσπέρου Ὠκεανοῖο·
> ἔνθα τε καὶ στῆλαι περὶ τέρμασιν Ἡρακλῆος
> ἑστᾶσιν, μέγα θαῦμα, παρ' ἐσχατόωντα Γάδειρα (62–5).

> But you, O Muses, tell its twisting paths
>   beginning in order from the western Ocean
> where near the boundaries the pillars of Heracles
>   stand, a mighty wonder, by furthest Gades.

Again, the sections on the Mediterranean, Africa (169–268), and Europe (269–446) are rounded off by six mythologically rich lines on Delphi (441–6), invoking Apollo and again the Muse, while also echoing the Homeric hymn to Apollo and Apollonius Rhodius:[37]

> Ἀλλ' ὁ μὲν ἰλήκοι · σὺ δέ μοι, Διός, ἔννεπε, Μοῦσα,
> νήσων πασάων ἱερὸν πόρον . . . (447–8)

> But may he show divine favour: and you, Muse, daughter
>   of Zeus, tell me
> the sacred way of all the islands . . .

Dionysius enhances the articulatory effect of this second invocation by opening the following section on islands (450–619) with seven lines (450–6) on Gades. We are thus taken back to the western point of departure that opened the description of the Mediterranean, Africa (174 ff.) and Europe (281 ff.). This is both didactically convenient and also appropriate under an emperor (see below) whose *patria*, Italica, was near Gades and whose adoptive mother and patron Plotina was actually from that city.

The third invocation to the Muses (650–1) signals the transition from Dionysius' general introduction to the shape of Asia to his catalogue of its peoples, so numerous that the Asian section alone (620–1152) balances in number of lines (as Dionysius suggests the land mass does in reality) those on the Mediterranean, Africa, Europe, and the Islands taken together (58–619). But Dionysius does not open and close his poem with the Muses. In his businesslike broaching of his theme he gives

[37] *H. Hom. Ap.* 165, Ap. Rhod. 2. 708.

himself a higher profile, recalling perhaps both Hesiod's *Theogony* and the Homeric hymn to Apollo:[38]

> Ἀρχόμενος γαῖάν τε χαὶ εὐρέα πόντον ἀείδειν
> καὶ ποταμοὺς πόλιάς τε χαὶ ἀνδρῶν ἄκριτα φῦλα
> μνήσομαι Ὠκεανοῖο βαθυρρόου· (1–3)

In beginning to sing of the earth and broad sea
and of rivers and cities and the countless tribes of men
I shall talk of the deep-flowing Ocean ...

At the poem's close, after a brief account of Dionysus' Indian expedition which introduces the eastern pillars of Dionysus (1164–5) to balance the western pillars of Heracles (63–4), he notes that he has talked of the most significant peoples of the earth but acknowledges mortal incapacity to enumerate all its inhabitants: only the gods who created the world and man in his various forms could do that (1166–80). Then he takes an emotional leave of his theme, again evoking a Homeric hymn in words and posture:[39]

> Ὑμεῖς δ' ἤπειροί τε καὶ εἰν ἁλὶ χαίρετε, νῆσοι,
> ὕδατά τ' Ὠκεανοῖο καὶ ἱερὰ χεύματα πόντου
> καὶ ποταμοὶ κρῆναί τε καὶ οὔρεα βησσήεντα.
> Ἤδη γὰρ πάσης μὲν ἐπέδραμον οἶδμα θαλάσσης,
> ἤδη δ' ἠπείρων σκολιὸν πόρον· ἀλλά μοι ὕμνων
> αὐτῶν ἐκ μακάρων ἀντάξιος εἴη ἀμοιβή. (1182–7)

But you, continents, and sea-girt isles, farewell
and waters of Ocean and the holy streams of the deep
and rivers and streams and gladed mountains.
For now I have sped over the swell of every sea,
now the twisting way of the continents: but may my hymns
bring me a fitting reward from the blessed ones themselves.

The Callimachean didactic poem is at the same time a hymn, its composer a celebrant as well as expounder of his material. That didactic aim is occasionally stressed, not without emphasis on Dionysius' own powers, as in the transition from the Mediterranean to Africa:

> Τοίη μὲν μορφὴ κυαναυγέος ἀμφιτρίτης·
> νῦν δέ τοι ἠπείρου μυθήσομαι εἶδος ἁπάσης,

---

[38] Hes, *Th.* 1, *H. Hom. Ap.* 1.
[39] *H. Hom. Ap.* 166 (cf. the echo of 165 at Dionysius 47).

ὄφρα καὶ οὐκ ἐσιδών περ ἔχοις εὔφραστον ὀπωπήν·
ἐκ τοῦ δ' ἂν γεραρός τε καὶ αἰδοιέστερος εἴης,
ἀνδρὶ παρ' ἀγνώσσοντι πιφαυσκόμενος τὰ ἔκαστα. (169–73)

Such is the shape of blue-glancing Amphitrite:
but now I shall expound the form of every continent,
so that even without seeing them you may have a distinct
     view
and thus may be honoured and more respected
when you utter everything in the presence of one who is
     ignorant.

Similarly the transition from north to south Asia:

'Ρηιδίως δ' ἄν τοι λοιπὸν πόρον αὐδήσαιμι
γαιάων 'Ασίης· ὁ δέ τοι λόγος ἐν φρεσὶν ἔστω,
μηδ' ἀνέμοις φορέοιτο πονηθέντων χάρις ἔργων.
Εἰ γάρ μοι σάφα τήνδε καταφράσσαιο κέλευθον,
ἦ τάχα κἂν ἄλλοισιν ἐπισταμένως ἀγορεύοις. (881–4)

Easily might I tell the remaining path
of the lands of Asia: and let the account stay in your mind
nor let the charm of the work I have laboured on be carried
     off by the winds.
For if you have clearly understood this way of mine
then with knowledge you may readily tell others.[40]

The *charis* that will assist the reader to remember the work is enhanced by carefully deployed purple passages. Mention of the African Nomads near the beginning of the African section allows nine lines elaborating the *topos* of their pre-agricultural way of life (186–94): this is balanced by a passage towards its end where the Egyptians are extolled as inventors of civilization, agriculture, and astronomy (232–7). The frozen, barren wastes of Scythia, at whose inhabitants Dionysius expostulates 'Impossible people, who have their dwellings in that country' (668), provoke an *ekphrasis* (664–78), later balanced by an even longer account of the riches of Arabia, whose aromatic treasures derive from Dionysus' release there from Zeus' thigh (927–53).

Many similar expansions, some of them introducing mythology, others natural history, endow the geographical

---

[40] Cf. Nicander, *Ther.* 1 ff. (ῥεῖά κέ τοι ...) and 4–7 (the respect his reader will gain among rustic peers).

framework with variety and allow a more lively or emotional tone. They must have enhanced the poem's eligibility for use as a school-reader through whose line-by-line explication *grammatici* could introduce pupils not only to geography but to central features of history and myth.

Some techniques are perhaps overworked. The pathetic triple repetition of a place-name is exploited four times. But at least three of these are carefully chosen. First Carthage:

> Τοῖς δ' ἔπι Καρχηδὼν πολυήρατον ἀμπέχει ὅρμον,
> Καρχηδών, Λιβύων μὲν, ἀτὰρ πρότερον Φοινίκων,
> Καρχηδών, ἣν μῦθος ὑπαὶ βοῒ μετρηθῆναι. (195–7)

After these Carthage embraces its lovely anchorage,
Carthage, city of Africans, before of Phoenicians,
Carthage, which legend tells was measured by an ox-hide.

Next comes the Tiber:

> Τοῖς δ' ἔπι μέρμερον ἔθνος ἀγαυῶν ἐστι Λατίνων,
> γαῖαν ναιετάοντες ἐπήρατον, ἧς διὰ μέσσης
> Θύμβρις ἑλισσόμενος καθαρὸν ῥόον εἰς ἅλα βάλλει,
> Θύμβρις ἐΰρρείτης, ποταμῶν βασιλεύτατος ἄλλων,
> Θύμβρις, ὃς ἱμερτὴν ἀποτέμνεται ἄνδιχα Ῥώμην,
> Ῥώμην τιμήεσσαν, ἐμῶν μέγαν οἶκον ἀνάκτων,
> μητέρα πασάων πολίων, ἀφνειὸν ἔδεθλον. (350–6)

After these is the dread people of the noble Latins,
dwelling in a lovely country, through whose midst
Tiber wending about casts its pure stream into the brine,
Tiber fair-flowing, most royal of other rivers,
Tiber, which cuts in twain beloved Rome,
Rome the honoured, mighty dwelling of my lords,
mother of all cities, wealthy shrine.

Then the river Rhebas:

> ἄγχι δὲ Βίθυνοι λιπαρὴν χθόνα ναιετάουσι,
> Ῥήβας ἔνθ' ἐρατεινὸν ἐπιπροΐησι ῥέεθρον,
> Ῥήβας, ὃς Πόντοιο παρὰ στομάτεσσιν ὁδεύει,
> Ῥήβας, οὗ κάλλιστον ἐπὶ χθονὶ σύρεται ὕδωρ. (793–6)

And nearby the Bithynians inhabit a rich land
where the Rhebas casts forth its delightful stream,
Rhebas, who marches beside the mouths of the Pontus,
Rhebas, whose water is the fairest that sweeps the earth.

Soon after we encounter the final example, Troy. Phrygia Minor, we are told,

$$
\begin{aligned}
&\kappa\epsilon\hat{\iota}\tau\alpha\iota\ \hat{\upsilon}\pi\grave{o}\ \zeta\alpha\theta\acute{\epsilon}\eta\varsigma\ \pi\acute{o}\delta\alpha\varsigma\ ^{"}\!I\delta\eta\varsigma, \\
&^{"}\!I\lambda\iota o\nu\ \hat{\eta}\nu\epsilon\mu\acute{o}\epsilon\sigma\sigma\alpha\nu\ \hat{\upsilon}\pi\grave{o}\ \pi\lambda\epsilon\upsilon\rho\hat{\eta}\sigma\iota\nu\ \check{\epsilon}\chi o\upsilon\sigma\alpha, \\
&^{"}\!I\lambda\iota o\nu\ \grave{\alpha}\gamma\lambda\alpha\grave{o}\nu\ \check{\alpha}\sigma\tau\upsilon\ \pi\alpha\lambda\alpha\iota\gamma\epsilon\nu\acute{\epsilon}\omega\nu\ \hat{\eta}\rho\acute{\omega}\omega\nu, \\
&^{"}\!I\lambda\iota o\nu,\ \hat{\eta}\nu\ \grave{\epsilon}\pi\acute{o}\lambda\iota\sigma\sigma\epsilon\ \Pi o\sigma\epsilon\iota\delta\acute{\alpha}\omega\nu\ \kappa\alpha\grave{\iota}\ ^{'}\!A\pi\acute{o}\lambda\lambda\omega\nu, \\
&^{"}\!I\lambda\iota o\nu,\ \hat{\eta}\nu\ \grave{\alpha}\lambda\acute{\alpha}\pi\alpha\xi\alpha\nu\ ^{'}\!A\theta\eta\nu\alpha\acute{\iota}\eta\ \tau\epsilon\ \kappa\alpha\grave{\iota}\ ^{"}\!H\rho\eta, \\
&\Xi\acute{\alpha}\nu\theta\omega\ \check{\epsilon}\pi'\ \epsilon\hat{\upsilon}\rho\upsilon\rho\acute{\epsilon}o\nu\tau\iota\ \kappa\alpha\grave{\iota}\ ^{'}\!I\delta\alpha\acute{\iota}\omega\ \Sigma\iota\mu\acute{o}\epsilon\nu\tau\iota.\ (815\text{--}19)
\end{aligned}
$$

> lies at holy Ida's feet;
> Ilion the windy is set beneath its flanks,
> Ilion, glorious city of heroes of long ago,
> Ilion, which Poseidon and Apollo built,
> Ilion, which Athena and Hera destroyed,
> upon the broad-flowing Xanthus and Idaean Simoïs.

The importance of Carthage, Rome, and Troy are clear: here are two great empires which had to fall to give way to the third, Rome; and just as Troy might seem to be the only begetter of Greek narrative epic so it is possible that Dionysius from learned Alexandria knew how important Carthage was to the Latin epic tradition. Moreover, it is interesting that he is ready to hail the imperial house as 'my lords': we may contrast his compatriot Appian a generation later for whom the Ptolemies were 'my kings'.[41]

Not surprisingly, this praise of Rome and the Tiber comes at the mid-point of the European section (269–446). It is linked to the later admiration of Ilion by the conjunction of city and river, and Ilion comes as close to the mid-point of the Asian section as the major division between north and south Asia allows. The use of this emotive technique a mere 19 lines earlier to describe the Rhebas is puzzling, and I shall argue elsewhere that it is to be explained as a tribute to the Bithynian origin of Antinous.[42]

I have so far focused entirely upon the poem to the neglect of the poet. This reflects the apparent anonymity adopted by the writer. Despite occasional intrusions in the first person, the poet seems to tell us almost nothing of himself. The closest we come

[41] Appian *Praef.* 38.
[42] In work in preparation on Hadrian.

to his personality is an outburst against travel in a Hesiodic
vein[43] that leads into a further praise of the power of the Muses:

'Ρεῖα δέ τοι καὶ τήνδε καταγράψαιμι θάλασσαν,
οὐ μὲν ἰδὼν ἀπάνευθε πόρους, οὐ νηὶ περήσας·
οὐ γάρ μοι βίος ἐστὶ μελαινάων ἐπὶ νηῶν,
οὐδέ μοι ἐμπορίη πατρώιος, οὐδ' ἐπὶ Γάγγην
ἔρχομαι, οἷά τε πολλοί, 'Ερυθραίου διὰ πόντου,
ψυχῆς οὐκ ἀλέγοντες, ἵν' ἄσπετον ὄλβον ἕλωνται,
οὐδὲ μὲν 'Υρκανίοις ἐπιμίσγομαι, οὐδ' ἐρεείνω
Καυκασίας κνημῖδας 'Ερυθραίων 'Αριηνῶν·
ἀλλά με Μουσάων φορέει νόος, αἵτε δύνανται
νόσφιν ἀλημοσύνης πολλὴν ἅλα μετρήσασθαι,
οὔρεά τ' ἤπειρόν τε καὶ αἰθερίην ὁδὸν ἄστρων. (708–17)

And easily might I describe for you this sea too [Caspian]
though I have not see its paths from afar nor crossed it by
    ship
for my life is not spent on black ships
nor do I inherit commerce from my father, nor to the Ganges
do I go, like many, across the Red Sea
heedless of their lives, that they may get unspeakable
    wealth,
nor do I have dealings with Hyrcanians, nor do I seek out
the Caucasian ridges of the Red Arianians:
but I am borne by the mind of the Muses, who are able
without wandering to measure the great brine
and mountains and continent and the ethereal path of
    stars.

This disclaimer can hardly refer only to travel to the further
reaches of Asia, as Bernays (1905, 3) wished, generally framed
as it is and followed by descriptions not only of the Far East but
of the much more accessible regions of Asia Minor and Syria.
Rather it emphatically dissociates the author from the investi-
gative explorer such as Herodotus, Megasthenes, or Posidonius
and sets him in a purely literary and scholarly tradition. But
neither it nor other utterances in the poem helped to locate the
poet in time and place until in 1884 Leue published his discovery of two acrostichs.[44]

---

[43] Hes. *Op.* 640–62, cf. also Theognis 249–50.
[44] Leue (1884). The further acrostich seen by Leue (1925), at 135–7 (οἷς) and 254–9
(τεχνοῖ) is not convincing, cf. Counillon (1981), himself proposing στένη at 307–11: it is
not clear what this acrostich is meant to communicate to the reader.

The first comes early in the poem (109–33), and is associated with the sea named by sailors after Pharos (115) and with the first of the only two extended similes in the poem (123–6): it runs

ΕΠΗ ΔΙΟΝΥΣΙΟΥ ΤΩΝ ΕΝΤΟΣ ΦΑΡΟΥ[45]

This confirms the statement of the *Life* of Dionysius in a four-teenth-century Chigi manuscript in the Vatican that Dionysius was from Alexandria, a statement we would otherwise have no good reason to prefer to others in scholia and lexicographers.[46]

The second is some 400 lines later, at 513–32, coextensive with Dionysius' description of the islands of the Aegean and marked at its close by the second extended simile of the poem:

ΘΕΟΣ ΕΡΜΗΣ ΕΠΙ ΑΔΡΙΑΝΟΥ[47]

The acrostich signature is in the didactic tradition: compare Nicander's signature in *Theriaca*, 345–53, and another Diony-sius, son of Calliphon, in his iambic geographical poem.[48] We also know from Vestinus' *Bomos* that acrostichs were in vogue under Hadrian. Although it took 17 centuries for a scholar to detect them, we must assume that Dionysius imagined his con-temporaries would be quicker off the mark. The second acros-tich fixes him certainly under Hadrian, and the reference to the god Hermes is probably to Antinous, which would put the lines' composition between AD 130 and 138.[49]

Conjecture may go further. Müller had already observed a notice in an eleventh century excerptor of the Ravenna geogra-pher concerning a description of Sybaris by a Dionysius who was librarian at Rome for 20 years and composed a hexameter *periegesis*. A Dionysius of Alexandria, son of Glaucus, is regis-tered in the Suda as having held an imperial post *a bibliothecis* as well as *ab epistulis* and in charge of embassies and rescripts. But this Dionysius is there stated to have flourished from Nero to

---

[45] The opening word of 110 in all MSS is μακρόν, giving EMH: Nauck (1889), 325, proposed to emend to πολλόν, and *ΕΠΗ* gives an easily intelligible sense which EMH does not (unless we understand πατρίς, as has been proposed).

[46] See the ed. of the *vita Chisiana* by Colonna (1957).

[47] Müller printed the reading of most MSS, Εὐρώπης δ' ἤτοι: to get the η of Hermes the reading of A, ἤτοι δ' Εὐρώπης, is required.

[48] Διονυσίου τοῦ Καλλιφῶντος, lines 1–23 in *Geog. Gr. Min.* i. 238.

[49] Counillon (1981).

Trajan, and to have succeeded his teacher Chaeremon, in Alexandria, presumably as head of the Museum. Not, therefore, our
writer: but conceivably his father, for manuscripts of the *Periegesis* call the writer Dionysius son of Dionysius, and Klotz
argued that Guido's puzzling description of his Dionysius as
Ionicus reflects a source where Dionysius was styled Διονυσίου,
and where the geographer was stated to be the librarian's son.[50]
It is a precarious foundation, but could be right. Upon it would
be constructed the following scenario. The elder Dionysius succeeds Chaeremon as head of the Museum when Chaeremon
goes to Rome to teach Nero philosophy, about AD 50. Through
his former teacher's influence Dionysius son of Glaucus is himself called to Rome under Nero and holds the procuratorial
posts listed in the Suda—perhaps totalling 20 years, rather
than spending 20 years *a bibliothecis* alone. His son Dionysius the
Periegete may know Rome from his childhood and feel attach-
ment to the imperial house (cf. 350–6 quoted above). But on his
father's retirement from imperial service under Trajan he
returns to their *patria*, Alexandria.

We cannot estimate when Dionysius' poem began to acquire
the vogue it enjoyed from late antiquity, when it was translated
by Avienus and Priscus into Latin, through to Byzantium, the
Middle Ages and early modern Europe, where it continued to
be a textbook in schools and Universities until the eighteenth
century.[51] The total silence on Dionysius in other second-
century writers does not prove neglect, any more than does the
silence on Lucian everywhere except in an Arabic translation of
Galen. It would have been interesting to know whether Dionysius' prayer for reward from the 'blessed ones' duly received
attention from Hadrian. The least that Dionysius must have
hoped for, if he did not already have it, was membership of the

---

[50] Guido's comment (c. 25 p. 466. 3 in the Pinder–Parthey edn. of the Ravenna geographer; also printed by Müller, *Geog. Gr. Min.* ii. xvi): '*de qua Sybari refert Iuvenalis satiri-
cus, latius tamen Dionysius Ionicus, qui Romae bibliothecarius per annos fuit viginti et orbem metro
heroico graeco carmine descripsit*' (there follows a rendering of Dionysius 378). The relationship between the librarian and geographer was suggested by Bernays (1905), 23–4,
argued for by Klotz (1909) (apparently unaware of Bernays's work) and accepted by
Gärtner in *Kleine Pauly* s.n. Dionysius no. 30.

[51] For the use of Dionysius as a school text cf. Jacob (1981) 56 ff. It was edited (and
adapted) by Edward Wells in an Oxford ed. of 1704 apparently intended to teach geography in the University.

Alexandrian Museum. If his father was indeed Dionysius son of Glaucus, he may already be a member of the Museum aspiring to higher things.

A word should be said about the other works that may be ascribed to Dionysius. The *Life* mentioned above (n. 46) attributes to him books on stones (*Lithiaka*) and says this attribution is accepted because they have the style of the *Periegesis*. One might add in its favour that in the *Periegesis* Dionysius mentions stones as the most noteworthy product of a number of regions.[52] Only two fragments survive. Other works, the *Life* notes, were ascribed to Dionysius by some and denied by others: *Diosemiai*, a *Gigantias*, and *Ornithiaka*: the *Bassarika*, by reason of their stylistic roughness, were generally ascribed to Dionysius of Samos.[53]

We now have some papyrus fragments of the *Bassarika* (once at least 14 books) and *Gigantias* (once at least 17). The former, more voluminous, are more different from the *Periegesis* than genre alone can explain, and both look like the work of the same hand. One of the papyrus fragments of the *Gigantias* is dated to the second half of the second century, and, like Dionysius Periegetes, both seem to know Nicander and be known to Quintus. That they are by our Dionysius is not perhaps as absurd as Livrea[54] insists, but more probably they are by another. A poem on giants, however, would not be out of place in Dionysius' lifetime, since one is ascribed by Philostratus to the Flavian and Trajanic sophist Scopelianus of Clazomenae.[55]

The *Ornithiaka* or *Ixeutika* are not preserved, but a prose paraphrase gives us a fair idea of the content of their three books. Fabulous behaviour, and indeed fabulous birds, place the work near to that of Aelian, while there are traces of what must have

[52] Electrum, 213, 317–19; crystal, 724; crystal and iaspis, 781–2; beryl, 1011–12. For the fragments of the *Lithiaka* see Müller, *Geog. Gr. Min.* xxvi: one actually quoted by a scholiast on *Periegesis* 714, the other (referring to Book 2) by Maximus on Dionysius the Areopagite *De myst. theol.* c. 2.

[53] Cf. Eustathius in *Geog. Gr. Min.* ii. 215. 6–14.

[54] For the fragments Heitsch (1963), no. xix pp. 60–77, is superseded by E. Livrea's edition (Rome, 1973), which includes *POxy.* 2815; for Quintus of Smyrna's probable knowledge of the *Bassarika* and *Gigantias* see Wifstrand (1933), 178–80, and *prolegomena* to Livrea's edn. 10 ff. Livrea emphatically rejects identification with the Periegete as does Keydell implicitly (in *Kleine Pauly* s.n. Dionysius no. 13) and Lesky (1966) explicitly (p. 816 n. 3).

[55] For Scopelianus' poem, *VS* I. 21, 518.

been purple passages of poetry, such as cliffs and canyons echoing the song of the swan.[56] The mixture of solid information and θαύματα makes ascription to the periegete attractive, as does the poet's claim to derive his knowledge from Apollo,[57] but we are in no position to make a serious judgement.

All this hexameter poetry seems to belong in a Hesiodic and Callimachean tradition. This continued to flourish into the third century. At the end of our period, between 177 and 180, a Cilician poet ('Oppian') dedicated his *Halieutika* in 5 books to Marcus and Commodus, and some 40 years later a Syrian poet whose work has been transmitted under the same name dedicated his *Cynegetika* in 4 books to Caracalla. Admittedly their scale was greater, following Callimachus' 4 books of *Aetia* rather than Aratus' *Phaenomena*, but their blend of learning and entertainment establishes them as successors to the didactic Dionysii.[58]

Epic narrating the deeds of kings and heroes is less well represented. Clearly mythological epic was written: fragments of a *Bassarika* and a *Gigantias* by a Dionysius have already been mentioned, as has Areius the Homeric poet from the Museum at Alexandria.[59] The *Gigantias* of Scopelianus and the prolific Severan father and son from Lycaonian Laranda, Septimius Nestor and Septimius Peisander, fall respectively before and after our period, but hint that the production of mythological epic was continuous in the three centuries preceding our first text to survive complete, the *Posthomerica* of Quintus of Smyrna,

[56] The prose paraphrase is edited by Garzya (1955) and as a Teubner text (with index verborum) *Dionysii Ixeuticon seu de aucupio* (Leipzig, 1963); again by M. Papathomopoulos, Ἀνωνύμου παράφρασις εἰς τὰ Διονυσίου Ἰξευτικά (Athens, 1976). Title and authorship are discussed by Garzya (1957), who shows that the ascription to Oppian in one group of manuscripts is conjectural and should be discarded in the light of clear ascription to a Dionysius in 1.1 (πανθ' ὅσα περὶ πτηνῶν τῷ ποιητῇ Διονυσίῳ συγγέγραπται) and 3. 25 (Διονύσιος δ' αὐτὰ παρὰ τοῦ τῆς Λητοῦς Ἀπόλλωνος διδαχθῆναί φησιν). Garzya also argues that on the analogy of Oppian's works the title should have been *Ixeutika* and that περὶ ὀρνίθων / ὀρνιθιακά, are unfounded (apparently neglecting the latter title in the *Vita Chisiana* and Eustathius, *Geog. Gr. min.* ii. 215. 6–14); and that the paraphrased work may have used Oppian's *Ixeutika* (5 books according to the Oppian *Life*, but only 2 in the Suda), though he seems also (mysteriously) to allow that both it and the *Lithiaka* could be by the Periegete. For the swan's song echoed see 2. 20.

[57] See 3. 25, quoted above n. 56.

[58] On the Oppians see most recently Bowersock (1985), with bibliography.

[59] Note too M. Decrius Decrianus, ἐπῶν καὶ μελῶν ποιητής, on a tablet published by Fraser (1959).

whose 14 books belong after the *Halieutika* of Oppian and before Triphiodorus, so probably between AD 200 and 250.[60]

Narration of the deeds of emperors, however, seems not to have been much favoured. A poem on the reigning emperor(s) is attested as a subject for competition at the Mouseia at Thespiae, and entries cannot have run to great length.[61] So too the only example to survive from the second century, by the Egyptian Pancrates, can hardly have been a full-length epic. One fragment and some information about its author have long been known from Athenaeus of Naucratis (15. 677 d–f). In a long discourse on garlands his character Ulpianus expounds the origin of the Alexandrian garland called 'Antinoeios'. Pancrates, an ἐπιχώριος, drew Hadrian's attention to the red lotus while the emperor was visiting Alexandria and said it ought to be so called because it had shot up from the ground when it drank the blood of the Moorish lion slain by Antinous in a hunt near Alexandria. Ulpian quotes a description in 4 lines of the lotus which echoes Homer's description of the flowers that sprang up during Hera's seduction of Zeus. A second-century papyrus published in 1911 gave us 40 hexameters, of which 30 are almost complete, in which Hadrian casts his spear at the lion and misses—deliberately, to test Antinous' mettle, and doubtless because he is familiar with the conventions of the Homeric duel. The lion attacks Antinous; then the clip fades, with clear traces of the lion's inevitable death at the hands of Hadrian. Hadrian's rescue of Antinous is predictable, and the successful outcome of the hunt is confirmed by Athenaeus' description and by the tondi on the Arch of Constantine which originally decorated a Hadrianic hunting-monument. A few line-ends and beginnings were contributed by another second-century papyrus published in 1927: they seem to come from Pancrates' opening and his description of the party assembling for the hunt.[62]

---

[60] For concise accounts of the Septimii and Quintus see R. Keydell s.nn. in *Kleine Pauly* iv (1975), 59.

[61] See *IG* vii. 1773, of *c.* AD 150–60, and *SEG* iii. 334, of *c.* AD 150–60 or after AD 169, attesting an epic poem honouring the emperor (as well as one honouring the Muses) as a subject for competition at the Mouseia at Thespiae: for details cf. Schachter (1986), 176–8.

[62] The fragments are in Heitsch (1961), no. xv, 51–3. For analysis of poetic echoes see F. Stoessl in *RE* xxxvi/2 s.n. Pankrates no. 5, 615–19. The tondos on the arch of

The fragments pretty certainly come from the poem of Pancrates, as the Oxyrhynchus fragment's first editor, Hunt, saw. It is turgid stuff, prodigal with simile and exploiting echoes of Homer and the Hesiodic *Shield* to build up a heroic encounter between Hadrian and the lion that recalls conflicts of Heracles and of Zeus with the Giants:

> τοῖ]ον ἐφεζόμενος δαμασήν[ο]ρα μίμνε λέοντα
> 'Α]ντίνοος λαιῇ μὲν ἔχων ῥυτῆρα χαλινόν,
> δεξιτερῇ δ' ἔγχος κεκορυθμένο[ν] ἐξ ἀδάμαντος.
> πρῶτος δ' 'Αδριανὸς προιεὶς χαλκήρεον ἔγχος
> οὔτασεν, οὐδὲ δάμασσεν, ἑκὼν. γὰρ ἀπήμβροτε σ[ίντου·
> ε]ὐστοχίης γὰρ πάμπαν ἐβούλετο πειρηθῆναι
> 'Α]ργειφοντιάδαο μεγηράτ[ου 'Αντι]νόοιο.
> θ]ὴρ δὲ τυπεὶς ἔτι μᾶλλον [ὀ]ρίνετο, ποσσὶ δ' ἄμυσσ[ε
> γαῖαν τρηχαλ[έ]η[ν] θυμούμ[ε]νος, ἐκ δὲ κονίη
> ὡ[ς ν]έφ[ος] ἱσταμένη φ[άος ἤ]χλυεν ἠελίοιο.
> μαίνετο δ' ὡς ὅτε κῦμ[α] πολυκλύστο[ι]ο θαλάσσης
> Στρυ[μ]ονίου κ[α]τόπισθεν ἐγειρομένου Ζεφύρ[οιο.
> ῥί]μ[φα δ' ἐ]π' ἀμφοτέροισιν ἐπώρορε ...

Mounted on such a horse did Antinous await the man-slaying lion holding the restraining rein in his left hand and in his right a spear headed with steel. First Hadrian cast his bronze-tipped spear, and wounded the beast without vanquishing it, for he deliberately missed the [predator?]: for he wished fully to test the aim of Argus-slayer Hermes, the lovely Antinous. But wounded the beast grew even more excited, and in his wrath tore at the rough ground with his paws, and the dust hung like a cloud and darkened the light of the sun; and he raged as does the wave of the thundering sea as the west wind from Strymon blows up behind it. Swiftly he lunged at them both.[63]

This is not the stuff of poetic immortality, but it did secure Pancrates membership of the Alexandrian Museum, and both his poem and his person were remembered for at least a century. It was probably composed in the immediate aftermath of the hunt, early in September 130, before the fatal trip up the Nile which was already under way in October, since it is hard to think that Pancrates risked this theme when Antinous was

Constantine were attributed to a Hadrianic hunting-monument by Bieber (1911), and their bearing on the hunt in Pancrates noted by Hoffa (1912). On that monument see Maull (1955).

[63] Fr. 2 col. ii (= *POxy.* 1085), 3–15.

already dead: if one believes he did, then the first months of 131 remain open.[64]

There may be more than this to the person of Pancrates. When the first papyrus was published Radermacher drew attention to the story in the Paris magical papyrus that an Egyptian from Heliopolis, Pachrates, had demonstrated to Hadrian a magical sacrifice with astounding properties: and in his *Philopseudes* Lucian tells of an Egyptian wizard Pancrates.[65] Though some vehemently distinguish the two, perhaps the hexameter poet who was honoured by membership of the Museum was the same as the wizard.

3. MELIC POETRY

I conclude with a brief glance at melic poetry—not simply such poems as the epigrams we have seen in metres that for archaic and classical Greece were melic, but poetry that was actually sung, such as Paion of Side's description *melopoios* implies. Like recitations of poetry, singing of various kinds of text must have bulked much larger in the experience of a second-century Greek than it does in our surviving witnesses. I look first at poetry that was certainly, or probably, choral.

Choirs sang *prosodia* in competitions and (in the framework of cult) hymns in honour of the Roman emperor and his household and of long-established divinities like Asclepius. The first two categories will clearly have required new compositions, but apart from one recent discovery our knowledge is limited to the names of victors in competitions and of *hymnodoi* and *hymnographoi*.[66] In worshipping traditional gods traditional texts will still

---

[64] Weber (who did not know the papyrus fragments) thought that the hunt took place after Antinous' death, as (less intelligibly) did Sijpesteijn (1969): *contra* Follet (1968), Lambert (1984), p. 257 n. 7. For a lively account of the events see Lambert (1984), 118–20, 153—4.

[65] Lucian, *Philops.* 34, cf. Radermacher (1916).

[66] Of victors in the *prosodion* at Thespiae we know Antiphon of Athens (cf. above n. 15) who shared a victory between AD 150 and 160 with a Thespian, Eumaron son of Alexander (*IG* vii. 1773); Eumaron is the sole victor recorded in a competition of the years AD 150–60, or after AD 169 (*SEG* iii. 334 = *BCH* xix (1895), 343. 11); two victors, Vipsanius Philoxenus of Thespiae and Callitychides of Thebes, are recorded for a competition which must fall between AD 161 and 169 or AD 176 and 180 (ibid. 344. 3–5; they also between them took prizes for the (hexameter) poem and (prose) encomia on the emperors and on the Muses). For a *hymnographos*, *IEphesus* 1149. For *hymnodoi* cf. my article in *ANRW* ii. xxxiii/1 (Berlin/N.Y., 1989), 221, n. 27.

have been sung,[67] but alongside these some new hymns were composed. One of these, a paean to Asclepius by Diophantus of Sphettus, probably the prytanis of AD 167/8, is chiefly written in *apokrota*, and so, like the hymn to Antinous discussed below, was perhaps intended to be sung by a citharode and not a choir.[68]

If that is so, our few choral fragments from hymns to traditional gods are, ironically, from the verse hymns to various deities composed by the great exponent of the prose hymn, Aelius Aristides. They belong to the first decade of his illness, AD 144–53, and were composed at the command of divinities, chiefly Asclepius, to assist his cure: and Aristides indeed claims that their performance by a chorus of boys brought relief.[69] This chorus, which he seems still to have maintained as late as AD 166, was presumably modelled to some extent on the *hymnodoi* attached to the cult of Artemis at Ephesus and to the imperial cult in Pergamum, Ephesus, and (from AD 123) Smyrna.

Although no hymn to an emperor survives, a hymn to Antinous has been discovered in the shrine of Apollo Hylatas at Courion in Cyprus, apparently inscribed by a citharode chosen to serve on an embassy, perhaps consolatory, to Hadrian.[70] It is not clear how this song was performed. It seems to begin with a first-person-plural verb, but thereafter the singer refers to himself in the singular and claims to have mounted a choral performance (l. 7). Moreover the metre, *apokrota* combined with paroemiacs, was a favourite with the citharode Mesomedes,[71] and might therefore suggest solo performances. Either, then, as Lebek proposed, the inscribed text was sung by the citharode

---

[67] The practice of singing 'classics' seems to be secured by the re-inscription of Sophocles' 'Paean to Asclepius', *IG* ii.[2] 4510, and the inclusion of that ascribed by Athenaeus 15. 702 A to Ariphron of Sicyon in the sequence of verse texts on *IG* ii.[2] 4533 (late second or early third century).

[68] *IG* ii. 4514, 10 + 10 *apokrota* followed by 4 hexameters. Of the hymns quoted in literary sources or found on papyrus collected in Heitsch, *GDRK* i. 155 ff., most are in hexameters, and none can be securely dated to our period.

[69] Aristid. *Hieroi Logoi* 4 (= 50 K). 38. For a fuller discussion see my article in *ANRW* II. xxxiii/1 (Berlin/N.Y., 1989), 214–20.

[70] First published by Mitford (1971), no. 104. For thorough discussion, and identification of the metre, see Lebek (1973).

[71] Cf. West (1982), 172–3.

Apokroton: ∪∪ − ∪∪ − ∪∪ − ∪ −
Paroemiac: ∪∪ − ∪∪ − ∪∪ − −

alone, to be followed by a choral song; or, as some believe archaic *kitharodia* was performed, the chorus merely danced while the citharode sang.

When we turn to solo performance it is clear that song accompanied by the *kithara* is in vogue,[72] and we are fortunate to have substantial remains of one of its leading exponents, perhaps its doyen, Mesomedes. He seems to span the reigns of Hadrian and Pius. The Suda asserts that he was a citharode from Crete and Hadrian's freedman—presumably, then, his full name was P. Aelius Mesomedes—and μάλιστα φίλος. Eusebius put Mesomedes' floruit in AD 144, and the Augustan History has the emperor Pius reduce the salary of the *lyricus*—a salary presumably granted to him by Hadrian. Among 'various works' the Suda ascribes a *Praise of Antinous*, which, for good or ill, has not survived. But as well as 2 poems preserved in the Palatine and Planudean anthologies, 13, originally from a single corpus, have been transmitted in various manuscripts, 4 of these with musical notation (which at least another 2 seem once to have had).[73]

The poems with musical notation are *prooemia* to the Muse (1*a*), and to Calliope and Apollo (1*b*); and hymns to the sun (2. 7–25) and to Nemesis (4). Another *prooemium* with no trace of musical notation precedes the hymn to the sun (2. 1–6). These three *prooemia* are not distinctive poetry, and it has been suggested[74] that they are earlier than Mesomedes and that he simply set the first two to new music.

There is much more to the hymn to Nemesis (3) which mixes the paroemiac with the *apokroton*.[75]

---

[72] A number of melic poets are known of whose compositions we cannot say whether they were citharodic, for choirs, or for some other sort of solo performance. These include the λυρικοὶ νόμοι of the sophist Hippodromus (Philostr. *VS* 2. 27, 620), the μέλη of Paion and the poetry of the Hermocrates of Rhodes encountered by Aristides at Pergamum *c.* AD 145 (Aristid. *Hieroi Logoi* 4 (= 50 K) 23). The varied talents of Q. Pompeius Capito and C. Iulius Longianus of Aphrodisias, honoured in AD 127 (above n. 22), presumably included melic compositions, and C. Cornelius Secundus Proculus honoured at Methymna (*IGR* iv. 6 = *IG* xii. 2. 519) as poet of μέλη may just belong in our period.

[73] Suda M 668, SHA *Pius* 7. 8. For texts see Heitsch, *GDRK* ii. 24–32. To his bibliography add Pöhlmann (1970), 12–31 who rightly argues that Heitsch 1*a* and 1*b* and 2. 1–6 are separate poems, and discusses transmission as well as printing texts with their musical notation.

[74] By Maas and Wilamowitz, cf. Pöhlmann (1970), 28.

[75] Cf. n. 71. The plural 'we sing' at 16 is not a good basis for Wilamowitz's view that 1–15 were sung by a solo performer and 16–20 by a chorus.

Νέμεσι πτερόεσσα βίου ῥοπά,
κυανῶπι θεά, θύγατερ Δίκας,
ἃ κοῦφα φρυάγματα θνατῶν
ἐπέχεις ἀδάμαντι χαλινῷ,
ἔχθουσα δ' ὕβριν ὀλοὰν βροτῶν
μέλανα φθόνον ἐκτὸς ἐλαύνεις·
ὑπὸ σὸν τροχὸν ἄστατον ἀστιβῆ
χαροπὰ μερόπων στρέφεται τύχα,
λήθουσα δὲ πὰρ πόδα βαίνεις,
γαυρούμενον αὐχένα κλίνεις.
ὑπὸ πῆχυν ἀεὶ βίοτον μετρεῖς,
νεύεις δ' ὑπὸ κόλπον ὄφρυν ἀεί
ζυγὸν μετὰ χεῖρα κρατοῦσα.
ἵλαθι μάκαιρα δικασπόλε
Νέμεσι πτερόεσσα βίου ῥοπά.
Νέμεσιν θεὸν ᾄδομεν ἀφθίταν,
Νίκην τανυσίπτερον ὀμβρίμαν
νημερτέα καὶ πάρεδρον Δίκας,
ἃ τὰν μεγαλανορίαν βροτῶν
νεμεσῶσα φέρεις κατὰ ταρτάρου.

Nemesis, winged balancer of life,
dark-faced goddess, daughter of Justice,
you who restrain with adamantine bridles
the frivolous insolences of mortals,
and spurning the destructive violence of mankind
drive out black envy!
Beneath your unceasing, traceless orbit
is spun the grey fortune of man
and unnoticed you walk in his tracks,
you bend the neck that is proud.
Beneath your arm you ever measure out life
and ever do you lower your eye to your bosom
as you control the scales in your hand.
Be gracious, blessed dealer of justice,
Nemesis, winged balancer of life.
Nemesis the deathless goddess we sing,
Victory with slender wings, all-powerful
infallible, and the assistant to Justice,
you who in displeasure at the pride of men
carry it down into Tartarus.

This hymn is traditional in thought and language and retains a sombre tone throughout. Equally serious are the hymns to Isis

(5) and the powers of the universe, perhaps Nature (4). A lighter tone is struck in a hymn to the Adriatic (6) in the same metre as that to Nemesis.

In a different genre a poem of some charm, composed in proceleusmatics, tells the fable of the rustic and the swan (10).[76]

Κύκνον ἐνὶ ποταμῷ
κάτεχεν ἄτερ βρόχου
παγόδετον ὕδωρ·
ὃν ἄμουσος ἰδών
αἰπόλος ἀγρότας
ἔθελε διολέσαι,
κεφαλὰν λιγύθρουν
τῷ σταχυοτόμῳ
δρεπάνῳ θερίσας.
κατὰ δ᾽ ὑδατοπαγοὺς
βαῖνε κελεύθου
βήμασι κούφοις,
Τιτὰν δὲ κύκνῳ
πυρόεντι βολᾷ
σύμμαχος ἐφάνη·
γίγνετο μὲν ὑγρόν
πάλι ποταμὸς ὕδωρ·
ἔπεσεν ὁ βούτας,
ὁ δὲ κύκνος ἀνέθορε
κἄμπτατο χαίρων.

A swan in a river
was caught without a snare
by the ice-bound water:
a rustic goatherd
no friend of the Muse
saw it and wanted to kill,
harvesting with his sickle
for cutting ears of corn
the head that sings sweetly.
Along the frozen path
of water he walked
with light steps,

---

[76] A more conventional verse for telling fables is to be found in the choliambic collection of Babrius, almost certainly from the last quarter of the first century AD, best consulted in B. E. Perry's *Babrius and Phaedrus* (Loeb edn., 1965), with discussion of date at pp. xlvii–lii.

and to the swan's aid the Sun
with his fiery dart
appeared as an ally:
once more the river
became flowing water:
the oxherd fell
and the swan leapt up
and flew off rejoicing.

Although Mesomedes is careless in some matters—in this a goatherd, an oxherd, or a reaper?—his language is often allusive as well as economical, and even without the music this swan-song makes a favourable impression. Less so two ingenious poems on sundials (7 and 8) and one on the chimaera (12). But two more deserve quotation. That on a mosquito (11) has the wit of a *chreia*:

'Ελέφαντος ἐπ' οὔατι κώνωψ
πτερὸν οὐ πτερὸν ἵστατο σείων,
φάτο δ' ἄφρονα μῦθον· ἀφίπταμαι,
βάρος οὐ γὰρ ἐμὸν δύνασαι φέρειν.
ὃ δ' ἔλεξε γέλωτος ὑφ' ἁδονᾷ·
ἀλλ' οὔτ' ἐδάην ὅτ' ἐφιπτάθης
οὔθ' ἡνίκ' ἀφίπτασαι, κώνωψ.

On an elephant's ear a mosquito
settled flapping its wing (no wing, to be sure)
and uttered the foolish remark: off I fly
for my weight is much more than your frame can endure;
and the elephant pleasantly laughed his reply:
but I didn't detect when you flew on to me
nor when you flew off, dear mosquito.

A lusher texture, reminiscent of erotic epigram,[77] pervades the set-piece description of a sponge (9):

Ἄνθος τόδε σοι βυθίων πετρῶν
πολύτρητον ἁλὸς παλάμαις φέρω
σμήνεσσι πανείκελον 'Ατθίδων
ἅτε κηρὸν 'Υμήττιον ἐκ πετρῶν,
ᾧ Γλαῦκος ἐν ὕδασι τέρπεται.
Τρίτωνος ὅδ' ἐστὶ χαμεύνα,

---

[77] No doubt love-songs formed a prolific genre of their own, but we have little evidence of its forms. Later we hear of a poet Celsus who devoted himself to such ᾠδαί, Philostratus *Ep.* 71.

τούτῳ παρὰ κύμασι παρθένοι
παίζουσιν, ἀγάλματα Νηρέως,
πώλων ὅδ’ ἀφρώδε’ ἀθυ⟨ρμάτ⟩ων
Ἐνοσίχθονος ἄσθματα λούει.
τοῦτον τάμε νηχόμενος δύτας
ἁλὸς ὕδασιν ἄτρομος ἐργάτας,
ἵνα σου κατὰ χιονέων μελῶν
λύσῃ μετὰ νύκτα, γύναι καλά,
κάματον τὸν ἐρωτοπαλαισμάτων

This flower I bring to you in my hands
with many holes from the deep rocks of the sea
the very image of a beehive, like a honeycomb
on Hymettus from the crags of Attica
which gives Glaucus pleasure in his waters.
This is the mattress of Triton,
with this by the waves do maidens
play, the pride of Nereus,
this washes the foamy panting
of colts, the playthings of Poseidon.
This was cut by a swimming diver
a fearless labourer in the waters of the brine
that from your snowy limbs
you might part, when night is over, fair lady,
the tiredness of love's wrestlings.[78]

The survival of Mesomedes' songs and music shows that he appealed not simply to his patron Hadrian but to a wider public. He is surely the tip of an iceberg. There must have been many citharodes whose songs gave pleasure to Antonine Greeks. *Kitharodia* figured in the Mouseia at Thespiae, and slightly later a Severan text from Smyrna documents citharodic victories in over 25 competitions in Rome and 17 Greek cities.[79]

---

[78] The translation assumes Ἀτθίδων in 3 (Wilamowitz, *Griechische Verkunst* (Berlin, 1921), 601). The general sense of the last line seems certain; we translate τὸν ἐρωτοπαλαισμάτων (D. A. Russell), *exempli gratia*, for τῶν ἐρωτικῶν ὀμμάτων.

[79] The Mouseia, *SEG* iii. 334. 30 and perhaps *IG* vii. 1773. 28, cf. Schachter (1986), 177 n. 5. The Smyrna text is *IGR* iv. 1432, the citharode C. Antonius Septimius Publius, and his victories are in Rome, Smyrna, Puteoli, Naples, Actium, Argos, Nemea, Pergamum, Delphi, Ephesus, Epidaurus, Athens, Sardis, Tralles, Miletus, Rhodes, Sparta, and Mantinea (he does not list minor *agones*). He also names his voice-trainer (φωνασκός) P. Aelius Agathemerus who was himself a κιθαρῳδὸς ἱερονίκης and μελοποιὸς ἔνδοξος, probably within our period: *IGR* iv. 1432. Note too that it is an illusion of *kitharodia* that Philostratus tries to create by his compositions for his *Heroicus* of *c*. AD 215 (208 K = 53 Lannoy, 213 K = 72–3 Lannoy), cf. *ANRW* II. xxxiii/1 (Berlin/N.Y., 1989), 222–3.

The popularity of Mesomedes' rhythms has even left its mark on Lucian, whose mock-tragedy *Podagra* follows him in mixing *apokrota* with paroemiacs for a 'choral' passage (87–111). We need not doubt Cassius Dio's story that Caracalla constructed a cenotaph for him, and may note that Dio expected his readers to recognize Mesomedes as 'the man who composed citharodic nomes'.[80]

I have offered a sketch, not a history: whether our material will ever allow the latter to be written is doubtful. We can be more confident in positive than in negative generalizations. Various species of epigram flourished, and some commemorative poems on stone grew into poems longer and grander than classical epigram. Some hexameter poems followed, and fewer seem to have flouted, Callimachean precepts, but our picture may be skewed by the greater capacity for survival of apparently useful didactic poetry. I have said almost nothing of dramatic poetry, but new tragedies and comedies were written and performed in competitions.[81] In melic poetry it is song accompanied by the *kithara* that seems to hold centre-stage, but again we are frustrated by the lack of examples of other melic texts we know to have existed. To explain why so little poetry survives from a period from which we have so much prose would require another paper. Quality is not the only factor, and poets of the Antonine Age deserve some congratulation for carrying the flag through an era in which prose had seized the literary highground.

[80] Cassius Dio 77. 13. 7, cf. Suda s.n. Mesomedes.

[81] e.g. the Mouseia at Thespiae, see the texts cited in nn. 61 and 66. Of imperial Greek tragedies a few trimeters may survive if the 5 iambics in Stobaeus iv. 22 (i) 3, 4 (p. 494 Hense) belong to the Tiberian epigrammatist Apollonides, cf. Gow–Page (1968), ii. 148 n. 2.

IV

The Second Sophistic: Some Problems of Perspective

GRAHAM ANDERSON

'Antonine Literature' is easily defined by the chronological
limits of a dynasty; but it is also tempting to characterize the
Antonine period as the climax of 'The Second Sophistic'.[1] No
one is likely to disagree, but it is not quite so clear with what we
are actually agreeing. Again, when we are singling out figures
in the cultural history of the Roman Empire it comes to us
fairly easily to say that Plutarch, for example, or Galen, or even
Tertullian 'flourished during the period of the Second Sophistic' or some such formula.[2] The expression has an air of precision about it: we are all expected to know what we mean, and
assume a similar knowledge in others. But we ought to be asking 'What Second Sophistic?' or 'Second Sophistic what?' In
trying to work towards an answer, I have set out to avoid any
spurious neatness or over-definition: the result has been a series
of only partially satisfactory projections, no one of which can
easily be made to include or exclude everything that we might
wish. But if nothing else, I hope that in questioning the term we
can stop and ask ourselves how wide or narrow our use of it is
intended to be. Only after we have some notion of what it is, or

---

[1] For historical and prosopographical treatment, Bowersock (1969), *passim*, with the
modifications of Bowie (1982); both offer more literary views in *CHCL* i.655–713 *passim*. For a literary map of the second and third centuries in general, Reardon (1971),
esp. 64–232 on the sophistic and its philosophical relations; on declamation in a Greek
context, Russell (1983). There is a useful cross-section of aspects, with a list of sophists,
in Bowersock (ed.) (1974). Sandbach's rather neglected article in *CAH* (1936) antici-
pates many of the points of recent debate in brief compass. I have offered a fuller treatment in *ANRW* II. xxxiii (forthcoming); and in a book entitled 'The Second Sophistic:
A Cultural Phenomenon in the Roman Empire', in progress.

[2] Of Plutarch: C. P. Jones (1971), 15; of Galen: Bowersock (1969), 66; of Tertullian:
Barnes (1971), 213 (with some subsequent hesitation in the 2nd edn, 333). Reardon
(1971), p. 15 n. 5, admits that the term is one of convenience, with possibly misleading
overtones.

might claim to be, can we perhaps begin to ask what contact
with it can imply.

I. SOME PROBLEMS OF DEFINITION

Lexical definition of the term sophist reflects the flexibility, not
to say the treachery, of the term itself. *LSJ* s.v. σοφιστής dis-
tinguishes three historical strata:[3] (I) a basic application
'expert', 'wise, prudent or statesmanlike man', current even
before the fifth-century Athenian Enlightenment, and naturally attractive to subsequent claimants to the title; (II) 'a
Sophist, one who gave lessons in grammar, rhetoric, politics,
mathematics for money, such as Prodicus, Gorgias, Protagoras';
under this (II. 3) is placed the 'later' usage, referring to 'the
ῥήτορες, Professors of Rhetoric and prose writers of the Empire,
such as Philostratus and Libanius'. The term was naturally
bedevilled with controversy throughout most of its history: it
could be used ironically of dubious claimants (I. 2), so that
'sophist' as a synonym for 'charlatan' or 'cheat' was already
current in the classical period (II. 2); this usage is no less
applicable in the early Empire. One notes problems of inclusion even in the fifth century: E. R. Dodds interestingly refused
Gorgias the title on the grounds that he did not claim to teach
virtue[4]—while citing the Platonic Socrates as observing that
people are apt to confound the roles of rhetor and sophist.[5] We
might also question *LSJ*'s catch-all 'and prose writers of the
Empire' as far too indiscriminate. While the choice of Philostratus and Libanius seems unexceptionable, both men are perhaps a little too close to their art and inclined to see sophists in
their own less-than-objective terms. Among the more unlikely
ranks of sophists one finds Pythagoras, the Seven Sages, Socrates, and Plato no less than Isocrates included by *someone*. And
whimsical Second Sophistic writers include such candidates as
Jesus Christ, Love, and the phoenix on its funeral pyre.[6] We

---

[3] For a much larger collection of references, Brandstätter (1894). Stanton (1973)
overstresses the pejorative use of the term.

[4] In the intro. to his edn. of Plato's *Gorgias* (Oxford, 1959), p. 7.

[5] *Gorgias* 465 c.

[6] Lucian, *Peregr.* 13; Ach. Tat. 5. 27. 4, 3. 25. 7.

might fall back on Dover's observation, when trying to explain
Aristophanes' treatment of Socrates *vis-à-vis* sophists: 'nothing
is more striking, in all departments of human life, than the
extreme subjectivity of differences. For everyone who under-
stands and cares about the difference between Bach and Rach-
maninov, the Labour Party and the Communist Party, Oxford
and Cambridge, or England and Scotland, there is another, to
whom the difference is of no interest or consequence.'[7] When
classifying sophists, that kind of subjectivity seems inevitable,
not least on the part of sophists themselves. The term 'sophistic'
also calls for brief comment. I take it to be a feminine adjective
qualifying τέχνη understood: the implied noun would cover not
only the notion of an art but also a profession, hence the possibility of collective application to a group of people. A natural
frame of reference for this use in classical literature would have
been the famous discussion of occupations with -ικός suffixes in
Plato's *Gorgias*, where Socrates faces an acknowledged master
of ancient sophistic at its most rhetorical, and associates irresponsible rhetoric with such arts as flattery and confectionery.[8]
The resonance of 'sophistic' is rather like that of modern forma-
tions in -(o)logy: it has the overtones of a profession and a science, even if it evokes similar suspicions. To have a science of
'making wise' (*LSJ* σοφίζω (1)) is the ultimate pretension: we
might translate 'the art of the formation of the intellectual' or
some similarly grandiose notion. It is surely the early association of the term 'sophist' with education that lies at the root of
its appeal, and also explains the shift of meaning, real or apparent, by Philostratus' time. Education was already bifurcating
from the period of Gorgias onwards, so that rhetors and philosophers took on separate identities within the lifetime of Isocrates; and with the efflorescence of scholarship and science in
the Hellenistic world it became difficult to emulate or reproduce the fifth-century polymath. The term would naturally
have been attractive to teachers of rhetoric; philosophers on the
other hand were much more likely to avoid a word which Plato
as well as the comic poets had associated with charlatanism.
The fact that 'the art of the formation of the intellectual' was

---

[7] In the intro. to his edn of Aristophanes' *Clouds* (Oxford, 1968), p. lii.

[8] e.g. 465 C, ὅτι ὁ κομμωτικὴ πρὸς γυμναστικήν, τοῦτο σοφιστικὴ πρὸς νομοθετικήν, καὶ
ὅτι ὁ ὀψοποιικὴ πρὸς ἰατρικήν, τοῦτο ῥητορικὴ πρὸς δικαιοσύνην.

now somewhat different, some seven centuries later, necessarily
reflects educational change; but it also reflects the reputation of
the original sophists for rhetorical display, and not all their
other talents had been lost; their successors still, in effect, prepared young men for statescraft as it in turn had come to be
conceived.

2. THE 'AUTHORITATIVE' PERSPECTIVE: PHILOSTRATUS' VIEW

Students of 'The Second Sophistic' must take the phrase at
source at the beginning of Philostratus' *Vitae Sophistarum*. After
the sophists of the fifth/early fourth centuries the would-be biographer mentions ἡ δὲ μετ᾽ ἐκείνην, ἣν οὐχὶ νέαν, ἀρχαία γάρ, δευ-
τέραν δὲ μᾶλλον προσρητέον ('the one after it, which should
not be called new, for it is old, but second').[9] We are told that
its exponents, starting with Aeschines, μετεχειρίζοντο τὰς
ὑποθέσεις οἱ μὲν κατὰ τέχνην, οἱ δὲ ἀπὸ Γοργίου κατὰ τὸ δόξαν
('they handled their subjects by rule, whereas the followers of
Gorgias handled theirs as they saw fit).[10] Philostratus' preference for calling his Sophistic 'Second' rather than 'New' is
justly suspected: he wants to have it both ways and trace his
term back to Aeschines, in the latter's capacity as founder of a
school; but he also wants the first luminary thereafter to be the
Neronian Nicetes; the term 'new' will force him to make an unnecessary choice. 'Not new, for it is old' already has that spe-
cious air of pedantic certainty to which sophistic writing is
prone as well as showing a consciously naïve parataxis. And to
claim that it is 'second' confers the suggestion, rightly or otherwise, of an equal and legitimate successor; we must be on our
guard. Philostratus' perspective is as elusive as his formulation:
the infamous gap in his chronology from Aeschines to Nicetes
can be understood in terms of a mannerism of ancient technical
writing.[11] Whether an ancient writer is tracing the history of

---

[9] *VS* 481 (for the *Vitae Sophistarum*) I follow Olearius' pagination, retained in
Kayser's Teubner (Leipzig, 1870) and in W. C. Wright's Loeb (1921).

[10] Ibid.

[11] For Philostratus' shortcomings, C. P. Jones (1974), pp. 11–16; for the problematic
layout, Anderson (1986), 10–13; for the *Gym.*, ibid. 269–72. cf. Lucian's technique in *De
salt.*, Anderson (1977).

gymnastics or pantomime, he will find it relatively easy to rattle off the name of the πρῶτος εὑρετής and a few associates, then jump more or less without apology to his own time, rather than trace systematic lines of scholarly development. Even if Philostratus had the information, and had it to hand, we must also allow for a widespread prejudice in the Greek world of the early Empire against Hellenistic history in general,[12] a cultural foreshortening of perspective which ignores a politically less glorious era. It may well be that Philostratus' dismissal of three apparent nonentities between Aeschines and Nicetes is the result of both these tendencies.

As far as Philostratus is concerned, Nicetes and his successors *are* 'The Second Sophistic'. We might accordingly define it as 'anyone or anything concerning the *Vitae Sophistarum* and the subject-matter there implied'. But again we should be wary. In the first place, if the second century is really to be an age of sophists, then Philostratus seems to present too few of them. This is evident enough from the use of the title in inscriptions to denote sophists unmentioned by him.[13] It is also clear enough from the number of cities wealthy enough to require the provision of prestigious higher education in an age of spectacular prosperity. It is hard to believe that Tarsus or Alexandria did not have its share of 'virtuoso rhetors with a big public reputation', to use Bowersock's convenient definition of the role of sophists in the Empire.[14] Some fewer than forty exhibits over a century and a half or so is scarcely a quorum, yet Philostratus does not speak of any criteria of selection: we are all too often simply assured that *x* or *y* is thought worthy of 'the sophistic circle'.[15] Moreover from those few we have to eliminate those whose careers were prematurely ended, and the number will be even smaller.[16]

There also seem to be some striking contrasts within the ranks of those Philostratus does select. In his notice on Heracleides of Lycia he seems to take it for granted that most sophists ran schools:[17] yet we know that Aelius Aristides did not, as he

[12] Cf. Bowie (1974), 174–95.
[13] For a few of these, Anderson (1986), p. 94 n. 50.
[14] Bowersock (1969), 13.
[15] e.g. *VS* 608 (Hermocrates); *VS* 625 (Heliodorus).
[16] e.g. Hermocrates again (*VS* 612); Hermogenes (*VS* 577).
[17] *VS* 614.

found to his cost when arguments were raised over liturgies;[18] the infant prodigy Hermogenes would have been too young to do so for most of his short performing career, though he may have been a teacher in his later years; Rufus of Perinthus has no pupils mentioned either, nor has the once-more relatively young Hermocrates.[19] The only irreducible requirement seems to be exhibition oratory outside the context of the law courts, not necessarily always extempore at that. Moreover the spread of interests and activities of individual performers has to be taken into account: many spent time in their local assemblies or the courts. This makes them in effect rhetoricians involved in the three traditional branches of oratory: epideictic, sumbouleutic, and forensic.[20] Philostratus' categorization, then, seems at least a little eccentric: do fewer than forty, many of them not wholly engaged in epideictic oratory, make up 'The Second Sophistic'? Or are they just the semi-skimmed cream of late Greek rhetoric?

3. TWO BORDERLINES: PHILOSOPHY AND LATINITY?

If we are not quite satisfied with Philostratus himself, we can perhaps look at what he himself was trying to look back on, the sophists of the fifth century BC and just beyond; we might then claim that anyone resembling them in the first three centuries AD could also be included. We are conditioned by our perspectives of Greek philosophy to regard the fifth-century sophists as symbols of a serious intellectual revolution, while those of the Empire are self-glorified schoolmaster-rhetoricians.[21] To some extent this notion is reinforced by Philostratus himself: Σοφιστὰς δὲ οἱ παλαιοὶ ἐπωνόμαζον οὐ μόνον τῶν ῥητόρων τοὺς ὑπερφωνοῦντάς τε καὶ λαμπρούς, ἀλλὰ καὶ τῶν φιλοσόφων τοὺς ξὺν εὐροίᾳ ἑρμηνεύοντας 'the ancients applied the term sophists not only to outstandingly eloquent and eminent rhetors, but to

[18] Aristid. 51. 87 Keil; Bowersock (1969), 39.
[19] VS 577 f.; VS 597 f.; VS 608–12.
[20] Cf. Sandbach (1936), 682: but we cannot always be sure that epideictic oratory was 'what pleased them most'; it pleased Philostratus most, in the context in which he was writing.
[21] For recent treatment of the latter, e.g. Solmsen (1975), Kerferd (1981), Kennedy, CHCL i. 472–76.

those philosophers who expressed their arguments with facility').[22] The unspoken implication is that the moderns are more discriminating, and do not normally regard philosophers as worthy of the title. Philostratus' first priority all too often seems to be to insist on the rhetorical integrity of his sophists, uncontaminated as far as possible by any serious involvement with philosophy. Hence for example his portrait of Herodes Atticus as the verbal purist and Athenian magnate;[23] only by chance does he actually come round to admit that his subject was entrusted by Marcus Aurelius with the assessorship for philosophical chairs,[24] and only by chance in Aulus Gellius can Herodes be seen to hold his own against a would-be philosopher. Only by chance, too, do we discover that Herodes clashed with the Quintilii in the judging of a musical contest at the Pythian Games.[25]

But it is also clear from Philostratus that he himself was not the only one to link old and new sophistic. Scopelian devoted himself to Gorgias, as Herodes cultivated Critias;[26] and in some cases at least we can surmise that imitation was not simply a verbal matter. The sophists of 'The Second Sophistic' show in the versatility of their interests that they have something of the general curiosity of their predecessors: if Dio's recitation of a Persian myth περὶ πολιτείας in Borysthenes is a doubtful example, then Aristides' account of his sojourn in Egypt is not:[27] it is not mere *mimesis* of Herodotus that prompts him to discuss the Nile floods, but intelligent correction.[28] We should also note Apuleius' serious if misguided interest in Platonic doctrine in the *De deo Socratis*, or Philostratus' efforts to project Platonic dialogue onto Apollonius of Tyana.[29] We must live with the suspicion that the two 'Sophistics' are not so far apart as Philostratus would have us believe, and that the change in sophists' treatment of philosophy reflects a change in the nature of philosophy itself: Lucian's *Hermotimus* is a witness to despair that all

[22] *VS* 484.
[23] For the latter Ameling (1983) now supplements Graindor (1930).
[24] *VS* 566.
[25] Gell. 1. 2. 6–12; *VS* 559.
[26] *VS* 518; 564.
[27] Dio Prus. 36; Aristid. 36 Keil.
[28] Aristid. 36 Keil.
[29] Philostratus *VA* 3. 18–49 *passim*, 6. 10–21 *passim*.

the doctrines of the dogmatic schools could be absorbed in a single lifetime. Moreover there was no shortage of rhetoric and professional one-upmanship in the old sophistic: Philostratus quotes a *bon mot* of Gorgias at the expense of Chaerephon that would have been at home in the age of Herodes.[30] Perhaps we should modify Bowersock's definition of a sophist and describe him in both periods as 'a performing *pepaideumenos* with a big public reputation'.[31]

We should also ask how in the Graeco-Roman milieu of the Empire any conception of a Second Sophistic can be related to Latin literature. Was there a 'Latin Sophistic'? There could almost by definition be no Latin 'Second Sophistic' in the sense that Roman history had scarcely enjoyed a 'First Sophistic' as such. To judge from Philostratus, we should indeed be quick to dismiss the idea: he makes much of the fact that Favorinus or Aelian, belonging to a Latin environment, none the less qualifies for inclusion in its insistently Hellenic ethos. Yet anecdotes in Aulus Gellius, Fronto, the Elder Seneca, the Younger Pliny, or Suetonius seem to imply a Latin rhetorical culture none too easily distinguished from that implied in Philostratus himself:[32] the enormous treatment of gesture alone in Quintilian should serve to confirm our suspicions.[33] The celebrities known to Seneca were already prima donnas with personalities—one thinks of the irrepressible Albucius Silus; and they could easily turn their hand to public or forensic activity.[34] Juvenal's famous caricature of the *graeculus esuriens* in Rome would fit a Philostratean sophist or a product of Gorgias with almost equal ease: *grammaticus, rhetor, geometres, pictor, aliptes,| augur, schoenobates, medicus, magus, omnia novit | Graeculus esuriens.*[35] Most of these occupations could have been essayed by a celebrated polymath like Favorinus as readily as by Hippias of Elis some seven centuries before;[36] Favorinus was in fact carica-

[30] *VS* 483.
[31] For the *pepaideumenos*, Reardon (1971), 3–30 *passim*.
[32] Now well explored e.g. by Fairweather (1981); Gamberini (1983); Champlin (1980). On Latin literature in general in the second century, Steinmetz (1982).
[33] 11. 3. 65–136.
[34] e.g. Sen. *Controv.* 7 *praef.*; Suet. *De rhet.* 6.
[35] 3. 76 ff.
[36] For his versatility, see especially Barigazzi (1966), testimonia *passim*.

tured by his enemy Polemo as dabbling in aphrodisiacs.[37] It is also evident enough from the letters of Fronto and the web of social relationships implied in them that a rhetorically based literary patronage was at work in the Antonine period on the Latin side as well as the Greek; it seems inconceivable that Fronto's rival in the case of Demostratus, the superlative Herodes, did not belong to similar networks in both cultures.[38] We might be tempted, then, to widen our definition of 'The Sophistic' in two ways: to take on board at least 'philosophic sophists' in Greek, and the Latin counterpart of *pepaideumenoi* in general.

4. HISTORICAL AND LITERARY PERSPECTIVES

A major divergence of perspective on virtuoso rhetors and their kind is well illustrated by the situation in the first century AD itself. It is at the very time when we are most inclined to accept the rise of sophists in the Greek world that our Latin sources seem most concerned to emphasize the famous 'decline of rhetoric'.[39] From the point of view of senators in Early Imperial Rome a shift to epideictic rhetoric is a turn for the worse. For the corresponding literati in a Greek environment the picture may have been rather different. Rhetors did not now have to engage in life-and-death opposition to military masters of the first century BC: addressing emperors over immunities or agrarian issues may have represented a distinct improvement from the perspective of the recovering East Mediterranean cities. Only if we bear two different historical traditions in mind can we come to terms with what is happening.

This leads us to a larger question: are we to treat sophists as Greek literature or as Roman history? The question seems self-evidently absurd as it stands, yet the studies of the last twenty years or so have tended to compartment their activities into one category or the other. Between Bowersock's *Greek Sophists in the Roman Empire* and Reardon's *Courants littéraires grecs* there is

---

[37] Ed. G. Hoffman, in *Scriptores physiognomonici graeci*, i (Leipzig, 1886), p. 162.

[38] On Fronto, Champlin (1980), *passim*; note especially the request for a procuratorship for his friend Appian, ibid. 98–101. On this aspect of Herodes cf. Bowersock (1969), 76–88 *passim*.

[39] e.g. G. W. Williams (1978), 6–51, Heldmann (1982).

surprisingly little contact, though both together employ most of the factors we are considering.[40]

We can deal first of all with the projection of sophists laid down by Bowersock. Here the picture has a distinct emphasis on public activity: the subjects are seen less for their literary output—that is dismissed in little more than a sentence[41]—as for their public persona, their friendships with consulars, their embassies to emperors, their private benefactions, and not least their coveted but contentious exemptions from public service. There are advantages in such a view. Consolidated by the resources of modern prosopography, it illuminates an aspect of sophists that many of them would by the nature of their profession have been delighted to flaunt. They are treated as social celebrities and luminaries centred on the *polis*. But that view has limitations too: Bowersock's sophists sometimes seem little more than the sum of their prosopographical contacts, and they are shackled to the treadmill of social mobility in an inexorable way. At some points at least even the picture of a sophist's society necessarily falls short. Bowersock has no chapter on the literary contacts of sophists: these may be men whose total impact on history is a name in Philostratus as a *kritikos* or a grammarian; and there is no chapter either on the sophists' domestic relationships, since Philostratus rarely identifies the freedmen, concubines, and others who provide the colourful scandal for which he has no little taste.[42]

The picture of sophists in society can be helpfully readjusted by noting that the civic activities of sophists are those of aristocrats in general.[43] Some such coveted honours as the post *ab epistulis graecis* do not by nature require a sophist, or indeed may be positively incompatible with the flamboyant individualism in which sophists delight.[44] The various city functions such as στρατηγὸς ἐπὶ τῶν ὅπλων are as much an indication of a sophist's political inclination and civic vanity as of his rhet-

---

[40] There is a useful short bridge between the two approaches in Bowie (1974).

[41] Bowersock (1969), p. 1, 'The quality of the second-century works we possess . . . is not high: they are often over-elaborated productions on unreal, unimportant, or traditional themes'; cf. p. 58, 'it could be argued without apology that the Second Sophistic has more importance in Roman History than it has in Greek Literature'.

[42] For the latter, cf. Anderson (1986), 58–63.

[43] Bowie (1982), *passim*.

[44] Cf. Bowie (1982), 43–49.

orical technique. Here we have however to guard against the kind of brinkmanship with which one is almost tempted to wish such figures as the Vedii Antonini of Ephesus into the ranks of sophists: 'The father and son of that name in the first half of the second century are not known to have been sophists,' writes Bowersock,[45] 'though they were doubtless men of superior education; but their huge benefactions were on a sophistic scale, and a recent inscription attests their presence on embassies to Roman emperors'. But benefactions and master-building do not a sophist make, even if the younger Vedius' daughter was married to no less a sophist than Damianus of Ephesus. One can, however, notice how often the very influential, politically involved sophists seem to have been involved in practice in the courts: Isaeus was content to avoid them, and so becomes for Pliny the younger a self-effacing sophist;[46] Nicetes, Scopelian, and Polemo are involved with them, and doubtless with the web of civic patronage that links the courts with wealthy satisfied clients.

So far, then, sophists in history. They have a no less elusive profile in literature itself. One becomes uncomfortably aware that the teaching activities of the schools are only a small and specialized part of the literary production of sophists or of the literary effort of the second and third centuries AD. One notes that Scopelian produced a Gigantomachy, Antiochus a History,[47] or Favorinus ten books of Pyrrhonic tropes;[48] while sophists could undertake editorial work, as in an ill-fated revision of Nicetes.[49] Aelian wrote *Epistulae rusticae*, while a host of miscellaneous opuscula fill out the *Corpus Philostrateum*.[50] Sophists were immensely wide-ranging if superficial literati, and such a label as '*Pepaideumenos* at work and play' would perhaps do justice to the versatility of sophistic literature. If the sophist is a species of the genus aristocrat, he is also a sub-species of the sub-genus littérateur.[51]

---

[45] Bowersock (1969), 47.
[46] Pliny *Ep.* 2. 3. 5. (Annum sexagensimum excessit et adhuc scholasticus tantum est ... Nos enim, qui in foro verisque litibus terimur ...).
[47] *VS* 518; *VS* 570.
[48] *VS* 491.
[49] *VS* 512.
[50] For the latter, Anderson (1986), 259–82.
[51] The first phrase from Bowie (1982), 53.

We can note the dichotomy, then, between literary and historical profiles of sophists. But these profiles can be matched. Philostratus often has more information than we give him credit for, and we have a valuable vignette of Scopelian transacting civic business and immediately going on to declaim.[52] We can seldom comment, however, on the proportion of time spent on what. Philostratus does give us one brief but telling aside to the effect that sophists spend most of their time teaching boys;[53] but in other cases he makes much of a performance which is only incidental to a diplomatic mission, as in Alexander Peloplaton's celebrated visit to Athens *en route* to join Marcus as *ab epistulis graecis*.[54] We are left asking whether either Alexander or Scopelian would have needed to earn his living by teaching as such, and so could have organised displays more or less as time or inclination dictated. We have to think of figures who may have spent their time in much the same dilettante fashion as the younger Pliny was often able to do. Neither Bowersock's nor Bowie's picture of the sophist emphasizes the time spent in what we might call salon-confraternity; there are hints enough in Philostratus,[55] but it is Aulus Gellius whose evocation of the salon-culture of Herodes Atticus or Favorinus shows us our species of contentious philologue in action on the gender of a rare word, the benefits of breast-feeding, or the criteria of authenticity for a play of Plautus.[56]

We do not know either how consistently most sophists took pupils, or how much time their pupils took. For some of the more eminent, one suspects, the professional chores must have fallen into the background; perhaps the 'school' as we tend to conceive it may have been little more than what present-day musicians understand by a 'master class', a celebrity dialogue of demonstration and counter-demonstration for the very few,[57] in which performers too often do little beyond their normal public exhibitions.

So far, then, 'historical' and 'literary' images of sophists.

[52] *VS* 518.
[53] *VS* 614.
[54] *VS* 571.
[55] e.g. *VS* 586 (both Herodes and Hadrian of Tyre).
[56] Gell. 4. 1. 1 ff.; 12. 1; 3. 3. 6.
[57] Cf. the description of Herodes' Clepsydrion, *VS* 585.

Where should we look to see both facets of this single phenomenon interacting with each other? One text of Apuleius neatly subsumes sophistic literature and history together. The sophist is addressing himself—in Latin—to the proconsul of Africa, Severianus—on the subject of one of the original sophists, Hippias of Elis.[58] Of all that he might have selected to say about Hippias, Apuleius has to choose the feature of his subject that most resembles paradoxography—Hippias' celebrated all-round self-sufficiency; and in particular the marvellous robe the sophist had worn at Pisa during the Olympic games, all hand made by himself including the jewellery; one is reminded of the murmur that went round the audience when the elegant Alexander Peloplaton made his début in Athens.[59] Apuleius can then glibly dismiss the element of 'do it yourself': he prefers to let craftsmen do all the other arts while he concentrates on rhetoric. He has turned Hippias' self-sufficiency on its head, and his attitude is typical. So is his ultimate purpose, to compliment Severianus: Apuleius assures us that he puts all his literary genius into a variety of genres, and all he would gladly dedicate to Severianus, whose moderation is the pride of the province, and whose son's impending praetorship can expect to be followed by the same high office as his father now holds.

Here Apuleius has combined a discussion of an eminent sophist and sophistic literary values with conventional compliment; he has produced a flourish of paradoxography in the service of patronage; and ancient literature and contemporary history stand cheek by jowl. We could analyse many another scene in the same way, such as the First Kingship Oration of Dio of Prusa, in which the Emperor Trajan is put by implication at the same crossroads as the mythical Heracles in the mould of the Allegory of Prodicus, still a sophistic *pièce de résistance* after so many centuries. Or we could note the scene in Philostratus of Herodes contemplating the Isthmus: a serious contemporary scheme of civil engineering is used to invoke Nero's failure, itself reminiscent of Xerxes' *débâcle*.[60] Ornamental literature embraces ornamental politics, to the satisfaction of both.

---

[58] *Flor.* 9.
[59] *VS* 572.
[60] *Dio* 1. 56–84; *VS* 551 f.

5. SOME SOPHISTIC PEOPLE?

What sort of figures should we bring forward in order to do
justice to the perspectives and factors we have been looking at?
I should suggest Dio of Prusa and Apuleius, if not as typical
sophists, then certainly as typically sophistic personalities and
products: I choose them partly because they contrive to elude
the terms of reference set by both Bowersock and Reardon, and
also because we have a sufficient œuvre for both to enable us to
form a much more varied picture, both literary and historical,
than a notice from Philostratus is inclined to provide.[61]

Dio is excluded by Bowersock on an interpretation of the
equivocal evidence of Philostratus;[62] and only touched on by
Reardon, presumably because the bulk of his activity falls
before the second century.[63] Unsurprisingly he seems to be included and excluded simultaneously by Philostratus himself.[64]
He has very obviously an intellectual and philosophical dimen-
sion; but his rhetorical skills and poses are no less a part of his
public persona.[65] He played too that role as a builder on which
the prominence of sophists and the assertiveness of cities is so
often based.[66] If Dio cannot be classified as a sophist, then
nobody can. No less can such a role be claimed by Apuleius:
one suspects that his exclusion from Philostratus is not so much
on grounds of being a Latinist, since in fact his sophistic performances could be bilingual.[67] It is rather that in belonging to
North Africa west of Naucratis he seems to lie outside Philostratus' relatively narrow quadrant of vision. We can see Apuleius
as a littérateur in the *Metamorphoses*, as a public performer in
the *Florida*, as an object of a kind of scandal from which sophists
were not excluded in the *Apologia*, and as socially at least the

---

[61] For discussion of Philostratus' notice, Desideri (1978), 35–7; Moles (1978), 95;
Anderson (1986), 99–102.

[62] Bowersock (1969), 110, includes Dio among those whom Philostratus 'could not
truthfully denominate sophists'.

[63] Reardon (1971), 10, seems to include him among philosophers, and advances
Aristides as the 'answer' to ancient worthies in rhetoric; but C. P. Jones (1978), 136–40
suggests some thirty items, by no means all philosophical, falling after 100 AD.

[64] *VS* 484, cf. 486–9.

[65] See especially Stanton (1973), 353–4; Moles (1978), 88–93 and *passim*.

[66] 47. 6 f., 48. 11, Pliny *Ep.* 10. 81 f.; C. P. Jones (1978) 112 ff.

[67] *Flor.* 26.

equal of the front runners in the sophistic rat-races of Philostratus.[68]

A further interesting case of literary versus historical interpretation can be found in the shifting fortunes of Lucian over the past few decades. There are those of us who see him as a scholarly manipulator of sophistic material, with a veneer of philosophy and a veneer of concern for the real world;[69] and there are those who see him rather as an acute observer of that world, who might occasionally make excursions into the world of the sophist's study.[70] But there is no contradiction between these perspectives: the world of the *Demonax* connects easily with the ethos of Philostratus. And the mention of Lucian in the Arabic Galen shows us at last a practical joker in a historical context:[71] Lucian emerges as the writer of a bogus pseudo-Ionic philosophical piece which he then persuades an eminent philosopher to comment on. The latter treats it as the genuine article, to his confoundment and no doubt Lucian's delight.

Lucian at least is a predictable subject of debate, on whom historians and literary scholars still incline to take sides. More surprising (to me, at least) is the assertion that Lucian and Aristides can be seen as rival and almost mutually exclusive embodiments of sophistic activity. That is rather like arguing that Heliodorus is the embodiment of the Greek novel while Achilles Tatius is not. In the case of Lucian and Aristides it is indeed true that the contrast is more extreme. Bowersock puts it like this:

Galen's eyewitness accounts of two distinguished literary contemporaries serve to illuminate their surviving writing and show Galen a perceptive observer. He saw in Aristides a man whose indomitable spirit triumphed over a body that was slowly wasting away. In Lucian he saw a malicious prankster who took pleasure in embarrassing serious people. There can be no doubt as to which of these two authors he judged the greater man, and his judgement was identical with the judgements of the subsequent generations of antiquity. The modern admiration of Lucian, often coupled with denigration of Aristides, is a

---

[68] For Apuleius as a sophist, Tatum (1979), esp. 135–59.
[69] e.g. Anderson (1976*a*) and (1982).
[70] Notably Baldwin (1973), C. P. Jones (1986).
[71] Strohmaier (1976), 118–19.

grave impediment to the understanding of Greek literature under Rome and Byzantium. Galen gives the correct perspective.[72]

It is not entirely clear from the above that Galen does not in fact set out to make a contrast between the two. And the context in which the physician writes on Lucian is against the latter half of Bowersock's view. Galen is making a comparison between the serious philosopher so easily duped by Lucian and an inexperienced physician who brings ridicule on himself by an elementary mistake. Sophists and their associates are often difficult to schematize, and so are their views of one another.

6. OUTSIDE THE SCHOOLS

We have noted, then, the sophist's ambiguous relationship to his Greek past and Graeco-Roman present; and his no-less-ambiguous relationships to historical and literary spheres. Can we add another penumbra of vagueness to the cultural context of sophists? We can say that they operate in an ethos just as intelligible and well-attested in the second century AD as it was in Aristophanes' *Clouds* or Plato's *Euthydemus*, an ethos in which an educational system and its political environment encourage a certain attitude of mind and related literary tendencies, certain intellectual reflexes and their accompanying resources of expression. It is difficult to arrive at an exact formulation to cover such an ethos: a sort of prefabricated smartness, a packaged sophistication, presenting a certain cultural mosaic. I can best sum it up by a glance at a much-forgotten and easily forgettable figure, Maximus of Tyre.[73] The forty *Dialexeis* present us with a thought-world which can be related to some aspects of most sophistic practitioners we know. The *dialexis* itself is a sort of essay or discourse, what a sophist will present when he is not put on the spot to work a *melete*. Maximus himself is not an inspiring performer, but he does know the raw materials, and

---

[72] Bowersock, *CHCL* i. 663. Earlier Bowersock had adopted a somewhat different formulation (1969), 1: 'Authors like Lucian and Aristides brilliantly mirror the world in which the sophists flourished' (though also hard on Lucian, ibid. 114 ff.).

[73] On Maximus, long-neglected, see now Koniaris (1983), Szarmach (1985), Trapp (1986).

demonstrates that versatile manipulation of them which we should feel entitled to demand of a 'virtuoso rhetor with a big public reputation'. We can illustrate from the end of *Or.* 14:

Ἂν δὲ ἐπὶ τὰς μοναρχίας ἔλθῃς, κολακεύει καὶ Ξέρξην Μαρδόνιος, βάρβαρος βάρβαρον, ἀνόητος ἀνόητον, δειλὸς οἰκέτης δεσπότην τρυφῶντα· τὰ δὲ τῆς κολακείας τέλη, ἀνίσταται ἡ Ἀσία, μαστιγοῦται ἡ θάλαττα, Ἑλλήσποντος ζεύγνυται, Ἄθως ὀρύττεται.

When you come to monarchy, Mardonius flatters Xerxes, the barbarian the barbarian, the fool the fool, the cowardly servant the fastidious master. And the goals of the flattery are these: Asia set in turmoil, the sea whipped, the Hellespont yoked, Athos excavated.[74]

Maximus' discourse is ostensibly about how to tell a flatterer from a friend: a hint in Herodotus 7.10 gives him the chance to connect even the declaimers' favourite stand-by to his subject. He then has the effrontery to wind up by turning to his own profession:

κολακεύει καὶ συκοφάντης ῥήτορα, λόγον λόγῳ ἐπανιστάς, καὶ ἐπιτειχίζων τὸ ἄδικον τῷ δικαίῳ, καὶ τὸ αἰσχρὸν τῷ καλῷ. κολακεύει καὶ σοφιστὴς φιλόσοφον· οὗτος μὲν κολάκων ἀκριβέστατος.

Even the fake informer flatters the rhetor, setting word against word, and putting up a fortification of injustice against justice, and evil against good. And the sophist flatters the philosopher: he is the most accomplished flatterer of all.

It is not too hard to decide whether Maximus belongs to this élite league of flatterers from whom he dissociates himself with so elegant a flourish.

It is clear enough that Maximus is forcing philosophy into a sophistic mould, however we choose to describe the latter. The result, as so often in sophistic literature, is the manipulation of motifs and *topoi* in ever-more-surprising combinations. When 'sophistic' takes possession of any given genre, the result is a distinctive texture which is something more than mere rhetorical elaboration. We might ask how such a texture functions in relation to another literary category. What do we mean, for example, when we talk about 'the sophistic novel'? It is tempting to put Chariton on one side as 'presophistic' and group Heliodorus, Achilles, and Longus together as 'sophistic', but

---

[74] On this commonplace, Lucian *Rhet. Prae.* 18 (Athos and Hellespont).

how clearly could we define 'sophistic' in this context?[75] A clumsily literal answer would be: 'The sort of thing we should expect the sort of people Philostratus calls sophists to write if they turned their hand to fiction'. Part of the distinction of these novelists is in their Atticizing ambitions, but that is not the heart of the matter; sometimes it is an air of ambitious assurance—virtuosity if we like to call it that—that marks the distinction: one could easily envisage large sections of Achilles or Heliodorus as suitable entertainment for a declamation audience;[76] in Chariton one might have to look a good deal further. But Longus is 'sophistic', yet in a different sense again; it is the rococo perfectionism of the miniature that lends this text its distinctiveness.[77] But attempts at neat characterization will only lead us on to further questions: what is it about Achilles that makes him 'sophistic' and no more, while Longus can be 'sophistic' and yet have a claim to commanding literary status at the same time?

As well as detecting and defining sophistic mannerisms we must also recognize their limits, and this brings us to a further pair of differing perspectives. In a classic treatment of Early Imperial archaism, Ewen Bowie puts the sophists besides historians and antiquarians as a manifestation of the archaizing tastes of the period.[78] Once more this offers helpful generalization, but that in turn must be applied with caution. It should be stressed that both parties have their contemporary facets as well: Arrian could write his *Expeditio contra Alanos* as well as the classic Alexander-History; Lucian could shrewdly characterize contemporary individuals as well as apparently timeless stereotypes; and even Aristides lived all his religious life, and a good deal of his political, in the present.[79] But more difficult to put into perspective is the fact that in some cases 'sophistic' and 'antiquarian' approaches to the world begin to diverge. In Plutarch, Pausanias, and even Athenaeus there is a strongly con-

---

[75] Reardon (1974), 26, noting that education is the common factor between novelists and the sophistic, and that elements of composition such as *ekphraseis*, letters, and monologues are a factor; but since the latter as he admits are encountered in Chariton, we are still not told what is distinctively sophistic about the three sophistic novels.

[76] e.g. Achilles, 1. 1. 2–13; 4. 13 f.; 5. 25. 2–26. 13.

[77] For the element of adoxography in Longus, Anderson (1984), 144.

[78] Bowie (1974), 168–95.

[79] Cf. Bowie (1974), 192; C. P. Jones (1986); Bowersock (1969), 36–41 and *passim*.

servative streak that does not fully align itself with everything that sophists might be supposed to embody.[80] Even Lucian's instructions to an aspiring rhetor, however glib or hypocritical, stress the importance of hard work and honest homework on Demosthenes and his kind, rather than the flashy epideictic archaism that contents itself with bombastic treatment of Xerxes.[81] It may even be ironic that Bowersock should wish to polarize Aristides and Lucian when the latter takes the very stand one would expect of the former. We might well wish to take refuge in Sandbach's formula of half a century ago: 'to us there seems endless gradation, which we cannot compress into categories'.[82]

7. CONCLUSION

To sum up: how does a wider, more integrated treatment of sophists affect our understanding of the cultural history of the early empire? It will show us a versatile philhellenic aristocracy for whom epideictic oratory in Greek is only a part of rather wider interests. The jewel in Philostratus' crown, Herodes Atticus, did not confine himself to an interest in Greek literature, or to rhetoric as opposed to philosophy:[83] the upward mobility in the Roman empire which Bowersock so well illustrates may go far to explaining why.[84] But there is perhaps a broader explanation. Versatility and its attendant curiosity are as powerful motive-forces in the formation of a sophist as archaizing Hellenism. And the word 'sophist' is as chameleon-like a term as Philostratus or any one of us may wish to make it. It is not just its connotations of grandeur and superiority that suit it to Philostratus' purpose, but its connexions with assumed authority: for Philostratus the philosopher admits his ignorance; the sophist says he knows.[85]

Philostratus' sophists are a sympton, then, of a much broader cultural phenomenon. They should not be seen in a vacuum in

---

[80] On the first two Russell (1972); Habicht (1985).

[81] *Rhet. Prae.* 9, 18.

[82] *CAH* xi (1936), 681 (of the distinctions between philosopher, sophist, and rhetor).

[83] e.g. Gell. 9. 2; 19. 12.

[84] Bowersock (1969), 28–9.

[85] *VS* 480.

which all Philostratus' statements are taken on trust.[86] We can perhaps try to adjust our perspective along some of the lines suggested by making a return visit to Russell's city of Sophistopolis,[87] a paradigm of the city-state as declaimers would have it. As Paideia's chariot touches down beside the Temple of Daedalus, we should note that the city is not totally given over to declaimers and their entourage; there is a Potters' Quarter where the sophists must learn at least enough philosophy to defend their city against the charges of the neighbouring city of Platonopoliteia. And a Roman proconsul is somewhere in the vicinity, ready to convey the loyal greetings of the metrosophistopolitans to their influential colonists in Rome or Carthage. The chief magistrates, or *Logophiloi*, are not exclusively sophists, though the latter take their share of governing and avoiding liturgies along with their fellow aristocrats. The religious life of the city is varied and vibrant; apart from worshipping their patron Peitho, they put strangers on trial for debasing her cult with magic rites, and someone has put out a prophecy that the doctor will reveal the doings of the trickster to the barbarians. Not everyone is attending declamations. Young people are leaving the city in pairs for day-trips to Lesbos or adventure-holidays in Egypt, where they will practise declamatory skills to more romantic ends. And encyclopaedic scholars crowd the libraries, deaf to the din of declamation outside. The city's history from its mythical founder Lalos the Krotoglot down to Gorgias has already been written; but the scholars are filling the gap between the city's capitulation to Alexander after a brave siege and the dazzling visit of Hadrian in modern times. I think we know and care enough about this city to follow their example.

[86] Against which C. P. Jones (1974). 11–16; Anderson (1986). 77–88 and *passim*.
[87] Russell (1983), 21–39.

V

Lucian's Introductions

H. G. NESSELRATH

Lucian's introductions (or *prolaliai*) and comparable pieces by other ancient writers have never been exactly showered with scholarly attention; in this century, apart from two recent short papers by Graham Anderson and Robert Bracht Branham, there are only two articles published in 1949 by Karl Mras and still earlier a Königsberg dissertation *De prolaliarum usu rhetorico* of 1911 by Aloysius Stock, who, taking Lucian's pieces as a starting-point, succeeded in outlining the general development of the form of *prolaliai* in antiquity. Short treatments of Lucianic *prolaliai* can, of course, be found in more general works on Lucian. Authors of these, like Jacques Bompaire and Christopher Robinson, tend to take a positive view of Lucian's introductions; not so Graham Anderson, who dismisses them as belonging to 'the slightest trifles among the vast amount of ephemera produced by the Second Sophistic'.[1] We shall have to take sides in this controversy; but first something has to be said about the genre or sub-genre (or whatever) of the rhetorical introduction of *prolalia* as such.

As Stock established, *prolalia* is not really an ancient term, for we find it only as a sub-title of Lucian's *Bacchus* and *Hercules* in the manuscripts, the oldest of which (Vaticanus 90 = Γ) dates from the tenth century, and in Thomas Magister (1270–1325).[2]

Parts of this paper were read and discussed in a Cologne seminar of Prof. Kassel's; a draft of it was read in Prof. Russell's seminar at Oxford. I would like to thank all participants for their critical and helpful suggestions, especially Prof. Kassel and Prof. Russell.

[1] Bompaire (1958), 288: 'Le genre, par son mépris des cadres rigides, . . . laissait une infinie liberté, et Lucien . . . a su en user pour introduire le meilleur de lui-même dans ces impromptus.' Robinson (1979), 8 (commenting on Lucian's *Zeux*.): 'One can reasonably say of this very neat and economic structure that Lucian has exploited his formal training with great skill to produce something other than a formal rhetorical exercise.' A similar opinion is held by Branham (1985), 243, in reaction to Anderson (1977*b*, 313).

[2] Stock (1911), 6–10; Thomas Magister, *Ecloga vocum Atticarum* p. 224, 1 Ritschl: λαλιὰ καὶ προσλαλιὰ καὶ προλαλιὰ δόκιμα, without, however, giving examples.

Probably, then, Lucian himself did not refer to his introductory
pieces as *prolaliai*, but rather as *dialexeis*, a term common in his
times and found quite often in the *Vitae Sophistarum* of Philostratus.[3] As *dialexis*, however, is vague in its meaning and is not re-
stricted solely to introductions, I shall continue to use the term
prolalia.

Not only did this term not exist in Lucian's times, but the
thing itself must then have been a quite recent development in
ancient rhetoric. Since the beginnings of a professional art of
speech, of course, rules had been laid down prescribing how
one could most effectively set about addressing one's audience:
that one should aim at arousing its good will and its attention
and interest, that one should try to come across as being modest
and not arrogant, and so on.[4] All these prescriptions, however,
dealt with introductory chapters as a firmly integrated part of a
whole, not with separate introductory pieces centred on themselves. That began to change when rhetoric as a whole changed
significance. By the end of the first century AD, when the Mediterranean world had already been living under Roman emperors for several generations, rhetoric had lost most of its original
functions in real life, in politics, and in the courts, and was now
more or less confined to higher general education and public
show performances. People even made it their profession to perform as orators and lived by this art, and Lucian was one of
them. For such performers it mattered less what they would say
than how they would say it; hitherto, the aim of an orator was
to sell people a certain political course or a certain judgment in
a law case—now, one would simply want to sell oneself. Therefore it was paramount to come across as being intelligent, educated, and eloquent from the very first moment; and it was
under these circumstances that introductory chapters tended to
gain importance and take on a life of their own.

As in most other developments, theory followed several steps
behind the actual emergence of *prolaliai* in lectures: the first
theorist to provide some more detailed advice on how to work

---

[3] Cf. the passages collected by C. L. Kayser in his edn. of Philostratus (Leipzig,
1871), vol. ii, p. vii nn. 42–4. On *dialexis* being well-nigh synonymous with *prolalia* see
Bompaire (1958), 286 n. 5, and the works of Kroll, Münscher, Schmid, and Hirzel
cited there.

[4] Cf. *Rhet. Her.* 1. 4. 6–7; Cic. *De inv.* 1. 15. 20, 16. 22; Quint. 4. 1. 5, 8–10, 33.

out an effective introductory piece seems to have been the rhetor Menander, about one and a half centuries after Lucian, and even Menander does not talk of a *prolalia*, but gives his instructions under the heading *lalia*; but he obviously considered *lalia* the form most appropriate for an introduction, as many of his rules for constructing a good *lalia* are in fact anticipated by Lucian's *prolaliai*.[5]

Yet Lucian was neither the first nor the only one to write and declaim such introductory pieces; Stock and Mras have pointed out that a number of Dio of Prusa's discourses have a quite similar character, and that in Lucian's own times the rhetorical addresses collected in the *Florida* of Apuleius can be considered as *prolaliai* (or excerpts from them), too; and references to introductory *dialexeis* of various sophists of the second century AD can furthermore be found in Philostratus.[6] So, in one respect, Lucian's introductions are just a typical product of their time; but on closer inspection they reveal some features that seem to be more of a mark of Lucian himself, in structure, content, and personal references.

First, structure: here we are on somewhat shaky ground, as, apart from the above-mentioned examples of Dio and Apuleius, there are only fragments left from the introductory speeches of other sophists. Yet Dio's introductions are something of a mixed bag, and it is not easy to detect regular and

---

[5] e.g. Men. Rh. 389. 12–13 Sp. (p. 116 R.–W.) χαίρει ... τὸ τῆς λαλιᾶς εἶδος ... τῇ τῶν διηγημάτων ἀβρότητι—compare the various διηγήματα in Lucian's introductions; in 389. 29 Menander calls the ξένη τῶν διηγημάτων ἀκοή an important means for producing ἡδονή (his examples are Herodotus' stories; but, of course, Lucian also shows a notable penchant for exotic things and in *Dips.* assumes a Herodotean attitude—see below). In 390. 19–391. 5 (p. 118 R.–W.) Menander demonstrates how the speaker may use a mythical or a historical exemplum to allude to his own situation or emphasize his wishes with regard to his audience; Lucian's proceedings in, e.g., *Zeux.* or *Bacch.* are quite similar. In 392. 18–22 (p. 122 R.–W.) Menander states that the speaker must know about famous musicians and other artists and their achievements; Lucian displays such knowledge in *Herod. Harm.*, and *Zeux.* (in 393. 5–16 a similar knowledge about poets is required—cf. Lucian's *Herod.*). The speaker is even to know about Okeanos and great streams (Men. Rh. 392. 26–8)—cf. Lucian's *Electr.*—and he is advised to give Dionysus and his companions a considerable part to play in his *lalia* (Men. Rh. 392. 24–6)—cf. Lucian's *Bacch.* At 393. 25 Menander makes it clear that *lalia* can either stand on its own or be part of a longer performance. The latter possibility gives a clue to how *laliai* placed at the beginning could develop into the sub-species of *prolaliai*.

[6] On Dio Prus. see Stock (1911), 41–66, and Mras (1949a), 74–7; on Apuleius, Stock (1911), 69–74, Mras (1949b), and (1949a), 81. On other sophists, Stock (1911), 85–94 (discusses Philostr. *VS* 572 and 579).

recurring patterns in them;[7] likewise, Apuleius seems to talk about whatever just comes into his head while preparing his listeners for what is going to follow.[8] Moreover, Dio's as well as Apuleius' introductions seem to have been one-occasion pieces and teamed up with only one specific follow-up speech, while Lucian's introductions conceivably could be (and probably were) employed several times; and this may be one reason why they exhibit clear and well-ordered (but never too rigid) structures that usually are well fitted to what their speaker wants to get across to his audience. Thus Lucian likes to develop two narrative or descriptive components at a time (e.g. the description of a picture combined with a little story or myth) and to round them off by applying their meaning to his own situation. The ordering of these components is always different: Lucian may put personal remarks about himself at the beginning, in

---

[7] Mras (1949a), 74, identifies Dio Prus. 42 and 57 as *prolaliai*. 42 is quite similar to Lucian's *Electr.* in that Dio warns his listeners not to harbour any overblown expectations about his *logoi*, while at the same time he slyly implies that they are indeed sought after. Unlike Lucian's *Electr.*, this piece contains no narrative parts. 57 is generally considered to be a *prolalia* to one of Dio's four discourses on kingship (1–4); its bulk is made up by a discussion of the meaning of Nestor's words in *Il.* 1. 260–74; only at the end (9–12) does Dio relate this to his own situation. In a way, Dio here compares himself to Nestor, as Lucian does to Zeuxis (in *Zeux.*) and Herodotus (in *Herod.*); but while Lucian tells stories, Dio gives a moralizing interpretation of a poet's words, a quite different procedure. In other cases Dio's *prolaliai* seem to be even more intimately connected with a specific follow-up speech than in the case just mentioned: von Arnim (1898), 438, had already classified the introductory sections of 12, 32, 33, and 35 as *prolaliai* as well; as the most important difference between the two authors he noted that Dio is fond of πλανᾶσθαι ἐν τοῖς λόγοις, as he himself called it (12. 16, and other passages discussed by von Arnim (1898), 439 ff.; cf. Mras (1949a), 75–7), while Lucian's train of thought is much straighter and more orderly.

[8] In *Flor.* 15, for instance, Apuleius starts with a geographical *ekphrasis* of Samos (p. 19. 11–20 Helm), which leads to the description of the sanctuary of Juno (pp. 19. 20–20. 5), where the statue of the young Bathyllus arrested Apuleius' attention (pp. 20. 6–21. 3). The claim that this statue does not represent Bathyllus but Pythagoras is refuted (p. 21. 3–7); but, having mentioned Pythagoras, Apuleius now launches into a very circumstantial report of that philosopher's life, studies, and travels (pp. 21. 8–22. 21), until he ends up with praising the Pythagorean emphasis on silence (pp. 22. 21–23. 9). That takes him on to Plato, the Academy and, finally, himself, who is now addressing, it seems, a high Roman official (p. 23, 9–16). In *Flor.* 16 it is the other way round: Apuleius wants to thank his audience for being honoured with a statue, but first has to account for a recent absence: he was afflicted by something quite comparable to what happened to the comic poet Philemon—and now Apuleius first launches into a characterization of Philemon's comic art (p. 24. 7–19) before he tells of his fateful accident (pp. 24. 19–26. 4), and then relates his own (p. 26. 5–24). Likewise in *Flor.* 9, a short mention of Hippias of Elis prompts a long digression on this sophist; the link between this digression and its application is much more tenuous than in Lucian's *prolaliai*.

the middle, or at the end (sometimes he uses several of these positions together), he may first describe a picture and then tell a story, or he may do it the other way round, or instead of a picture he may present a second story; his personal remarks may only be an afterthought, or they may set the frame for the whole piece right from the beginning. Thus not one of the eight little works that I am going to comment upon here[9] exactly resembles another; and the rhetor Menander may have had in mind such richness of variation when he stated: ἔστιν ἀρίστη τάξις τῆς λαλιᾶς τὸ μὴ κατὰ τῶν αὐτῶν βαδίζειν συνεχῶς, ἀλλ' ἀτακτεῖν ἀεί (391, 22–4 Sp. = p. 120 R.–W.).

Second, content: this area has (as far as I can see) up to now received the least attention (with a few notable exceptions); when dealing with Lucian's introductions at all, scholars have tended to concentrate on what Lucian reveals about himself, the implication being, of course, that the stories he tells are not really worth closer attention. It may be these, however, that intrigued his audiences most. The stories and pictures that Lucian presents in his *prolaliai* are extraordinarily varied, and he could not have told them without having either a wide range of reading or a remarkably vivid imagination or both; for they take us to the Olympic festival, to the swans of the River Po, to the poisonous snakes of North Africa, to an important battlefield in Asia Minor, to a mysterious old god in Gaul, and to magical fountains in India (to say nothing, as yet, about the

[9] These eight (*Bacch.*, *Herc.*, *Electr.*, *Dips.*, *Herod.*, *Zeux.*, *Harm.*, *Scyth.*) are those that Max Rothstein (1888), 116 ff., had already classified as *prolaliai*, excluding three other pieces that time and again have been proposed as additional members of the group (e.g. by Reardon (1971), p. 165 n. 20): *Somn.* was recently defended by Anderson (1977*b*) p. 314 n. 5, as being a *prolalia*, while Bompaire (1958), p. 288 n. 5, is more sceptical; in fact, *Somn.* clearly is a special-occasion piece (written for Lucian's return to his native Samosata) and, unlike any other of Lucian's introductions, ends with a moral appeal to his listeners, especially the young. In the case of *Dom.*, Bompaire (1958), p. 288 n. 5, argued for, and Anderson (1977*b*), p. 314 n. 5, against, its inclusion among Lucian's introductions; but for *Dom.* as well as for *Prom. Es* (see below), Rothstein's observations (1888), 117, are still valid: 'certissimum est alienos ab hoc genere [sc. prolaliarum] esse libellos De domo et Prometheum minorem qui suum habent consilium neque ullo modo ad aliam orationem sequentem spectant'; *Prom. Es* even seems to be addressed to someone other than Lucian's usual audiences, namely to an acquaintance who has kept to the more serious (i.e. forensic) side of the rhetorical profession (cf. ch. 1 p. 85. 11–12 M.): ὑμεῖς ... ὁπόσοι ἐν δίκαις εὐδοκιμεῖτε ξὺν ἀληθείᾳ ποιούμενοι τοὺς ἀγῶνας). Stock (1911), 28–32, considered *Somn.* a true *prolalia*, but wanted to exclude *Scyth.* and *Harm.* arguing that they were letters—for which, however, no certain indication can be found.

pictures). Quite a number of these things cannot be read about
in any other ancient Greek or Latin text; did Lucian simply
invent them, or did he find them in books that are forever lost
to us? Whichever he did (probably both), one gets the impression that he took more pains in finding, selecting, and arrang-
ing subject-matter for presentation to his listeners than did the
greater part of his fellow sophists who mostly confined themselves to declaiming over and over again themes taken out of
the classical reaches of Greek history and myth. Lucian,
obviously, enjoyed fascinating his audience with exotic and
unusual themes; and if they did have a more common look
sometimes, he tried to present them in a uncommon way (e.g.
Dionysus' conquest of India in *Bacchus*).

Third, references by Lucian to himself and his work: without
the introductions, we would know even less about Lucian's life
and career than we do. It could be dangerous to make one's
introductory address too personal: Philostratus relates how the
sophist Philagrus got a very unfavourable reception in Athens
when he included a lament for his recently deceased wife in his
introductory *dialexis* (*VS* 579). Lucian never presented himself
so heavyhandedly; in those introductions which he seems to
have written earliest (see below) he carefully avoided any reference to himself that might have seemed too personal; only after
he had become somewhat more known and familiar to his
audiences did he let some personal feelings or reactions to his
listeners' expectations come into his words; and more than once
he tried (or at least feigned) to correct preconceptions of his
audience which seemed wrong to him.

In these personal remarks there even seems to be perceptible
a gradual change and development of Lucian's attitudes to his
art and his audiences that might be a possible guide for establishing a relative chronological order of the eight introductory
pieces. It is always a precarious undertaking to construct such a
chronology on so tenuous a basis; we can, however, attain a
somewhat greater amount of probability, if we combine
Lucian's remarks about himself and his art with the development of his skills in structuring his *prolaliai*, a development that
is quite perceptible: *Hercules* and *Bacchus*, works of Lucian's old
age, are arguably also the best in arrangement and presentation. Taken together, these observations encourage me to pro-

pose the following order for the eight little works: *Herodotus sive Aetion* (which must probably be taken closely together with *Harmonides* and *Scytha*). *De dipsadibus, De electro, Zeuxis sive Antiochus, Hercules, Bacchus.*

1. *Herodotus sive Aetion*

This is probably the most loosely structured piece within the set; it even contains one clumsy inconsistency of a sort that is not found in the other introductions. Apart from that, however, *Herodotus* already has most of the typical features of Lucian's *prolaliai*.

The situation is this: Lucian is about to perform for the first time (it seems) at a big and important regional assembly in the province of Macedonia.[10] Speeches given on such occasions were reckoned among the λόγοι ἐπιβατήριοι,[11] and one of their main themes was a praise of the city where the speaker had newly arrived; and just such a praise of city and of the people assembled there is what we find at the end of *Herodotus*, combined with an expression of self-conscious doubt on Lucian's part whether he will measure up to the situation. How then did he dare to come here and present himself on such a grand occasion, one might ask. It is to explain this that Lucian begins his talk with the story of how the great Herodotus, setting out from his native Caria together with his writings, came to mainland Greece and, wanting to get rich and famous as quickly as possible, went straightway to the Panhellenic Games at Olympia and recited his *Histories* there (*Herod.* 1).

Herodotus' ploy succeeded beautifully—in Lucian's story, that is; for we have every reason to doubt that Herodotus' way to fame was as straight and simple as this. Herodotus probably was at Olympia at one time or another,[12] possibly even when

---

[10] Hall (1981), p. 457 n. 52, cites Mommsen and Gallavotti who opt for Thessalonica as the meeting-place of this assembly; but Jones (1986), p. 11 n. 25, prefers Beroea, with some reason.

[11] Men. Rh. 377. 31–378. 3 Sp. (p. 94 R.–W.): Ἐπιβατήριον ὁ βουλόμενος λέγειν δῆλός ἐστι βουλόμενος προσφωνῆσαι ἢ τὴν ἑαυτοῦ πατρίδα ἐξ ἀποδημίας ἥκων, ἢ πόλιν ἑτέραν, εἰς ἣν ἂν ἀφίκηται, ἢ καὶ ἄρχοντα ἐπιστάντα τῇ πόλει.

[12] On Herodotus and Olympia see F. Jacoby, *RE* Suppl. 2 (1913), 274.

games were held there; but it is highly unlikely that he went there immediately after leaving Halicarnassus and with a complete set of his *Histories* in his pocket—all our other sources on Herodotus' life militate against such a straightforward and simple conception. All Lucian needed to know to make up this story was a knowledge of Herodotus' birthplace and of the Olympic Games as one of the best opportunities in Greece to show off one's strength and skill not only of body, but of mind as well. Everything else in Lucian's story is probably due to his fertile imagination, which worked out every detail so that in a comparison it could be well applied to Lucian's own situation (which he does at the end of the piece). In this application, however, one incongruity remained: In *Herod.* 1 Lucian characterizes the Olympic festival assembly as the very élite of Greece (ἀπανταχόθεν ἤδη τῶν ἀρίστων συνειλεγμένων), only to devaluate it later when he proceeds to compare the spectators at Olympia (συρφετώδης ὄχλος, ἀθλητῶν μᾶλλον φιλοθεάμονες, ἐν παρέργῳ οἱ πολλοὶ τὸν Ἡρόδοτον τιθέμενοι, 8) to the festival assembly he himself is now going to address. This is quite awkward; but the awkwardness is somewhat diminished by the fact that Lucian has put other things in between: not only short references to other famous men who sought and found fame in Olympia, like the sophists of old, Hippias and Prodicus and Polus and a fourth one, whose name has been corrupted in the manuscripts,[13] καὶ ἄλλοι συχνοί; but also one more detailed account of how the painter Aetion so impressed the *Hellanodikas* Proxenidas by exhibiting his painting *The Marriage of Roxana and Alexander the Great* that Proxenidas married off his daughter to Aetion in turn. Lucian makes the description of this painting

---

[13] The mysterious Ἀναξιμένης ὁ Χῖος: no sophist or writer of this name and origin is known elsewhere. C. Müller (*FHG* II. 43) proposed to read Ξενομήδης ὁ Χῖος, but Xenomedes' home was Keos, not Chios; see Jacoby in the notes to the commentary on *FGrH* 442 (vol. iii/b, p. 178). There, Jacoby argued against the alteration of Lucian's text ('Der unbekannte A. war gewiss ein sophist, wie die mit ihm genannten . . .'). That was in 1955; 29 years earlier, in *FGrH* 72 (Anaximenes of Lampsacus) T 10, Jacoby himself had proposed to read Ἀναξιμένης ⟨ὁ Λαμψακηνὸς καὶ Θεόπομπος⟩ ὁ Χῖος, but these historians of the 4th cent. BC do not really fit between two sophists of the 5th, Prodicus and Polus. Moreover, Ἀναξιμένης has no really old manuscript authority; according to Macleod's apparatus, Γ has Ἄναξης (without accent) and V Ἀνάξης, which probably means that already in Γ's ancestor something between Ἀναξ- and -ης had become illegible and that, having no really suitable candidate to put in, one should probably write Ἀναξ⟨　⟩ης ὁ Χῖος today.

the centre of his story, and it is indeed the most beautiful part of this *prolalia*.

At least one problem, however, attaches to this part: Lucian's transition from Herodotus and the sophists to Aetion is somewhat artificial and in one point, apparently, even quite misleadingly phrased. Lucian introduces Aetion by way of an antithesis: 'Why do I give you the names of these old sophists and writers and historians, when they say, τὰ τελευταῖα ταῦτα, that Aetion . . .?' Already in the nineteenth century controversy arose around τὰ τελευταῖα ταῦτα and its meaning and implications. Karl Otfried Müller[14] understood the three words as 'what happened lately' and inferred that Aetion must be a painter of a time only shortly before Lucian's own. All other passages, however, where Aetion is mentioned (including two by Lucian himself: *Merc. Cond.* 42, *Im.* 7) suggest that Aetion in fact belonged to the second half of the fourth century BC— which is admittedly a bit early for τὰ τελευταῖα ταῦτα, if we understand it as Müller did; but can we understand it differently? K. B. Stark, H. Brunn, and H. Blümner[15] took it as

---

[14] Müller (1830), 212 = (1835), 240 = (1848), 250. Also Bompaire (1958), 516, takes τὰ τελευταῖα ταῦτα as meaning 'dernièrement' and thinks that this chronological error ('Aétion vivait à l'époque hellénistique') was caused by Lucian's 'fidélité impudente aux sources' (515; see also below n. 16).

[15] See Stark (1852), 41; Brunn (1859), 244 ff. = (1889), 164 ff.; Blümner (1867), 44. A year earlier, however, Blümner (1866), 46, had still rejected this solution and, suspecting a corruption in Lucian's text, proposed to read ὅπου τὰ τελευταῖα ταῦτα ⟨ἐγένετο or εἴδομεν.⟩ καὶ ᾽Αετίωνά φασι—a desperate and not convincing remedy. In the following year, Blümner came round to Stark's and Brunn's opinion, because he thought that in *Laps.* 6 Lucian had employed a construction very similar to the offending one in *Herod.* 4, namely: καὶ τί σοι τοὺς παλαιοὺς λέγω, ὅπου καὶ ᾽Επίκουρος κτλ. (p. 361. 1 Macleod). But the two sentences are not as similar as they might seem at first sight: in *Laps.*, Epicurus is contrasted with Pythagoras and his followers, and there is enough of chronological distance between them to make Pythagoras appear truly παλαιός compared to Epicurus; moreover, there is no τὰ τελευταῖα ταῦτα here causing the real headache. Sommerbrodt (*Neue Jbb. für Philol. u. Päd.* 87, (1863), 625) wanted to delete ταῦτα after τὰ τελευταῖα, but this will not do, as Blümner rightly remarked, because Lucian employs the expression τὰ τελευταῖα ταῦτα also in *Peregr.* 1. In (1872), 137 ff., and in his edn. (Berlin, 1889) Sommerbrodt went even further, ejecting the whole of καὶ τὰ τελευταῖα ταῦτα from the text; but following this logic, one would probably have to delete ἐκείνους after τοὺς παλαιούς too and might as well rewrite the whole sentence. Recently C. P. Jones (1986), p. 157 n. 50, has interpreted τὰ τελευταῖα ταῦτα again as 'lastly' or 'finally' and supported this with *Peregr.* 4—but there we only have τὰ τελαυταῖα without ταῦτα, while in *Peregr.* 1 τὰ τελευταῖα ταῦτα is not only summing up, but also has the connotation of 'what happened lately'; so the problem in *Herod.* 4 remains.

meaning 'finally' (introducing the last item in a sequence) and rejected Müller's argument; but the sharp chronological antithesis which is clearly there in Lucian's words (τοὺς παλαιοὺς ἐκείνους – τὰ τελευταῖα ταῦτα) can hardly be explained away so easily. I am inclined to consider two solutions: either Lucian took his list of oratorical performers and artists who were successful at Olympia out of a source for which Aetion really still belonged to τὰ τελευταῖα ταῦτα, or Lucian himself introduced this antithesis to put as much emphasis as possible on Aetion and his picture so that he might be better justified to describe it. Both of these possibilities should be seriously considered. In Lucian's writings there are a number of passages where he inexplicably seems to know historical facts only up to the first part of the third century BC,[16] which would make sense if he depended there on a source dating from that time; on the other hand, Lucian clearly was very eager to bring Aetion's picture into his text at all costs and just for its own sake, without taking much heed whether his argument would be furthered by such an inclusion; that is shown by the fact that Lucian lets Aetion and his picture drop out of sight almost immediately once the description is finished; so far as the concluding sentences of this *prolalia* are concerned the *ekphrasis* of Aetion's painting might never have come into it. By including it nevertheless, Lucian obviously wanted to display his skills in bringing such a work of art right before the eyes of his audience just by his words and he was so successful that he even inspired Renaissance painters to transform his description back into painting.[17]

---

[16] Helm (1906), *passim*, has collected such passages in order to show that for all of them Lucian depended on Menippus of Gadara; his conclusions, however, were attacked by McCarthy (1934), 28–49, and, more recently, by Hall (1981), 80–94, who demonstrated that Lucian need not have been so dependent on Menippus to get hold of such historical allusions. This, however, still does not explain why Lucian several times talks about things as being still extant when in fact they were not. Some of the most striking anachronisms of this kind occur in *Icar.* (cf. Helm (1906), 96 ff.); and one quite comparable to τὰ τελευταῖα ταῦτα in *Herod.* 4 is found in *Pro im.* 23 where Lucian mentions τὴν οὐρανίαν Ἀφροδίτην, a sculpture ὃ ἐποίησεν Πραξιτέλης ἐν Κνίδῳ οὐ πάνυ πολλῶν ἐτῶν, Praxiteles being an artist from *c.* 400 BC! Blümner's effort ((1866), p. 45 n. 65) to explain away this peculiarity is unconvincing. So while we may admit that not every anachronism in Lucian must derive from Menippus, the fact that Lucian commits anachronisms remains; and explaining τὰ τελευταῖα ταῦτα in *Herod.* 4 by saying 'chronological exactness scarcely seems to have been his main concern', as Hall (1981), p. 480 n. 35, does, may not be sufficient.

[17] See Foerster (1886), 19 ff. (on Sodoma's picture and on a preliminary drawing by

Two other introductory pieces, *Harmonides* and *Scytha*, may well belong to the same Macedonian sojourn in Lucian's travels, for they are quite similar in theme and content (in *Scytha*, 9, Macedonia is explicitly named as the scene of action); but both seem addressed not to crowds but to individuals of important standing, whose favour Lucian obviously hoped to win. In both pieces he deals with the same question as in *Herodotus* (how to acquire fame and favour as quickly as possible) but uses different exempla to illustrate his point: in *Harmonides* that of the young flute-player Harmonides, who asks his teacher, the great Timotheos of Thebes, what he should do to earn a quick reputation. Timotheos advises him to seek recognition by important individuals (*Harm.* 1–2). Harmonides himself dies, before he can put this advice into practice, but Lucian intends to make good use of it and, having come to this point in his introduction, launches into an effusive flattery of the man he addresses (*Harm.* 3). He follows the same procedure in *Scytha*, but this time his introductory story (or rather stories, for there are really two; and the first one moreover contains a short *ekphrasis* of a funerary monument) is more elaborate, telling how the Scythian Toxaris became a citizen (and afterwards even a healing spirit) in archaic Athens, and how he introduced his younger compatriot Anacharsis to Solon, when Anacharsis came to Athens as well. The rest of the piece is once more a feast of flattery for the addressees (father and son of the first family in town), only this time it is presented a little more indirectly: Lucian judiciously puts it into the mouth of the many people who, or so he pretends, directed him to these two men when he asked to whom he should present his skills (*Scytha*, 10). In all three of these introductions—*Herodotus*, *Harmonides*, *Scytha*— Lucian comes across as still very much an apprentice who is for the first time confronted with the task of winning a friendly constituency and benevolent backers.[18] In *Herodotus* his skills of

Raffael that one of his pupils used as a model for a painting in the Palazzo Borghese at Rome); Botticelli, too, seems (partially, at least) to have been inspired by Lucian's description of Aetion's picture in his 'Mars and Venus' (see Robinson (1979), 69).

[18] Jones (1986), 168 ff. agrees with this early dating of the three little pieces. Hall (1981), 34 ff., is more inclined to date *Herod.* and *Scyth.* (she does not commit herself on *Harm.*) 'in the winter of 165/6', but does not rule out an earlier dating.

structuring are not yet fully developed, but his ability to produce a beautiful *ekphrasis* is already there (as well as in *Scytha*),
and able storytelling can be found in all three.

2. De dipsadibus

The three *prolaliai* so far considered all deal with Greek themes
and settings: Olympia, Thebes, Athens. It is in *De dipsadibus*
that Lucian for the first time leaves the boundaries of Greece
and takes us to a very different place, namely to Southern
Libya (i.e. the desert regions of North Africa) with its harsh cli-
matic conditions and its dangerous snakes. He starts with a
thrilling evocation of the sand, the dryness, the desolation, and
the unsufferable heat of these regions.[19] After the *ekphrasis* of the
desert itself, Lucian proceeds to describe the activities of the
only humans who temporarily dare to visit these desolate parts:

---

[19] A somewhat similar geographical ekphrasis is quoted by Philostratus (*VS* 574)
from a *dialexis* of Alexander Peloplaton: Ἀραβία γῆ δένδρα πολλά, πεδία κατάσκια,
γυμνὸν οὐδέν, φυτὰ ἡ γῆ, τὰ ἄνθη. οὐδὲ φύλλον Ἀράβιον ἐκβαλεῖς, οὐδὲ κάρφος ἀπορρίψεις
οὐδὲν ἐκεῖ φυέν, τοσοῦτον ἡ γῆ περὶ τοὺς ἱδρῶτας εὐτυχεῖ. One wonders, however, if Alexander could have gone on much longer like that (Lucian could, as *Dips.* shows), and his
phrasing, compared to Lucian's, sounds rather artificial; see Norden (1898), 411.
    We have a North African setting and theme, too, in Dio Prus. 5 (a Λιβυκὸς μῦθος);
but again there are important differences from *Dips.*: like Lucian, Dio wants to tell
about a θηρίων . . .γένος χαλεπὸν καὶ ἄγριον (6), but from the very start he makes it clear
that his story is a *mythos*, an invention, while Lucian at least pretends to relate something real; and Dio, again, from the start looks for a moral in his *mythos*, while Lucian
has no other aim but entertainment and self-presentation. After introductory remarks
about the doubtful use of such *mytheumata* (1–4), Dio first tells of the hunting habit of his
mysterious creature (5–7) and then lets himself get drawn into an *ekphrasis* of the dangerous Syrtis (8–11); Lucian proceeds just the other way round (first geography, then
the animal, and no proem), and his object of *ekphrasis* is the desert, not the Syrtis. After
the Syrtis, Dio at last describes the fantastic appearance of his creatures (12–13) and
their method of ensnaring and killing (and eating) humans; Lucian, in a similar passage, stays within the realm of scientific biology, while Dio transgresses into fantasy.
Now Dio develops a first moral of his tale (16–18), then gives a sequel to the original
story (18–21), then a sequel to the moral as well (22–3), and after that still another
addition to the story (24–7) which ends quite abruptly without a moral this time (but
one could very easily think of one); Lucian's *dipsas*-tale has no moral whatsoever
attached, only a cunning application to flatter the audience. So, while Dio's Λιβυκὸς
μῦθος may in a very general way have inspired Lucian to develop a similar theme,
Lucian clearly chose different subject-matter and a different way of presenting it.

the wild Garamantes who during the winter season, when the heat is not totally stifling, set out to hunt in the desert, trying to catch wild asses, big ostriches, apes, and sometimes elephants. All these animals in such utterly destitute places? Lucian tries to explain away this improbability with the remark that only these animals are able to stand those desert conditions. Still the reader might not be convinced. Lucian has used all his skill in ch. 1 to draw an impressive picture of total desolation, and now there are not only asses, ostriches, and apes, but even elephants to be found here?

A look at Lucian's possible sources for his *ekphrasis* of North Africa may show what caused this apparent contradiction. Already Herodotus[20] in his account of Libya describes the African desert in stark and powerful terms; his division of Libya into four different regions extending each from west to east and following one upon the other from north to south[21] is likely to lie at the bottom of Lucian's location of the sandy deserts of Southern Libya and the adjacent dwellings of the Garamantes. Northernmost is found ἡ οἰκουμένη or παραθαλάσσιος Λιβύη, after it there is ἡ θηριώδης, followed by an ὀφρύη ψάμμου, a 'ridge of sand', which is the region where a string of oases can be found and among them that of the Garamantes; and finally, ἡ ἔρημος Λιβύη, which is southernmost and totally devoid of water and vegetation and animal life. Who would not think that this is the region Lucian has in mind while drawing up his *ekphrasis* of the desert in *Dips.* 1? But Herodotus explicitly denies that any living thing can be found in this desert *south* of the Garamantes, and on the other side he enumerates all the animals that the Garamantes hunt according to Lucian's description (*Dips.* 2), when he discusses the whereabouts of the θηριώδης Λιβύη which lies *north* of the Garamantes' dwellings. If Lucian's only source on Libya had been Herodotus, we would have to assume that he mixed up the θηριώδης and the ἔρημος zone that Herodotus talks of.

---

[20] 4. 185. 3 ὑπὲρ δὲ τῆς ὀφρύης ταύτης τὸ πρὸς νότου καὶ ἐς μεσογαίαν τῆς Λιβύης, ἔρημος καὶ ἄνυδρος καὶ ἄθηρος καὶ ἀνομβρος καὶ ἄξυλός ἐστι ἡ χώρη καὶ ἰκμάδος ἐστὶ ἐν αὐτῇ οὐδέν. cf. also 2. 32. 4 τὰ δὲ καθύπερθε τῆς θηριώδεος ψάμμος τέ ἐστι καὶ ἄνυδρος δεινῶς καὶ ἔρημος ἀπάντων.

[21] 4. 181; in 2. 32. 4–5 Herodotus enumerates only three zones.

It is, however, not necessary to make this assumption. Herodotus' distinction of four succeeding zones is very schematic and does not wholly correspond to the real geographical situation of North Africa;[22] already in antiquity other writers gave a modified picture closer to reality. The elder Pliny, for instance, tells us that immediately to the south of the coast of the Greater and Lesser Syrtis there is sand and snake-infested territory, then mountainous regions teeming with wild animals, still further inland *elephantorum solitudines, mox deserta vasta ultraque Garamantes* ... (*NH* 5. 26). So desert and animals for hunting and even the snakes that Lucian will later on evoke in his piece are really to be found north of the Garamantes, in what Herodotus calls ἡ παραθαλάσσιος and ἡ θηριώδης Λιβύη. This is confirmed by Lucian himself when he relates that a friend of his saw the funerary monument of a man killed by a *dipsas*-snake right on the coast of the Greater Syrtis (*Dips*. 6). Probably, then, Lucian relied on such sources as Pliny used for his account of the hunting activities of the Garamantes and the presence of the snakes; but it may very well be due to the influence of Herodotus that in the first chapters of *De dipsadibus* Lucian generates the (incorrect) impression that the Garamantes actually went south into the desert to hunt. *De dipsadibus* has a markedly Herodotean flavour also in other respects: Lucian in fact assumes something like the spirit of Ionian ἱστορίη when he discusses the medical explanation for the lethal effect of the *dipsas*'s poison (ch. 5) and when, by way of a digression, he informs his readers on the appearance and the use of the big ostrich-eggs that are pictured on the monument he had described (ch. 6–7).

By including such digressions, Lucian does not show any hurry to come to the point he wants to make in this introduction; by lavishly showering his listeners with interestingly presented facts on marvellous and exotic things, he keeps building up expectation about what all this is going to lead up to. After he has talked like an accomplished geographer and biologist about the North African desert, its human inhabitants, its dangerous snakes, and, finally, about the most dangerous of them all, the *dipsas*, Lucian almost offhandedly remarks that he has

---

[22] Herodotus himself already deviates somewhat from his earlier schematic description when discussing the differences in animal life between the eastern and western parts of the θηριώδης zone in 4. 191. 2–192. 3.

never seen one single bit of all these things;[23] and by this statement he probably wants his audience to admire even more his
skills of rhetorical display. And still he goes on telling fascinating details about the *dipsas*, not missing the opportunity to
present the picture and verse inscription that his friend found
on the above-mentioned funerary monument.[24]

Only now does Lucian finally come to the real *raison d'être* of
his little Libyan *logos* (9). Several times already (4, 6, 8—each
time somewhat differently) he has described the unbearable
torments a man bitten by a *dipsas*-snake has to suffer, namely
his unquenchable thirst. With an unexpected but skilful turn of
thought he now asserts that his own thirst for having this very
audience again and again listening to him is just as unquenchable; they are like a pure and translucent water for him in his
thirst, and nowhere (or so he pretends) would he find any
better. So here again we see a big lump of flattery dispensed at
the end of a *prolalia*; it must be noted, however, that Lucian has
already become more subtle than in his embarrassingly direct
onslaughts of flattery in *Herodotus*, *Harmonides*, and *Scytha*. In *De
dipsadibus* he never leaves the thirst-and-water metaphor, and
his transition from storytelling to metaphorically praising his
audience is witty and ingenious.

3. *De electro*

In *De dipsadibus* we see a Lucian who is apparently quite familiar with the audience he is speaking to, having addressed them
before; in *De electro* we find him once again in a new place with
new listeners, but for the first time with already a kind of fame
preceding him, for in the last chapter of this piece (6) he is
apparently trying to dampen expectations somewhat—which
implies that there really were such expectations.

De electro is very short—in fact the shortest piece among all
Lucian's *prolaliai*—but it none the less contains two little stories

---

[23] *Dips.* 6 (p. 322. 5–7 Macleod): ἐγὼ μὲν οὖν οὐδένα τοῦτο πεπονθότα εἶδον . . . οὐδὲ
ἐπέβην τῆς Λιβύης τὸ παράπαν εὖ ποιῶν. After hearing about all these strange and dangerous things everyone in the audience would probably be in sympathy with this piece
of smug self-congratulation (εὖ ποιῶν) on keeping away from such places of trouble.

[24] 'Tota nimirum de cippo et epigrammate narratiuncula ficta est a Luciano', as
Preger (1891), p. 232 n. 284, remarks.

(mythical ones, this time) and their application to the speaker;
they are set in the frame of an allegedly real incident in
Lucian's life. Thus for the first time the author puts himself a
bit more into the limelight. This, and the fact that Lucian by
now has a certain reputation to cope with (see above), suggests
that *De electro* stands somewhere in the middle of his career.
There is yet another thing which we have not found before in
his *prolaliai*:[25] *De electro* is shot through with a subtle ironic
humour. The author pretends to have been a naïve and gullible
believer in the old myths about Phaethon and his sisters and
about the sweet-singing swans, and he tells how in both instances he was rudely cured of his beliefs by some very down-to-
earth inhabitants of the region where he had hoped to see these
mythical wonders with his own eyes: Phaethon's sisters turned
into poplars shedding tears of amber, and melodious swans,
both supposedly to be seen on the banks of the River Po (here
identified with the mythical Eridanos).

Lucian strikes an ironical chord in the very first line, beginning: 'As to amber, the myth will have convinced you too, of
course, that . . . .' By putting so much ridiculous confidence in
myth, Lucian cunningly hints that neither the seemingly
straightforward presentation of the mythical story he is about
to tell nor his own posturing as its faithful believer are to be
taken too seriously; what Lucian in fact tries to do is to establish
a tacit understanding with his audience (or at least the more
enlightened part of it) that he is just play-acting. After these
hints, then, Lucian fully assumes the role of a true believer: he
piously summarizes the main points of the story of Phaethon
and the Heliades, and does not forget to add how much he had
hoped that one day he himself would be able to come to the
River Po and get rich by collecting all that precious amber
dripping down from the maidens-turned-poplars . . . . And then
a remarkable element of farce comes into the story as Lucian
(seemingly embarrassed) has to confess how his beautiful hopes
were destroyed: he actually got to the River Po (he tells us) and
asked the rowers who were taking him upstream where to find
poplars and amber; but, as they seemed not to understand a
single word of his question, he gave them a summary of the

---

[25] Apart from the momentary flash of wit in *Dips.* 6 (see n. 23).

myth—only to have these people answer that never in their life did they see anyone like Phaethon drop out of heaven nor any poplars shedding amber tears; would they otherwise toil and row him along if they could lay their hands on riches so much more easily? All this adds up to a wonderful joke, as Lucian succeeds in presenting his unsophisticated rowers as being at the same time stupid and smart, not comprehending what he is making a fuss about, but nevertheless showing his hopes to be utter nonsense by a very down-to-earth reason. Lucian still keeps up his humorous tongue-in-cheek tone when he describes his own embarrassed silence after he had to take this rebuke, and his disappointment when realizing that his hopes of amber had vanished into thin air.

And even now (in front of what must have been an audience already chuckling with pleasure) Lucian continues with the pose of the naïve stranger and asks his rowers about the famous singing swans which—or so he has been told—can be found on the River Po as well; and as he obviously fears that he might be cut short again with unbelieving questions, he hastens to add that according to myth these swans once were attendants of Apollo, living here at the river and being very fond of music, and that after being turned into swans they are still supposed to dwell here and sing.

As we might expect, Lucian has no more luck with his second tale than with the first; his rowers make it abundantly clear that the few swans they ever noticed about the river made only a harsh croaking noise instead of singing. Apart, however, from bringing about a second failure for poor Lucian, his swan-tale has the further interest for us that nowhere else in extant ancient literature do we find it related in quite this way. The story of Kyknos, the friend of Phaethon, who because of his grief for the latter's death was turned into a swan, is well known from several accounts, most of all probably from the *Metamorphoses* of Ovid,[26] and in the same work Ovid tells stories of two other Kyknoi who are changed into swans.[27] But always in these stories only one Kyknos is concerned (moreover he is not connected with Apollo) while Lucian talks of a collective

---

[26] *Met.* 2. 367–80; see Bömer, ad loc., and Adler (1922).
[27] *Met.* 7. 371 ff.; 12. 64 ff.

transformation of a number of people who already in their human state are intimately connected with Apollo. Now swans were widely believed in antiquity to be holy birds of this god;[28] in some stories they even draw his flying chariot to the Hyperboreans and back.[29] But here, again, we find nothing about their once having been humans, which according to Lucian they were, nor are they connected with the River Po. So it might have been Lucian himself who combined various elements of these traditions and myths about swans and made them into a new tale of his own:[30] from the story of Phaethon and Kyknos he took the element of metamorphosis and the connection with the River Eridanos / Po, and from the belief in swans as holy birds of Apollo he took the plural number and the connection with the god. There was at least one intrinsic reason for Lucian to modify the traditional Kyknos story: after his rowers had so ridiculed his Phaethon story, he could not really present Kyknos as a friend of Phaethon's to them.

It is only in the last chapter (6) of *De electro* that Lucian puts down the mask of the naïve believer in mythical superstitions and becomes himself again. Out of the story he just told about himself and his ridiculous disappointment he now fashions a warning against overblown expectations his audience might have about his coming performance; this warning enables him not only to appear as a paragon of modesty himself, but to lash out against his fellow sophists as well, who are not so modest (or so he suggests). All in all, this little piece of well-constructed rhetoric gives a very favourable impression of its author: not only does it show his skills in retelling old mythical stories with subtle irony—skills worthy of the author of the *Dialogues of the Gods* and *the Sea-Gods*—but also his capacity for self-deprecating humour; and there is no more apprentice's timidity in the way Lucian modestly, yet also self-assuredly, distances himself from

---

[28] Sappho fr. 208 V.; Ar. *Av.* 769 ff.; Plat. *Phaed.* 85 AB; Call. *Hymn. Ap.* 5; Call. *Hymn. Del.* 249 ff.; Cic. *Tusc.* 1. 73.

[29] Alc. fr. 307c V. (see Page (1955), p. 249 n. 3).

[30] Pausanias 1. 30. 3 relates a story that comes quite near to Lucian's swan-tale (Λιγύων τῶν 'Ηριδάνου πέραν ὑπὲρ γῆς τῆς Κελτικῆς Κύκνον ἄνδρα μουσικὸν γενέσθαι βασιλέα φασίν, τελευτήσαντα δὲ 'Απόλλωνος γνώμῃ μεταβαλεῖν λέγουσιν αὐτὸν ἐς τὸν ὄρνιθα), but Pausanias, too, talks only about one Kyknos. Servius, likewise, *ad Aen.* 10. 189 says that Kyknos, Phaethon's friend, had got the gift of singing from Apollo in his lifetime and after his death was turned into a swan by the god.

other sophists. He obviously no longer needs to flatter his listeners effusively (as in *Herodotus, Harmonides, Scytha,* and even *De dipsadibus*) in order to establish a good relationship with them.

4. *Zeuxis sive Antiochus*

Lucian's next introduction, *Zeuxis sive Antiochus,* in a way starts where *De electro* ends—with the problem of a reputation based on debatable premisses. As in *De electro,* Lucian again gives his piece a very personal frame, dwelling, in fact, more on himself than in any other of his *prolaliai;* but while in *De electro* he appeared in front of a new audience for the first time, he now addresses listeners whom he is already well acquainted with (he even calls them φίλοι, ch. 1), and his problem with them is not one of having to lower their expectations but of correcting a wrong impression many of them seem to have got about the main virtue of his art: they think that it is the newness and boldness of his themes that makes his productions so admirable; but to him that is not really the most important thing—quite the opposite. And so he reveals his reactions to their one-sided perception (2), demonstrating how embarrassed and sad he is about it.

Thus we in fact get something almost like a lament (and a hidden reproach) from Lucian this time—a quite unusual and even bold beginning for a sophist who depends on the goodwill of his audience. We may assume that Lucian could afford to start like that when his fame was quite established and the peculiar features of his work (as compared to that of other sophists) were known, too, at least to a certain extent. Lucian deals with these unusual features at other places as well, most notably in *Prometheus es in verbis;* there, however, he pretends to be more dissatisfied with himself than with the people who praise the unusualness of his productions, but in the end shows himself more or less resigned to the course he has once chosen; in *Zeuxis* it is really with his listeners that Lucian says he is annoyed. He even hints how severely he might react to their misperception by telling them a story about the painter Zeuxis which, besides, gives him another welcome opportunity to demonstrate his skills in the *ekphrasis* of a picture.

Zeuxis, as Lucian tells us, once painted a very unusual subject: a beautiful female Centaur together with her two little
ones suckling at her breasts and her husband a little way off.
Lucian lavishes three chapters (4–6) on what really is a fine description, and right in the middle of it (5) he states what he
admired most in Zeuxis picture (and what obviously he himself
would like to get praised for as well): ἐν μιᾷ καὶ τῇ αὐτῇ ὑποθέσει
ποικίλως τὸ περιττὸν ἐπεδείξατο τῆς τέχνης—'he gave a many-
sided demonstration of the special quality of his art in one and
the same subject' (353. 14 Macleod). Zeuxis, however, fared as
badly as Lucian did when exhibiting his art (ch. 7): people only
had eyes for the unusualness of the subject and did not even
notice how finely it had been executed by the painter. And so
Zeuxis, not willing to put up with this ignorant slighting of his
art, ordered his assistant to wrap up the picture and store it
away.

By relating this Lucian subtly hints that he might well do the
same as Zeuxis and not go on presenting his works to an incom-
prehending public; but then he himself judges Zeuxis' reaction
as ὀργιλώτερον ἴσως (8) and thus makes it clear that he will not
imitate it; instead, he adds another story, that of Antiochus I
and his victory over the Galatians, to demonstrate that one can
in fact react humbly to the fact that an element of novelty can
be most helpful under certain circumstances and may therefore
not be such a bad thing after all. It is not necessary here to retell
in every detail the tale about Antiochus and the sixteen elephants that gave him victory, the Galatians never having seen
such animals before; it is enough to say that after being able to
show off his talents in describing Zeuxis' picture Lucian here
provides himself with a wonderful opportunity to tell an excit-
ing story, and he makes the most of it. Incidentally, this story is
not to be found elsewhere in any Greek or Roman historian,
which, however, does not necessarily mean that Lucian simply
invented it;[31] he may have quite deliberately searched for a his-

[31] Had Lucian made it all up by himself, he might have fitted in the details of Antiochus' story more neatly into his argument; as it is, there remain some loose ends which
make it probable that Lucian took it over from somewhere else. In the three cases that
Lucian compares with each other in this piece (his own, that of Zeuxis and that of
Antiochus), all three protagonists experience the effects of καινότης and τὸ παράδοξον;
but while Lucian and Zeuxis had hoped to impress people more by skilfully demon-

torical example[32] (as remote as it may seem to us) that fitted agreeably into the train of his argument. However that may be, the Antiochus story enabled Lucian to conclude his remarks about the unusual aspects of his literary work on a more upbeat note than the Zeuxis example would have been able to provide: while Zeuxis ends up angrily sulking at his ignorant spectators, Antiochus modestly recognizes the importance of the element of unexpectedness that the elephants gave to his battle-plans. Antiochus' modesty thus sets the tone as Lucian returns to directly addressing his audience. In fact Lucian now recognizes that the unusual features of his productions might really be a factor worth taking into account (ὥσπερ ἐστί, καινὸν καὶ τεράστιον δοκεῖ αὐτοῖς, ch. 12); but he still hopes that his listeners will be able to see its other virtues as well—he is now even quite confident that they will, being γραφικοὶ καὶ μετὰ τέχνης ἕκαστα ὁρῶντες. And with this little injection of flattery, accompanied by a humble wish (εἴη μόνον ἄξια τοῦ θεάτρου δεικνύειν), this introduction ends; it seems that Lucian is again at peace with his audience.

Zeuxis sive Antiochus exhibits the same kind of rhetorical showpieces as *Herodotus sive Aetion*, the first of Lucian's introductory

---

strating their art than by presenting something new, and were consequently disappointed by the public's onesided response, Antiochus never tried to overcome the Galatians by using art (the art of strategy), judging his situation hopeless; only when his faithful adviser Theodotas counsels him to throw the Galatians into disarray by effectively deploying his 16 elephants, does some τέχνη come into the game; after victory, however, Antiochus not once remembers the artful Theodotas, but only commemorates his brute elephants as essential for his victory. Thus the relationship between τέχνη and τὸ παράδοξον in the example of Antiochus is quite different from that in the example of Zeuxis and Lucian's own, and one might say that the comparisons Lucian draws between the three cases are not totally compatible with one another. This, however, would probably not have detracted much from the effectiveness of Lucian's presentation of this piece to his audience. When Lucian remarks that Antiochus experienced something similar to Zeuxis' experience with the female Hippokentauros (8, p. 354. 24–6 Macleod) he probably means that both (and Antiochus more willingly than Zeuxis) were to discover how important τὸ καινὸν καὶ τὸ παράδοξον turned out to be in their respective cases. At the beginning of the last ch. (12, p. 356. 27: Ὥρα τοίνυν με σκοπεῖν μὴ καὶ τοὐμὸν ὅμοιον ᾖ ᾿Αντιόχῳ) Lucian is still somewhat unhappy that his efforts might have no more merits than Antiochus' elephant victory, but at least he is now more prepared than in the beginning to accept the obvious importance of the element of καινότης in the perception of an audience; and up to a certain extent it was Antiochus' story and experience that prepared the ground for this partial change of heart.

[32] Bar-Kochva (1973) treats Lucian's *Zeux.* in fact as a quite reliable source for Antiochus' victory over the Galatians.

pieces considered here; but in *Zeuxis* both of these show-pieces are much better integrated into the whole arrangement. In *Herodotus* the Aetion episode does nothing to further the argument and is consequently ignored in Lucian's finishing remarks; in *Zeuxis* both the Zeuxis story and the Antiochus story illustrate Lucian's possible reactions (rejection or acceptance) to someone praising καινότης in his works, and Lucian alludes to both stories (ἐλέφαντες – θήλεια ἱπποκένταυρος, ch. 12) when he turns back to discussing his problems with his audience. In *Herodotus* a timid Lucian had to resort to massive flattery to justify his first appearance before those Macedonians; in *Zeuxis* flattery is just an added spice that comes in fleetingly at the end, after Lucian has in telling words vented his frustration at the one-sidedness with which his earlier performances were received, and after he has expressed himself more personally than ever before. We may have doubts about the seriousness of such remonstrances—it may all be a kind of play—but we cannot doubt that a man who expresses feelings (be they real or feigned) with such consummate ease and who illustrates them with rhetorical means perfectly at his command, is at a high point in his career.

5. *Hercules*

With the *prolalia* entitled *Hercules* we enter Lucian's old age; Lucian, in fact, compares his years to those of the Gallic Hercules he describes (ch. 7), and him he calls γέρων ἐς τὸ ἔσχατον (1). We hear, furthermore, that Lucian quite a time ago had actually ceased giving oratorical performances and that only now has he considered re-entering the lecture circuit. Yet *Hercules* does not give us the picture of a man wasted away by old age, but of one whose rhetorical capacities are still there in full and undiminished vigour and who is conscious as well as confident of his powers; Lucian even hints at one point that right now his abilities might well be at their highest peak (8). He adds some customary words of cautious prayer for success at the end of this introduction, but otherwise he is far from being afraid that these latest efforts at displaying his talents might seem ridiculous, and he exudes every degree of confidence that his efforts will carry success. With this confidence, Lucian can make the connection of old age and eloquence the very theme of this introduction.

To illustrate this theme Lucian might have chosen a very familiar figure of Greek myth, namely the Homeric hero Nestor; instead, he again opts for something remarkably exotic and thus typically Lucianic: a strange picture of an old Celtic god called Ogmios who in some respects looks like Hercules and in others not. After establishing the curious identification Hercules–Ogmios (right at the beginning of 1), Lucian immediately sets about describing the outward appearance of this strange creature; and we gradually become aware that we are again encountering one of Lucian's favourite rhetorical devices, the description of a picture. There follows an explanation of its extraordinary features by an old and learned Celt who—so we are told—approaches Lucian as he is still wondering at what he sees.[33]

Up to the present day scholarly debate has not conclusively answered the question whether Lucian here is describing a real picture,[34] and if so, whether it could have been an authentically Celtic one.[35] So far, not one painting (or sculpture) really

---

[33] Friedländer (1912), 79, fittingly compares the Celt's appearance in *Herc.* with the beginning of the *Tabula Cebetis*, a work Lucian twice (*Merc. Cond.* 42; *Rhet. Praec.* 6) expressly mentions as a model for himself.

[34] The authenticity of the Ogmios picture is doubted or rejected by Blümner (1867), p. 82 n. 1, Matz (1867), 6, Reinach (1913), 53 ff., and Caster (1937), p. 362 n. 58. The picture was taken for real by Friedländer (1912), 79, Koepp (1919), 42, Egger (1943), 291, Martin (1946), 361, Benoît (1952), Hafner (1958), 144, Le Roux (1960), 210–13, and Lesky (1970), 117. Pernice (1939), p. 275 n. 2, and Bompaire (1958), 726, remain undecided.

[35] Both Koepp (1919), 69–73, and Hafner (1958), 149, see the picture as a Greco-Roman creation, but come to widely different conclusions as to what it was to show: according to Koepp (1919), 72, it allegorically depicts 'einen sonst unbekannten . . ., in seinem Wesen nicht erkennbaren gallischen Gott . . ., in dem man die Zaubergewalt der Rede verehrte', no Ogmios and no Hercules at any rate; and Hafner (1958), 149, thinks that the figure shown is not Hercules (still less Ogmios), but Geras, personified Old Age, who has taken over Hercules' weapons after having overcome him somehow. But we have no traces of such a victory of Geras elsewhere; in other pictures (cf. Waser, *RE* vii/1, 1240–2) Geras is a frail and withered little man; if Lucian had seen a figure with such a physique in a picture, could he really have mistaken him for Hercules? Even those, however, who detect an authentically Celtic representation in Lucian's description present a bewildering array of varying interpretations: Egger (1943), 300, and Benoît (1952), 153, see a kind of Celtic Hercules *Psychopompos* represented, Martin (1946), 389, the divine ancestor of the Celtic nation (the golden chains symbolizing

comparable to the one Lucian describes[36] has been unearthed in former Celtic territory; and as to the Celtic coins that at one time were associated with Lucian's description, it has been quite convincingly shown that they probably have nothing to do with it.[37] Still, not everything Lucian tells here can be invention: the stem of the name Ogmios appears again in the name of the Irish god Ogma and in Ogam (or Ogom), the name of a sacred Celtic alphabet;[38] so there really seems to be some connection between Ogmios and intellectual capacities like writing or artfully speaking (things that are both encompassed by the word *logos*), and the old Celt's interpretation of Ogmios as a god of *logos* in *Herc.* 4–6 may not be too far off the mark after all. Moreover, the fact that Renaissance painters and engravers like Raffael, Dürer, and Hans Frank actually found it possible to translate Lucian's description into a picture encourages one to believe that he did indeed have some work of art in mind.[39] There may have been more of a Greco-Roman allegory in it than of genuinely Celtic traits, and the old Celt's interpretation of the picture may be misleading in some points; but on the whole it seems unlikely that Lucian should have made up such a strange thing totally on his own, without getting at least some

genealogical connections); Reinach (1913), 54, while gravely doubting the authenticity of the picture, nevertheless thought that Lucian's description might be based on reminiscences of the idol of a Celtic warrior-god, surrounded by severed heads; in the view of Le Roux (1960), Lucian's Ogmios represents only one aspect of a mysterious god possessing various magical 'constraining' qualities. Older opinions are conveniently summarized by Egger (1943), 292 ff.

[36] Koepp (1919), 69–71; Hafner (1958), 145; Bompaire (1958), 726, critically comments on Benoit's efforts (1952) to find such similarities in still-existing archaeological objects.

[37] Koepp (1919), 64–7; Hafner (1958), 146.

[38] So far, no general agreement has been reached about the etymological origins of Ogmios / Ogma / Ogam: Egger (1943), 302–4, whose discussion of the problem is still of value, postulates an original Celtic stem (ogm- ?) meaning 'to lead' and comparable to *agere*, ἄγειν; but Le Roux (1960), 209–11, regarding Egger's material as insufficient, points out (after others; see her notes) that up to now no satisfying Celtic etymology for Ogmios exists, and prefers to regard Ogmios as a name of ultimately Greek origins (to be compared with ὀγμεύω, ὄγμος) which was taken over by the Gallic Celts (to denote an indigenous religious concept, however) and then handed along to their Irish cousins; see also Martin (1946), 363.

[39] The drawings of Raffael and Dürer can be found in Koepp (1919), pl. IV. 1 and 2; the engraving of Hans Frank in Hafner (1958), pl. 25; Dürer's and Frank's in Egger (1943), 305 ff. See as well the discussions of Jahn (1868), 349 ff., Egger (1943), 304–5, and Le Roux (1960), 216–18.

inspiration in the Celtic West where he had spent some time travelling and performing earlier in his career.[40]

Anyway, the picture of Ogmios that Lucian describes fits his purpose excellently; this is to provide an explanation for how he became convinced that it would be a good thing to get into rhetorical performances once more. His story of how he encountered Ogmios and the old learned Celt is interesting enough to arouse the curiosity of his listeners[41] (probably somewhere in the Greek East, where Celtic gods must have appeared extremely exotic), and Lucian rounds it off with a splendid little display of his literary erudition: within a few lines we get verses from the *Iliad*, partly turned into prose, a quotation from Anacreon not found elsewhere, and a famous half-line from Herodotus,[42] all fitted neatly into Lucian's own remarks, so as to convince his listeners how easily these quotations come to him, and to give them the impression that the old orator in front of them is still capable of mastering all the tricks of his trade. On the other hand Lucian prudently avoids the danger of appearing boastful or conceited; in his last sentence he makes it clear that the goodwill of his audience really means something to him, and that only with their approval his hopes of appearing as a vigorous and experienced veteran orator will become reality.

6. *Bacchus*

A similarly high, but not overblown, attitude of quiet self-confidence and a similar degree of mastery in dealing with an audience are shown in what may be Lucian's last *prolalia*, *Bacchus*. Lucian seems to address this piece to people he has already visited in earlier times; in fact, he tries to reawake reminiscences of those times and promises to live up to his former standards (5). At the same time he has to deal again (as in *Zeuxis sive Antiochus*) with some apparent misconceptions which at least

---

[40] On Lucian's travels in Gaul see *Apol.* 15 and *Bis Acc.* 27.

[41] Bompaire (1958), 727, well describes how Lucian in 1–3 step by step heightens the attention of his listeners.

[42] Ch. 7, p. 22. 7–9 Macleod: *Il.* 8. 103–4; ch. 8, p. 22. 13–15: Anacreon *PMG* 379; ch. 8, p. 22. 15: Hdt. 6. 129. 4; in p. 22. 27 an *Odyssey* quotation follows: *Od.* 18. 74.

some parts of his audience seem to harbour about his productions, thinking them merely comic and funny and nothing more (5). To combat this, Lucian this time does not opt for the *ekphrasis* of a picture or the retelling of an historical example, but resorts to myth, not posing, however, this time as a gullible believer (as in *De electro*), but performing as a subtle and skilful narrator, with the same strength of vivid imagination as in the *Verae Historiae*. Lucian chooses to retell a myth which had been common and familiar at least since Hellenistic times, but he tells it from a quite uncommon point of view, as R. B. Branham[43] has already well pointed out: Dionysus' invasion of India is seen through Indian eyes (we have no real parallel to this in other extant literature). What the Indian scouts monitoring Dionysus' advance describe to their king is a wild pageant consisting mostly of excited women behaving in a very peculiar way, and a few male creatures behaving no less peculiarly. The unusual viewpoint Lucian has chosen enables him to describe the invaders (who, of course, were familiar even to the most uneducated Greek) in hilarious detail,[44] deliberately omitting all names so that his listeners can do some delightful guesswork about the identity of the commanders and officers of the Bacchic army. Only when he proceeds to describe the actual battle-preparations of both sides does Lucian finally leave his Indian viewpoint and give the names of the leaders of the invading troops: Dionysus himself, old Silenus, bewildering Pan, and the reckless Satyrs—not to forget the raving Maenads, who now at last get their proper name, too. While working up to the climax of battle and the rout of the Indians, Lucian does everything to magnify the element of paradox in his story: while other accounts of the myth usually present the Maenads as just one contingent of Dionysus' army among several others,[45] Lucian makes them the real bulk of the Bac-

---

[43] Branham (1985), 241 f.

[44] Cf. the description of Pan, Silenus, and the Satyrs in *Deor. Conc.* 4, which is similar to the one in *Bacch.*, but shorter and not so carefully crafted, because Momus, the speaker, takes it that all of Dionysus' companions are known to the gods he addresses.

[45] Diod. 2. 38. 6 (= Megasthenes *FGrHist* 715 F 4) ἱστοροῦσι δ' αὐτὸν καὶ γυναικῶν πλῆθος μετὰ τοῦ στρατοπέδου περιάγεσθαι; 4. 2. 6 and 4. 4. 2 (from tales that Diodorus says the Greeks relate about Dionysus, see below); Polyaen. 1. 1. 3 (Dionysus lured his enemies to attack him by showing them only his women troops at first, and then he defeated them by sending in the male components of his army). Closer to Lucian's

chic forces, adding only a few male officers. Silenus, Pan, and the Satyrs in the role of these officers cannot be found before Lucian's times either (that, however, may be the result of the loss of so many works from Hellenistic times; Hellenistic poetry may already have had something similar). Only Lucian's contemporary Polyaenus[46] has the god Pan as an under-*strategos* of Dionysus. The paradox of this army is fully brought out when Lucian describes the orthodox martial deployment of it before battle;[47] Maenads elsewhere are, of course, not exactly known as paragons of military discipline. When Silenus' ass sounds off his martial war-cry,[48] a further hilariously incongrous note comes in; and by the time Lucian reached the end of this story, he must have had his audience chuckling with pleasure.

Now, however, he turns serious and reveals what he wanted to demonstrate by telling this story: just as the Indians reacted prematurely and wrongly when hearing about the strange appearance of Dionysus' army, so people tend to react wrongly when confronted with Lucian's *logoi*. There may be something unusual about them, but they are no mere laughing-stock; just as the Maenads brandished dangerous iron barbs previously hidden under harmless ivy, so Lucian's works may reveal on closer inspection something more serious than mere jokes. Once more, then, Lucian has to cope with the problem of the right appreciation of his work (compare *Zeuxis*); only this time he is not so much concerned with the outward form and art that he wants to see appreciated in his productions as with their

account of Dionysus' women army and his ruse of concealing the iron tips of their weapons with ivy is a tale that Diodorus ascribes to some unspecified 'mythographers' (3. 63. 1–2), presumably of Hellenistic times. In this tale, Dionysus (the third one of this name) collects an army from the θίασοι γυναικῶν that he spent his youth with at Nysa, and sets out to conquer the world (3. 64. 6); some of his opponents he overcomes by using the trick of the ivy-covered spear-tips (3. 65. 5). Similarly, in a tale that Diodorus imputes to Libyan sources (3. 74. 1), the third Dionysus selected women soldiers like the first one had employed Amazons (3. 74. 2).

[46] Polyaen. 1. 2; in Diod. 4. 4. 3 we see Silenus as a trusted *paidagogos*, caretaker, and teacher of Dionysus, accompanying him on his campaigns.

[47] Cf. Branham (1985), 241.

[48] The cry of the ass even terrified the Gigantes during their attack on the Olympian gods (see Ps.-Eratosth. *Catast.* 11 (p. 92 Robert); Hyg. *Astr.* 2. 23; Schol. Germ. *Arat.* p. 71 Breysig). Kuhnert (1909–15), 510, regards this as 'Erfindung alexandrinischer Dionysosepiker'; whether Lucian got his war-cry of Silenus' ass from here or whether he found it already in a lighthearted account of Dionysus' Indian campaign (likewise from Hellenistic times), must remain an open question.

content. We can hardly gauge how serious Lucian is in claiming that there is more in his pieces than meets the eye;[49] perhaps he is only trying to heighten his listeners' attention; but if so, he has at least chosen an original way to do it, not resorting to flattery, but appealing to his audience to try harder and use more of its intelligence. He even exhorts them to act as if they were present at an initiation ceremony for the mysteries (5, p. 18. 15–20 Macleod); if they do, he implies, they will enjoy his performance just as much as they did in former times.

At this point, Lucian might have concluded this introduction, but he decides to direct the attention of his listeners to something else, namely his appearing before them in spite of his advanced age. For that purpose he again takes them to India, this time to a marvellous place, where three fountains with magical powers exist. After a short *ekphrasis* of the place itself (6) Lucian concentrates on the third of the fountains, which belongs to Dionysus' old companion Silenus, and describes the surprising effect its water can have on an old man when he drinks from it at the time of a certain yearly celebration: speechless at first, he soon acquires a clear delivery and fluent speech that will keep going until the sun sets on that day and the magic subsides; but if by then he has not yet come to the end of his magically inspired discourse, he will pick it up again and continue from exactly the same point a year later if he drinks again from Silenus' fountain (7).

So Lucian finishes his last *prolalia* with a most extraordinary tale. Nowhere else (as far as I can see) in Greek or Roman texts do we hear again of this magical fountain nor even of the Indian tribe in whose country it is supposed to exist: The Μαχλαῖοι Ἰνδοί, although Lucian gives them a quite specific location (on the eastern bank of the River Indus), are mentioned only here. This fact prompted Eduard Schwartz to change their name into Μαλλαῖοι, but the trouble is that this name is nowhere else to be found either. Only the Μαλλοί (Mâlava in the Mahabharata) provide a name that comes near (but is still a way off from Μαχλαῖοι). The Malloi are a people who played a considerable part in the Indian campaign of

---

[49] He could have had works in mind like *Herm.* or *Nav.*, where in fact one might discern something serious behind an entertaining façade.

Alexander the Great,[50] and afterwards they even got a place among the mythical enemies of Dionysus when the god set out on his Indian conquest.[51] The fact that Lucian has begun this last *prolalia* of his with just this story of Dionysus lends some support to the assumption that the Malloi may lie behind Lucian's Μαχλαῖοι; but we cannot really be sure, for the name Μαχλαῖοι also suspiciously looks like being possibly derived from μαχλός, giving these Indians a more than dubious reputation.[52] So the possibility remains that Lucian himself simply invented the Μαχλαῖοι and their magical fountains; the author of the *Verae historiae* obviously had an astonishingly fertile imagination, while at the same time he was remarkably able to make even the most fantastic places he described look real, and one may never be sure where Lucian's inspiration from whatever sources stops and where his freewheeling imagination takes over. Even in his last sentence in *Bacchus* he leaves us with a mystery. He explicitly states that his tale about Silenus' fountain and its curious effects on old men is to be understood as a humorous allusion to his own condition—but he refuses to tell us how exactly we are to apply this hint. Does it simply mean that old Lucian now puts himself and all he is going to say under Silenus' patronage and thus cunningly reduces his own responsibility for the success or failure of his performance? Or do the implications go further? A hundred years ago, Adolf Thimme thought that Lucian also wanted to have the most astonishing feature of Silenus' fountain applied to himself (namely that after drinking from it one continues a speech at exactly the same point where one had to interrupt it a year ago, 7), and so he suspected that this *prolalia* actually served to introduce the second book of Lucian's *Verae historiae* to his listeners. This probably goes too far;[53] but Lucian would have been delighted that his last remarks were taken so seriously.

[50] See Arr. *Anab.* 6. 3–20; *Ind.* 4. 10 and 19. 8; Diod. 17. 98. 1; Plut. *Alex.* 63. 2; Plut. *De Alex. Magn. fortuna* 1. 2 (*Mor.* 327 B); Curt. Ruf. 9. 4. 5.

[51] Steph, Byz. p. 430. 9 Meineke s.v. Μαλοί = Dionysius, *Bassarica* fr. 11 Livrea (see above p. 79 and n. 54).

[52] Cf. the beginning of 7: ῍Α μὲν οὖν πάσχουσιν οἱ παῖδες ἐπειδὰν πίωσιν, ἢ οἷα οἱ ἄνδρες τολμῶσι κατεχόμενοι τῷ Πανί, μακρὸν ἂν εἴη λέγειν . . .

[53] Bompaire (1958), p. 288 n. 1 and 698, however, accepts the argument of Thimme (1888); Helm (*RE* xiii/2, 1731, l. 60 ff.) is more sceptical. See now Anderson (1976*b*), 262–4, with convincing arguments that no such relationship exists.

To sum up: Lucian's introductions are a series of charming and (in most cases) carefully and convincingly structured texts that on the whole give a very favourable impression of his rhetorical powers (and probably did so already in antiquity). They show that his skills in describing a picture or telling an interesting story or bringing something exotic vividly before our eyes were at his command throughout his career, and that, moreover, he improved at integrating these showpieces into the developing portrayal of himself that his audiences were to get by these introductions. Starting with heavy doses of flattery, he later on became more subtle in addressing his listeners, the strokes of his self-portrayal became more distinct and individual, and still today Lucian's comments about the unorthodox aspects of his work (καινότης and παραδοξολογία, see *Zeuxis* 1, *Bacch.* 5, *Electr.* 6) and how he wanted them to be appreciated give us valuable insights in Lucian's aims and attitudes. The two *prolaliai* he probably wrote last show how successfully he combined imaginative storytelling with a witty and thoughtful application to himself. While his remarks probably do not reach the depth of thought Robert Branham wanted to detect in them, the *prolaliai* are, on the other hand, surely not the totally contemptible by-products of an irrelevant rhetoric that Anderson declares them to be.[54] By-products, in fact, they probably were for their author, who produced them most of all to win and retain the interest and favour of his listeners; but by-products artfully made, which still today convey to us an intriguing portrait of the man who wrote them, and of his talents.

---

[54] Anderson (1977*b*), 313. It probably goes too far to search deeply for 'literary functions' in these pieces, or to inquire 'what they reveal of the τέλος of Lucian's art' (Branham (1985), 237). More to the point (though perhaps still formulated in too highbrow a fashion) is Branham's statement that 'the prologues are used to mediate between Lucian the performing artist and his audience by highlighting important features of his art and defending them against potential criticism and misunderstanding' (240). All Lucian probably wanted to attain by his introductions was to come across as an interesting, intelligent, and enjoyable rhetorical entertainer and (perhaps) as someone who had something more in store than the usual sophist's fare; and in getting this across he probably succeeded.

VI

Plato's *Phaedrus* in Second-Century Greek Literature

M. B. TRAPP

Few works were more firmly entrenched in the 'cultural syllabus' of Hellenic *paideia* by the second century AD than Plato's *Phaedrus*. Its rich range of subject-matter—love, the soul, beauty, human destiny, the cosmos, rhetoric, dialectic, teaching, and writing—combined with its literary and stylistic brilliance made it an object of intense and sustained interest to rhetors and philosophers alike, the best single justification for regarding its author as, in Cicero's words, 'non intellegendi solum sed etiam dicendi gravissimus auctor et magister'.[1] It must have been hard for the *pepaideumenos* to emerge from his education, whether rhetorical, philosophical, or both, without having been invited to study and admire this dialogue, and without having come to regard it as a proper model for imitation in his own literary products. My main aim in what follows is to illustrate the consequences of this state of affairs in surviving second-century Greek literature—to show just how and where in the work of the period the *Phaedrus*' potential as an object of classicizing *mimesis* was in fact realized.

I. DIO *Oration* I AND THE LOCUS AMOENUS

Just over half way through his first oration *On Kingship*, Dio of Prusa turns away (with becoming reluctance) from the theme of Zeus and his administration of the cosmos. It is too vast a topic for the present occasion and would require too detailed an exposition. He will end instead, he says, with a myth—or

This essay has benefited greatly from criticism and comment; my thanks to the participants in the Oxford seminar (especially Mark Edwards), to my Birkbeck (now King's) colleague Roland Mayer, and above all to this volume's editor.

[1] *Or.* 3. 10.

rather, with a sacred and edifying *logos* told in the guise of a myth—which he once heard from an old woman of Elis or Arcadia, during the period of his exile:

καὶ δὴ βαδίζων ὡς ἀφ' Ἡραίας εἰς Πῖσαν παρὰ τὸν Ἀλφειὸν μέχρι μέν τινος ἐπετύγχανον τῆς ὁδοῦ, μεταξὺ δὲ εἰς ὕλην τινὰ καὶ δυσχωρίαν ἐμπεσὼν καὶ πλείους ἀτραποὺς ἐπὶ βουκόλι' ἄττα καὶ ποίμνας φερούσας, οὐδενὶ συναντῶν οὐδὲ δυνάμενος ἐρέσθαι, διαμαρτάνω τε καὶ ἐπλανώμην μεσημβρίᾳ σταθερᾷ. ἰδὼν οὖν ἐπὶ ὑψηλῷ τινι δρυῶν συστροφὴν οἷον ἄλσος, ᾠχόμην ὡς ἀποψόμενος ἐντεῦθεν ὁδόν τινα ἢ οἰκίαν. καταλαμβάνω οὖν λίθους τέ τινας εἰκῇ ξυγκειμένους καὶ δέρματα ἱερείων κρεμάμενα καὶ ῥόπαλα καὶ βακτηρίας, νομέων τινῶν ἀναθήματα, ὡς ἐφαίνετο, ὀλίγον δὲ ἀπωτέρω καθημένην γυναῖκα ἰσχυρὰν καὶ μεγάλην, τῇ δὲ ἡλικίᾳ πρεσβυτέραν, τὰ μὲν ἄλλα ἄγροικον στολὴν ἔχουσαν, πλοκάμους δέ τινας πολιοὺς καθεῖτο. (1. 52–3)

Making my way from Heraea in the direction of Pisa along the banks of the Alpheus, I managed to keep on course for a time. Somewhere along the road, however, I came into wooded and rough country, crossed by a number of tracks leading to various cattle- and sheep-pastures. Meeting nobody and unable to ask the way, I became lost and by high noon was wandering helplessly. So when I caught sight of a clump of oaks, like a grove, on a rise in the ground, I made for it in hopes of catching sight from it of a road or a house. There I found a collection of stones roughly set together, along with what seemed to be the offerings of herdsmen: hides of sacrificial animals hung up, and clubs and staves. Seated at a little distance away there was a woman, strong and tall though advanced in years, dressed in rustic fashion, but with long grey hair.

This old woman, Dio learns, is a priestess of Heracles and a prophetess. She prophesies to him, foretelling a speedy end to his wanderings and to the reign of the tyrant who has exiled him.

"Συμβαλεῖς δέ," ἔφη, "ποτὲ ἀνδρὶ καρτερῷ, πλείστης ἄρχοντι χώρας καὶ ἀνθρώπων· τούτῳ μήποτε ὀκνήσῃς εἰπεῖν τόνδε τὸν μῦθον, εἰ καί σου καταφρονεῖν τινες μέλλοιεν ὡς ἀδολέσχου καὶ πλάνητος. οἱ γὰρ ἀνθρώπων λόγοι καὶ τὰ πάντα σοφίσματα οὐδενὸς ἄξια πρὸς τὴν παρὰ τῶν θεῶν ἐπίπνοιαν καὶ φήμην. ὅσοι γάρ ποτε σοφοὶ καὶ ἀληθεῖς κατ' ἀνθρώπους λόγοι περὶ θεῶν τε καὶ τοῦ σύμπαντος, οὐκ ἄνευ θείας τε βουλήσεως καὶ τύχης ἐν ψυχῇ ποτε ἀνθρώπων ἐγένοντο διὰ τῶν πρώτων μαντικῶν τε καὶ θείων ἀνδρῶν. οἷον ἐν Θρᾴκῃ τινὰ λέγουσιν Ὀρφέα γενέσθαι, Μούσης υἱόν, ἄλλον δὲ ποιμένα ἐν ὄρει τινὶ τῆς Βοιωτίας αὐτῶν ἀκοῦσαι τῶν Μουσῶν· ὅσοι δὲ ἄνευ δαιμονίου κατοχῆς καὶ ἐπιπνοίας λόγους τινὰς ὡς ἀληθεῖς παρ' αὐτῶν ἐκόμισαν εἰς τὸν βίον, ἄτοποι καὶ πονηροί." (1. 56–8)

'One day,' she said, 'you will meet a powerful man, ruler of a great empire and of many men. Do not hesitate to tell him this tale of mine, even if there are those who are going to despise you as a babbler and a tramp. The words of men and all their cleverness are worth nothing in comparison with utterances inspired by the gods. All the many wise and true sayings about the gods and the universe that have ever circulated among men found their place in human souls by the gods' own will and dispensation, through the medium of the inspired prophets of early times: Orpheus, for example, who they say lived in Thrace, the son of a Muse; and another, a shepherd on one of the mountains of Boeotia, who heard the Muses themselves speak to him. But all those who have claimed to circulate true accounts from their own resources, without divine possession and inspiration, are presumptuous and wicked. Listen, therefore, to the tale I have to tell.'

The tale, which occupies the whole of the rest of the oration, is the tale of the education of Heracles and of his choice between the two peaks—the Peak Royal and the Peak Tyrannous—which need not be repeated here.

The most obvious literary model exploited in this second half of Dio's *Oration* 1 is Prodicus' fable of Heracles at the Parting of the Ways, as retold by Xenophon in *Memorabilia* 2. 1. Dio's is just one of the many developments and adaptations of this fertile allegory with which later Greek and Latin literature is so liberally strewn.[2] Mimesis of Xenophon's Prodicus, however, accounts only for the content of the old priestess's myth; there are other models for its frame. The priestess herself—a *mantis* with a message for the man who is now relaying it to his present audience—is a grandchild of Diotima, the γυνὴ Μαντινική, whose teachings are reported by Socrates in the *Symposium*. And the circumstances of her encounter with Dio are modelled on the encounter between Socrates and Phaedrus in the *Phaedrus*.

Dio and the priestess meet by a sacred grove, decorated with offerings: compare the famous grove of *Phdr.* 230 B. They meet at high noon (μεσημβρίᾳ σταθερᾷ): compare *Phdr.* 242 A (μεσημβρία ἵσταται ἡ δὴ καλουμένη σταθερά). Dio's path to the grove by which they meet takes him along the banks of a river: compare *Phdr.* 229 A. The prophetess speaks under the

---

[2] e.g. ps.-Diogenes, *Ep.* 30; ps.-Philo, *De Merc. Mer.*, *passim*; *Tabula Cebetis*, *passim*; Lucian, *Somn.* 6–16; Galen, *Protr.* 2–5; Clement, *Paed.* 2. 10. 110; Themistius, 22. 280 A ff.; Julian, *Or.* 2. 56 D; Basil, *De Leg. Gr. Lib.* 5. 55–77; Cic., *Off.* 1. 32. 118; Ovid, *Am.* 3. 1. 1 ff.; Quint., 9. 2. 36; Silius Italicus, *Pun.* 15. 18–128.

influence of divine inspiration, as Socrates affects to in *Phdr.*
235 C and 241 E. She discusses the nature of inspiration itself
and asserts the superior value of its products, as Socrates does in
Phdr. 244 A–245 A.

Furthermore, it may not be entirely coincidental that this
whole Phaedran passage in Dio's oration follows hard upon—
and is given as substitute for—a discussion of Zeus and his
government of the cosmos. For Zeus the great leader in his
winged car, marshalling the hosts of the gods through the
heavens, is famously Phaedran too; and, as will be seen in due
course, that whole section of the dialogue could properly be
taken as an allegory of the cosmos. But whether or not one
accepts this further link, there can be no doubt about the
Phaedran resonance of the grove and the mid-day meeting.
The correspondence is not exact, but that is no objection, for
the divergences are pointed and purposeful. Plato's encounter
took place in the elegant, domesticated charm of the well-
groomed Attic countryside, amid images and offerings dedicated to the Nymphs and to Achelous. Dio's takes place in
Dorian territory (he goes out of his way to draw attention to the
priestess's Dorian accent);[3] and it takes place in trackless, open
country, by a shrine decorated with the rough, improvised
offerings of peasants to Heracles. The latter episode is surely
meant as a piquant transposition of the former, trading on the
familiar antithesis of Attic and Ionian elegance with the
harsher ethos of the Dorians.[4]

Dio, indeed, seems to have had a definite taste for describing
philosophical encounters in ways that draw on the precedent of
the *Phaedrus*. We shall see it at work again in another of his epideictic dialogues, *Oration* 36, where I shall argue that the meeting of Dio and Callistratus outside the walls of Borysthenes
draws similarly and equally knowingly on the Platonic prototype. But these transpositions, from elegant Attica to the wilder
climes of Elis and the shores of the Black Sea, were not
manœuvres executed in isolation. In thus fixing on the opening
pages of the *Phaedrus* and its rustic setting as material for imitation, Dio was following established precedent and making his

---

[3] 1. 54, δωρίζουσα τῇ φωνῇ. Cf. Hermogenes *De Ideis* 491 Sp. where the Dorian
accent is said to give σεμνότης, and see Gow on Theocr. 15. 88.

[4] e.g. Maximus, 37. 4 IK, 32. 3 B, 33. 2 CD.

individual contribution to a trend that has left many more traces besides.

Grammatici and *rhetores* had long since singled out the dialogue's opening for its particular charm and for its felicity as an example of Plato's skill in the plain style. Dionysius of Halicarnassus praised it on both counts in his essay on Demosthenes, his enthusiasm untarnished by his equally firm disapproval of the other, more 'dithyrambic' portions of the same dialogue.[5] Indeed, it looks very much as if, in praising Plato's plain style as a whole, he allowed his own critical language to be shaped by this particularly admired example: Plato's writing in this register, he says, is διαυγής, ὥσπερ τὰ διαφανέστατα τῶν ναμάτων— echoing the description of the stream at *Phdr.* 229 B; and he echoes the description of the grove of 230 B (along with *Rep.* 401 C) when he speaks of an aura resembling a breeze ἀπὸ τῶν εὐωδεστάτων λειμώνων. Two centuries later we find Hermogenes again singling out the grove of 230 B as one of the several paragons of sweetness, γλυκύτης, contained within the dialogue, along with the appeal to the Muses of 237 A and the poetic flourish of 241 D 1.[6] But it was not only in the schools of rhetors and grammarians that pupils had their attention directed thus. One of the two certain fragments of Harpocration's commentary on the dialogue shows that the description of the grove had attracted notice from philosophers too. Socrates, he said, in characterizing his surroundings so elaborately, was deliberately trying to outdo the earlier and shorter description given by Phaedrus in 229 B.[7] Harpocration's aim here seems to have been to rescue Socrates's words from a charge of irrelevance or fussiness. He looks for his solution to the manifest competitiveness of other parts of the dialogue: as Socrates will later set himself up as a rival to Lysias and his script for the non-lover, so here, allegedly, he sets himself up as a rival to Phaedrus.[8]

---

[5] *Dem.* 5–7.

[6] Hermogenes, *Id.* 2. 4 (ii. 358. 24 ff.; 363. 15 ff.; 364. 10 ff. Sp.). The appeal to the Muses is also cited by Men. Rhet. (iii. 334. 5 ff.; 335. 6 ff. Sp.) as a model for cletic hymns in prose.

[7] Harpocration, in Hermias *Comm. in Phdr.* 32. 1 ff. Couvreur. For a discussion of Harpocration's commentary, Dillon (1971).

[8] For the perception of competitive rivalry as an essential element in the dialogue, see also Maximus, 18. 5 G. Hermias, 9. 11 ff. Couvreur, Hermogenes, *Id.* 2. 10 (ii. 403.

Given this scholastic signposting—not to mention the distinction of its object—it is no surprise to find the Phaedran
grove adding lustre to more compositions than just the two by
Dio already mentioned. Some care is admittedly required in
sorting out what should and should not be allowed to count
under this heading. The Phaedran grove is just one instance of
a larger class of *loca amoena* and was by no means the only available classical model. Plato himself also offered the cave and
grove at the beginning of the *Laws*, and Homer such celebrated
set-pieces as the Cave of the Nymphs in *Odyssey* 13.[9] None the
less, there remain a good number of cases whose phrasing or
surroundings tie them firmly to the specific model of the
Phaedrus.

Two good early examples are provided by Cicero, in the *De
oratore* and the *Brutus*, both of which of course share with the
Phaedrus the topic of rhetoric. In *De or.* 1. 7. 28 the evocation is
direct and explicit: the sight of a plane-tree evokes a paraphrase
of Plato from Scaevola, together with the suggestion that the
present party should follow Socrates's example in their choice
of a place for their conversation. In *Brutus* 6. 24 the allusion is
lighter: Cicero, Brutus, and Atticus sit down for their discussion
in the grounds of Cicero's Tusculan villa 'in pratulo propter
Platonis statuam'. Also early, though of unspecifiable date, is
the hilltop grove outside the walls of Abdera where the supposedly mad Democritus is encountered by Hippocrates in ps.-
Hippocrates, *Epistle* 17.[10] Here the identity of the occupant, the
extra-mural location, and the collocation of plane-tree, nym-
phaeum, and stream all tie the description closely to its Platonic precedent. From the second century, besides Dio, there is
a trio of imitations guaranteed as specifically Phaedran by their
connection with the theme of love, and in two of the three cases
also by a direct acknowledgement in the phrasing: Plutarch,
Amatorius, 749 A (where Plutarch's speaker comments on the
extreme frequency of such imitations); Achilles Tatius, *Leucippe*

21 ff.), and the rather smug manipulations of Aristides, 28. 142–4. On a purely technical level this aspect of *Phdr.* allowed it to be held up by rhetors as a useful example of
the exercise of *antirrhesis*: so Theon, *Progymn.* (ii. 70. 15 ff.); cf. Plutarch, *De rect. rat. aud.*
40 E. Modern commentators find not competitiveness but significant irony in Socrates'
words: Rowe (1986), 135 and 141 (see also nn. 51, 55, and 56 below).

    [9] *Od.* 13. 102 ff. On the whole topic, Curtius (1953), 185 ff.
    [10] 17. 6–8, p. 299 Hercher.

and Clitophon, 1. 2. 3; and ps.-Lucian, *Amores*, 31. These will be discussed in more detail below. But echoes of this kind are not tied uniquely to the theme of love, as can be seen from other works from the Lucianic corpus: certainly *De domo* 4, where the reminiscence is explicit, and accompanied by other, supporting references to Phaedran wording and concepts;[11] certainly also *Anacharsis* 16, where the withdrawal to a shady spot is tied to the *Phaedrus* by another of its catch-phrases, γυμνῇ τῇ κεφαλῇ;[12] perhaps also *Navigium* 35 and *Philopatris* 3, though here the relationship is more distant.

It is possible that Plato's *locus* also had its influence on Christian writing of the period, as other elements from the dialogue certainly did. Justin Martyr, in the opening stages of his *Dialogue with Trypho*, recalls a meeting with an aged Christian in a lonely place not far from the sea.[13] This old man, playing Socrates to Justin's opinionated youth, convinces him of the mortality of the human soul and declares that the truth of the doctrine is guaranteed by Holy Writ.[14] It has recently been suggested that this whole episode should be read as a knowing and deliberate reversal of the setting and the argument of the *Phaedrus*: the reference to scriptural authority counters Plato's insistence that books are an inadequate vehicle for truth;[15] the argument for the mortality of the soul contradicts the dialogue's single most celebrated doctrine (ψυχὴ πᾶσα ἀθάνατος);[16] and the lonely, sea-shore setting substitutes a landscape of uncertainty and desolation for the serene and cultivated charm of the banks of the Ilissus.[17] The suggestion is an attractive one, even though the reversal (if such it is) is managed without any direct verbal reminiscences of the original. Like Dio in *Orations* 1 and 36, Justin would be deliberately altering the tone of the setting to suit a different interview and a different revelation;

---

[11] The idea of a flow of beauty (251 BC and 255BD); wings (246 and 251 B–D); and an echo of the wording of the appeal to the Muses in 237 A.

[12] 243 B; also echoed by Clement, *Protr.* 7. 76. 6, and Maximus, 40. 6 F.

[13] *Trypho*, 3. 219 E ff.: ἐπεὶ ἔδοξέ ποτε πολλῆς ἠρεμίας ἐμφορηθῆναι καὶ τὸν τῶν ἀνθρώπων ἀλεεῖναι πάτον, ἐπορευόμην εἴς τι χωρον οὐ μακρὰν θαλάσσης.

[14] *Trypho*, 7. 224 D ff.

[15] *Phdr.* 275 CD.

[16] *Phdr.* 245 C 5, cited by Hermogenes, *Id.* 1. 6 (ii. 291. 15 ff.) and Plutarch *De procr. an.* 1016 A; also inscribed (along with αἰτία ἑλομένῳ θεὸς ἀναίτιος) on a herm of Plato discovered in Tivoli in 1846 (Richter (1965). ii. 166, no. 8, with fig. 906).

[17] Edwards (1987), 270–2.

unlike him, he would be pushing beyond elegant variation to pugnacious and pointed reversal.

2. DIO *Oration* 36: CHARIOTS AND THE COSMOS

Dio's *Oration* 36, which we have already had occasion to mention, is another of his epideictic dialogues. In it, for the benefit of an audience of his fellow Prusaeans, Dio recalls a visit he once paid to Borysthenes—a frontier-post of Hellenism on the shores of the Black Sea—and a discourse he delivered there on the nature of the cosmos. A long introduction (1–27) sets the scene: it consists of a preliminary conversation with young Callistratus outside the city walls by the banks of the river; a prudent withdrawal (in the face of the threat of an enemy attack) to the temple of Zeus; and the beginnings of a disquisition on the true city, from which Dio is quickly diverted by an intervention from the venerable and cultivated Hieroson. The discourse itself, in which Dio turns from the mortal to the cosmic city (as requested by Hieroson), occupies the whole of the rest of the work (28–61). From first to last this is a dialogue shot through with Platonic, and above all with Phaedran, imitation. Its debt to the setting of the *Phaedrus* has already been mentioned and will be spelled out shortly; but it will be more convenient to begin by examining its main constituent, Dio's discourse on the cosmos.

Before it starts, a number of earlier remarks have already brought Plato and his elevated prose style to mind. Most significantly (26–7), old Hieroson has declared his own devotion to the philosopher and has exhorted Dio to imitate his noble diction, ὡς δύνασαι ἐγγύτατα τείνων τῆς τοῦ Πλάτωνος ἐλευθερίας περὶ τὴν φράσιν. He has also expressed his excitement at the prospect of Dio's performance with the somewhat Phaedran phrase ἀνεπτέρωμαι δαιμονίως. From the start, therefore, we are set up to expect a discourse with a strongly Platonic flavour, and are perhaps also put on our guard for echoes of one particular dialogue. Our expectations are, however, not immediately answered. The first eleven sections of the discourse (28–38), are (at least at first hearing) Stoic rather than Platonic—

an exposition of the doctrine of the fellowship of gods and men in their common cosmic home.[18]

Matters change, though, at 39, as Dio turns from exposition of philosophical doctrine to a myth of the Magi, which he claims to convey the same message in allegorical guise. Plato and the *Phaedrus* now come rushing to the fore. The underlying doctrine is still Stoic, but the myth in which it is now clad is a myth of Zeus the charioteer, τέλειόν τε καὶ πρῶτον ἡνίοχον τοῦ τελειοτάτου ἅρματος. And Dio launches into it—no doubt with Hieroson's encouragement still ringing in his ears—in fine Phaedran style: τὸ δὲ ἰσχυρὸν καὶ τέλειον ἅρμα τὸ Διὸς οὐδεὶς ἄρα ὕμνησεν ἀξίως τῶν τῇδε οὔτε Ὅμηρος οὔτε Ἡσίοδος ...

These words (ch. 40) are a deliberate and obtrusive echo of Plato's in *Phaedrus* 247 C. Plato in that passage is of course talking of the ὑπερουράνιος τόπος beyond the outer circle of the material cosmos, but Dio has transferred them to the chariot of Zeus. It soon becomes clear that this transfer is no casual matter. Rather, it is symptomatic—an advance warning—of the way Dio is now to transpose this celebrated image from Plato's myth wholesale for his own purposes. For Dio's (or the Magi's) chariot of Zeus is not, as it was for Plato, an image for one constituent of a larger whole; it is itself the whole cosmos. This Zeus drives a car with four horses, not two, and those horses are the four elemental spheres. Thus at the very outset of the myth, Dio both underscores his debt to the imagery of the *Phaedrus* and at the same time declares himself for a bold re-working. Inevitably the adaptation that follows strays a long way from its prototype: first in the description of the bizarre way the chariot runs, with the inside horse motionless in the middle as the others race around it; and still more in the extension of the image to cover the doctrines of *ekpyrosis* and *apokatastasis* (47–57). Yet even with this degree of adaptation, contact is not entirely lost with the details of the prototype. Each of Dio's elemental horses is assigned its own distinctive character and aspect, echoing the contrasting descriptions of the two Platonic horses in *Phaedrus* 253 DE (36. 43–7); the Earth-Horse, Hestia, is said to sit still in its central position χαλινὸν ἀδάμαντος

---

[18] Compare *SVF* iii. 333–9; Diogenes Laertius, 7. 138; Musonius, 42. 8 ff.; and Epictetus, 1. 9. 4.

ἐνδακόντα, echoing *Phaedrus* 247 A and 254 D (36. 46–7); and the
description of the sweating of the Horse of Water echoes *Phaedrus* 254 C (36. 49). It all involves some considerable shifts
between the old and the new homes of these individual details,
and the Phaedran borrowings are combined with much material derived from other sources, but the central affinity is clearly
visible.

From the myth and the discourse on the cosmos we may now
turn back to the earlier portions of the dialogue; for there too
Dio has drawn on the *Phaedrus*.

First of all, there is the matter of the setting. Although Dio
and his audience prudently adjourn for their main business to
the (thematically appropriate) temple of Zeus, they begin outside the walls of Borysthenes, in the surrounding countryside.
As the account begins Dio is strolling in mid-morning, along
the banks of the river Hypanis: καὶ δὴ καὶ περιεπάτουν περὶ
πλήθουσαν ἀγορὰν παρὰ τὸν Ὕπανιν (36. 1). He there encounters
a group of Borysthenites, quickly joined by the young Callistratus, a handsome eighteen-year-old devoted to λόγοι καὶ
φιλοσοφία, and renowned for the number of his lovers. It is with
Callistratus that he begins his conversation, on the topic of the
relative merits of two classic poets, Phocylides and Homer. This
is certainly Platonic imitation of some kind; Dio is establishing
himself as the Socrates of the episode.[19] But we can surely be
more specific: it is again towards the *Phaedrus* that he is looking,
just as in *Oration* 1. The extra-mural location, the indication of
the time of day (even if not the same), and the proximity to a
river all match, as also does the character of Callistratus
(Phaedrus-like in his juvenile charms and his concern for *logoi*),
and the initial topic of conversation (the skill and sagacity of
well-known writers). As in *Oration* 1, Dio aims to please by a
sophisticated transposition, from the cultivated centre to the
more rough and ready periphery of Hellenism.[20]

Secondly, we should look at the opening paragraphs of Dio's
first discourse, before the interruption from Hieroson (18–19).
Dio here begins with a declaration on the importance of definition. By way of an example, he offers a specimen definition of

---

[19] For Dio's use of the Socratic persona, Moles (1978), 96–100.
[20] Compare also 36. 9 ff., 16 ff. and 24 ff. for Dio's play with the notion of the Hellenism of the frontiers in this oration.

the term 'man', before turning to his real subject, the true city. Once again, there can be no denying the generally Platonic colour of these paragraphs. Dio is again casting himself in the role of Socrates and recalling his quest for definitions. The phrasing too is Platonic, in such clauses as λέγω δὲ ὁποῖόν τι καὶ καθ' ὃ μηδενὶ τῶν ἄλλων ταὐτόν. But again, I would suggest that we have here another specifically Phaedran reminiscence. For Socrates in the *Phaedrus* begins *his* first speech with an almost identical point, stressing the need to define the subject of any discussion at its outset (237 BC). Moreover, *Phaedrus* 237 BC is actually quoted by the second-century Platonist Albinus in his *Isagoge* (1), which suggests that it had some general currency as a useful formulation of the point at issue.

Thirdly, there is 22, also from the first, aborted section of Dio's discourse. This seems to echo two further Phaedran passages, again from the myth. Ἀγαθὴν μὲν γὰρ ἐξ ἁπάντων ἀγαθῶν πόλιν οὔτε τις γενομένην πρότερον οἶδε θνητὴν οὔτε ποτὲ ὡς ἐσομένην ὕστερον ἄξιον διανοηθῆναι—so Dio on the good city, again recalling Plato's introduction to the ὑπερουράνιος τόπος in *Phaedrus* 247 C: τὸν δὲ ὑπερουράνιον τόπον οὔτε τις ὕμνησε πω . . . οὔτε ποτὲ ὑμνήσει κατ' ἀξίαν. Then also Dio's description of the courses of the gods: τῶν μὲν ἡγουμένων τε καὶ πρώτων θεῶν ⟨   ⟩ χωρὶς ἔριδος καὶ ἥττης . . . τῶν μὲν φανερωτάτων πορευομένων ἑκάστου καθ' ἑαυτόν . . .[21] Here the echo is twofold, as Dio plays both on the general description of the *poreia* of the gods in *Phaedrus* 246 E ff. and on the celebrated *sententia* of 247 A 7 (φθόνος γὰρ ἔξω θείου χοροῦ ἵσταται).[22]

Finally, there are Dio's words in 33-5, on the value of poetic testimony to the nature of Zeus and the cosmos. Poets as a class are allowed only a limited importance: they are said to be attendants of the Muses, not full initiates, and are therefore not to be looked to for more than obscure hints of higher truth. The only exceptions Dio allows by name are Homer and Hesiod, both of whom are said to have enjoyed the occasional brief flash

---

[21] The text given by the MSS seems defective here. A participle balancing πορευομένων is required between θεῶν and χωρὶς in the second extract, and in the first the word θνητὴν is awkward and should perhaps be expelled.

[22] Compare Lucian, *Prom.* 18; Clement, *Strom.* 5. 4. 19. 2; 5. 4. 24. 2; 5. 4. 30. 5; 7. 2. 7. 2; 7. 7. 49. 4; Maximus, 41. 3 A; Plutarch, *Quaest. conv.* 679 E; *De prim. frig.* 954 F; *Non posse* 1086 F; *Comm. in Hes.* fr. 10 (= 31 Sandb.).

of true inspiration. Now, the wording here is not markedly Phaedran, but the topic is. Poetic inspiration is allowed a real, but very limited value as a route to higher truth in the discussion of the species of *mania* in *Phaedrus* 245 A, and both Socrates and Dio conjure up the picture of poets 'at the gates' (Dio 36. 33; *Phdr.* 245 A 6). And Socrates is also made to play with the concept of inspiration, in a characteristically ironic way, in *Phaedrus* 235 C and 241 E.

In considering Dio's *Oration* 1, we saw how his exploitation of the opening pages of the *Phaedrus* was symptomatic of a more widespread trend in literary composition, supported and partly conditioned by the teaching of grammarians, rhetors, and philosophers. The contribution of the *Phaedrus* to *Oration* 36 is on a larger scale and more pervasive, but the same point holds. We have already noted in passing how the echo of *Phaedrus* 237 BC in 36. 18–19 can be paralleled in a second-century philosophical handbook. Still easier to parallel is the last of the allusions to be discussed above, to Plato's handling of the topic of madness and inspiration. Though not singled out in any surviving text from the scholastic milieu, this was clearly a celebrated set-piece. The author of the pseudo-Lucianic *Demosthenis encomium*, like Dio, co-opts the image of the gates of poetry (5). Plutarch alludes to the whole doctrine in *De virt. mor.* 452 B and paraphrases it at length in *Amatorius* 758 D ff. And Aelius Aristides evokes the passage no less than eight times in his *To Plato; In Defence of Oratory* (*Oration* 2)—a marvellous display of professional chauvinism in which inspiration is claimed for the art of speech as well as for the art of poetry, and Plato cudgelled with his own clubs.[23]

It is however in his exploitation of what follows the classification of kinds of madness—the analysis of the soul and the myth of its journey through the cosmos in *Phaedrus* 245 C ff.—that Dio is most manifestly swimming with the tide. In the philosopher's school this passage counted as one of the principal sources and authorities for Plato's doctrine of the soul (along of course with the *Phaedo* and the *Republic*), while also providing useful information about his teaching on Fate and on human happi-

---

[23] 2. 34 (244 A); 35 (244 D); 42 (244 B and 275 B); 46 (244 B); 49 (244 A); 52 (244 A–245 B); 58 (245 B); 164 (244 C); cf. also 44 (275 C); 137 (269 D); 156 (236 B); 459 (269 D).

ness.[24] At the same time, it served grammarians and rhetors as a model of literary grandeur (σεμνότης).[25] And when we turn to look for other literary exploitations in second-century writing, the haul is enormous.

At a relatively superficial level, individual details and phrases from the myth are often found drafted in to add surface sparkle to works of pure rhetorical entertainment: so Aristides 3. 680, 28. 114 and 142, 42. 4; and Lucian *Pisc.* 22, *Bis acc.* 33, *Rhet. prae.* 26, *Prom.* 18, *Sacrif.* 8 and 10—Lucian having a particular taste for elegantly familiar allusions to great Zeus in his winged car. But the myth was also a repertorium of imaginative detail for more serious, philosophically oriented writing. Christian and non-Christian authors alike cite and adapt it again and again in their discussions of the nature of soul, human and cosmic, both in isolated snatches and in the construction of elaborate mythical structures of their own.

Among the non-Christians—as was long ago pointed out by Roger Miller Jones—one of the most notable and consistent contributions made by this section of the *Phaedrus* is to the *locus* of the 'flight of the soul': descriptions of the real or metaphorical travels of the soul through (and sometimes out of) the cosmos, either during philosophical contemplation or after the final severing of body and soul at death.[26] The habit of drawing on the *Phaedrus* for this purpose (along with the complementary myths of the *Phaedo* and the *Republic*) is first seen in surviving Greek literature in the essays of Philo Judaeus.[27] In the second century it is continued in Plutarch's myths in the *De facie* and the *De genio*, and in a series of smaller-scale exploitations in the *Dialexeis* of Maximus of Tyre.[28] But by no means all evocations of the myth of the *Phaedrus* fall into this category. Many are allusions to or adaptations of the equally celebrated images of the soul's wing and the soul-chariot.[29]

---

[24] Alcinous, *Didaskalikos*, 4 (246 E); 5 (246 A); 25 (245 C–E) and 26 (248 C); also ps.-Plutarch, *De fato*, 568 C ff. (248 C).

[25] Hermogenes, *Id.* 1. 6 (ii. 290. 23 ff.; 291. 15 ff.; 294. 20 ff. Sp.); ps.-Hermogenes, *Heur.* 4. 11 (ii. 255. 22 ff.). Note also Men. Rhet.'s citation of the myth as a model for *hymnos physiologikos* (iii. 337. 7 ff. Sp.).

[26] R. M. Jones (1926).

[27] e.g., *Opif. mundi* 69 ff.; for a fuller list, see R. M. Jones (1926).

[28] *De genio*, 591 C ff.; *De facie*, 943 CD; 943 CD; Maximus, 10. 3 B; 10. 9 C; 11. 10 DE.

[29] Maximus, 1. 5 C; 41. 5; Plutarch, *Quaest. Plat.* 1004 C; 1008 C; *An seni* 786 D; *Virt. mor.* 445 C; *Tuenda San.* 125 B; *Vit. Ant.* 932 B.

Christian exploitation of the *Phaedrus* myth, which is symptomatic of a much more general debt to pagan philosophizing
literature,[30] also involves both the borrowing of individual
images and more wholesale appropriations. Zeus in his winged
car is invoked by Athenagoras and by the author of the *Cohortatio* attributed to Justin; the wings of the soul by Tatian and the
heretic Basilides.[31] But by far the greatest and most consistent
debtor is Clement of Alexandria, who borrows from this section
of the dialogue some thirty times in the *Protrepticus*, the *Paedago-
gus*, and the *Stromateis*.[32] This and other cases prove Clement to
have known the *Phaedrus* intimately and to have been influenced by it in a way that went beyond conscious borrowing,
to a state in which its images, phrases, and concepts came to his
pen unbidden when he turned to certain topics.[33] In Jean
Daniélou's words, the myth alone provided him with the
language to re-express in a cultivated manner 'the whole of
Christian theology, from Man's Fall to his restoration by
grace'.[34]

If we now return to Dio's *Oration* 36 and set it against this
background of widespread literary exploitation, it is clear how
little eccentricity there was in his choice of the *Phaedrus* as the
model for a philosophizing myth. Indeed, the choice was even
more firmly conditioned by established tradition than the parallels so far given have suggested. Although the re-use of the
myth itself has been seen to be conventional, one might still feel
that the way the image of the chariot is transferred from soul to
cosmos strikes an individual and original note. In fact, on
further investigation, this too turns out to have its precedents.
Both Plutarch and Philo before him know that the πτηνὸν ἄρμα

[30] See in general Daniélou (1973), chs. 2 and 4.

[31] Athenagoras, *Legatio*, 23; ps.-Justin, *Cohortatio*, 31 (referring the image not to Plato
but to Ezekiel 10: 18); Tatian, *Oratio*, 20; Basilides, *ap.* Hippolytus, *Refutatio*, 7. 22.

[32] *Protr.* 4. 56. 4 (247 C); 6. 68. 3 (247 C); 10. 89. 3 (254 D); 10. 106. 3 (248 C); 12. 121.
1 (246 A ff.); *Paed.* 2. 10. 86. 2–3 (250 E and 254 D); 2. 10. 89. 2 (254 C–E); 3. 2. 14. 1
(246 A ff.); 3. 11. 53. 1–2 (247 B ff.); *Strom.* 1. 1. 4. 3 (248 B–E); 1. 15. 67. 4 (247 C); 1. 28.
176. 2 (250 C); 3. 3. 13. 1–2 (248 C ff.); 3. 13. 93. 3 (248 C); 5. 1. 14. 2 (248 C ff.); 5. 3. 16.
1–3 (247 C); 5. 4. 19. 2 (247 A); 5. 4. 24. 2 (247 A); 5. 4. 30. 5 (247 A); 5. 8. 53. 1 (247 B);
5. 11. 73. 2 (250 C ff.); 5. 13. 83. 1 (246 C); 5. 14. 138. 3 (250 BC); 7. 2. 5. 6. (246 E); 7. 2.
7. 2 (247 A); 7. 3. 20. 8 (248 C); 7. 7. 40. 1 (246 BC); 7. 7. 46. 8 (247 B); 7. 7. 49. 4 (247 A);
also *Quis dives* 42. 6 (254 d).

[33] For a detailed consideration of Clement's use of *Phdr.* in his *Protr.* see Butterworth
(1916).

[34] Daniélou (1973), 121, with a reference also to Origen, *Contra Celsum*, 4. 40.

of *Phaedrus* 246 E can, if desired, be taken as an allegory of the whole cosmos and its harmonious revolutions.[35] The elaboration of the details of the cosmic chariot in *Oration* 36 may indeed be Dio's own work, but the interpretation of Plato on which it is based is not.

3. THE RIGHT TRUE END OF LOVE: THE *Phaedrus* AND *Logoi Erotikoi*

Mention has already been made in passing of uses of the myth and the *locus amoenus* in such texts as Plutarch's *Amatorius* and Achilles Tatius's *Leucippe and Clitophon*. The literature of love as a whole is another field in which the influence of the *Phaedrus* was extensive, both among the novelists and in works with greater intellectual pretensions.

With the novelists, the greatest density of allusion comes where one might have expected, in the *Leucippe and Clitophon*: in the description of the *locus amoenus*, μύθων ἄξιος ἐρωτικῶν, where Clitophon and the narrator meet, in 1. 2. 3; in the reference to the philosophical concept of love in the debate (the '*dubbio amoroso*') at the end of Book 2; and in three passages, based on *Phaedrus* 251 BC and 255 BD, which speak of the creation of love by the outflow of beauty from the beloved into the lover's soul via his eyes (1. 4. 4, 1. 9. 4, 5. 13. 4). Longus too makes noteworthy, if intermittent use of the dialogue, echoing 255 D in 1. 22. 4 and 249 D in 2. 7. 1, and perhaps being helped to the cicada-episode of 1. 25–6 by 259 AC.[36] Xenophon of Ephesus, like Achilles Tatius, co-opts the notion of the 'flow of beauty' twice, in 1. 3. 2 and 1. 9. 6–8. Chariton, if I am not mistaken, has a distant echo of 242 B–243 D in 8. 1. 3.[37]

In all these cases the *Phaedrus* is being used to infuse either a modicum of philosophy, or a little of the stylistic sweetness for which it was so admired by the rhetors.[38] The total debt, however, is not enormous. If we wish to find examples of a more

---

[35] Philo, *Quaest. in Gen.* 3. 3, p. 181 Markus; *Quis rer, div.* 301; Plutarch, *Quaest. conv.* 740 B; cf. also Numenius, fr. 12 des Places. On this tradition of exegesis, in which Plato's words are applied to the Platonic-Stoic World Soul, Boyancé (1952) and (1963).

[36] Hunter (1983), 32 (with n. 43 on p. 109) and 56–7.

[37] ἐπεὶ δὲ καλῶς ἀπελογήσατο τῷ ἔρωτι Χαιρέας, echoing Socrates' reference to the Palinode in 243 A ff.

[38] Cf. Hunter (1983), 96–7.

thorough-going imitation in this area, of a kind to set beside the two orations of Dio already discussed, it is again to the traditions of philosophical and quasi-philosophical writing that we must turn.

Surviving titles testify to the growth of a rich tradition of dialogues and essays *On Love* from the fourth century BC onward.[39] Given the almost total loss of Greek philosophical literature of the Hellenistic period, it is a tradition which—very conveniently for the purposes of this survey—first becomes visible to us in three works of the second century: the pseudo-Lucianic *Amores*, the *Amatorius* of Plutarch, and Maximus of Tyre's *Dialexeis* 18–21. Each of the three (as no doubt the earlier works now lost) draws heavily on a wide range of pre-existing literature, historical as well as philosophical, verse as well as prose. In the philosophical sphere, moreover, they rely as much on Plato's *Symposium* as on the *Phaedrus*. However, as we shall now see, the *Phaedrus* does exert a considerable influence on all of them, and on every level from casual decoration to basic structure. The contrast with the relatively sparse use of the dialogue by the novelists is marked.

The pseudo-Lucianic *Amores* is a dialogue on the relative merits of homosexual and heterosexual love. Its core is a debate between one Callicratidas and one Charicles, held in the temple of Aphrodite on Cnidus, which is recalled by the narrator for his friend Theomnestus. Not surprisingly it is in the speech of Callicratidas, the champion of homosexual love, that Phaedran debts are most marked, beginning with the following rather mannered conceit in its second paragraph (31):

εὐξαίμην γάρ, εἴπερ ἦν ἐν δυνατῷ, τὴν ἐπήκοόν ποτε τῶν Σωκρατικῶν λόγων πλατάνιστον, Ἀκαδημίας καὶ Λυκείου δένδρον εὐτυχέστερον, ἐγγὺς ἡμῶν ἑστάναι πεφυκυῖαν, ἔνθ' ἡ Φαίδρου προσανάκλισις ἦν, ὥσπερ ὁ ἱερὸς εἶπεν ἀνὴρ πλείστων ἀψάμενος χαρίτων· αὐτὴ τάχα ἂν ὥσπερ ἡ ἐν Δωδώνῃ φηγὸς ἐκ τῶν ὁροδάμνων ἱερὰν ἀπορρήξασα φωνὴν τοὺς παιδικοὺς εὐφήμησεν ἔρωτας ἔτι τοῦ καλοῦ μεμνημένη Φαίδρου ...

I might wish, were it possible, for that plane-tree which once overheard Socrates's words, most favoured of all the plants in the Academy and the Lyceum, to stand growing beside us now—the tree beside which Phaedrus reclined, as related by that revered author with all the extraordinary grace at his command. It might well, like

---

[39] Wilhelm (1902), 55–75.

the oak at Dodona, have let a holy voice break forth from its boughs, in praise of the love of boys, recalling even now the fair Phaedrus . . .

Rather precious, but the love-sick plane is an agreeable idea none the less, and the whole passage is a shade more cunning than at first appears. It recalls principally *Phdr.* 230 BC, but contrives to blend that reminiscence with an allusion to a quite separate passage, 275 B, in the reference to the oak of Dodona.

As Callicratidas then proceeds to develop his case, further Phaedran details creep in. In 37, the distinction is drawn between a higher and a lower form of love—a distinction indebted to the *Symposium* as much as to the *Phaedrus*, but with a definite Phaedran tinge to the language, in the use of the char-ioteer metaphor and of the vocabulary of inspiration (οὐδὲ ἐνὶ πνεύματι τὰς ἡμετέρας ψυχὰς ἐρεθίζων). In 38 ff. there is an elab-orate comparison between the vicious sophistication of women's lives and manners and the virtuous simplicity of boys; this draws—for the general concept rather than for any specific phrase or detail—on contrast between the lover and the non-lover in the first speech of Socrates (especially 239 CD).[40] In 46 we get a quotation from Sappho, inspired by her invocation by Socrates in *Phdr.* 235 C. And in 48 the discussion of the creation of reciprocal love, like an image in a mirror, echoes *Phdr.* 255 BC (*eros* and *anteros*).[41]

Phaedran reminiscence is not, however, confined solely to the speech of Callicratidas. His opponent Charicles, when he made his speech (19–28), had also referred to the famous model, though with scorn rather than respect. In 24 he pointed out acerbicly that the supposedly lovable Phaedrus was really a traitor to his teacher Lysias, and that his indulgent treatment by Plato was just one more example of homosexual special-pleading. And before that, in the description of the temple pre-cinct and the bower in which the discussion takes place, we have had a clear evocation of the *locus amoenus* by the Ilissus, crickets and all (12 and 18).

The second amatory text, Plutarch's *Amatorius*, is altogether a more sophisticated dialogue than the *Amores*, and at the same

---

[40] This part of Socrates' first speech is also echoed by Maximus, 22. 3 F (239 C), and by Plutarch, *Amat.* 752 C, 749 F, *De adul. et am.* 51 D.

[41] Cf. Plutarch, *Vit. Alc.* 193 D.

time deeper and more consistent in its exploitation of the *Phaedrus*. It begins with a framing passage in which Plutarch's son, Autobulus, agrees to tell his friend, Flavianus, of a conversation his father once had on Mount Helicon, above Thespiae, on the subject of love (748 E–749 B). The conversation itself, which then follows, can be divided into four 'acts': the first three set in the Muses' shrine, the fourth and last on the road back to Thespiae. Act I is primarily a discussion of the merits of homosexual and heterosexual love, between Pisias and Protogenes on the one hand, and Anthemion and Daphnaeus on the other; the occasion of the debate—kept fairly constantly in view—is the dilemma of the young man Bacchon over an offer of marriage from a rich widow. The act ends with a contribution from Plutarch himself in favour of the heterosexual option (749 B–754 E). Act II is an interlude, in which events in the town below—the abduction of Bacchon by the widow—force the departure of a number of the participants (754 E–756 A). Act III, the climax of the dialogue, is dominated by Plutarch and his explanation of the divinity and the true nature of Love (during which the heterosexual/homosexual distinction largely drops out of view, 756 A–766 D). Act IV is a kind of diminuendo conclusion, as the participants, now on their way back into town, return to the topic of heterosexual fidelity (766 D–771 E).

Phaedran here, before we even get down to details, is the overall structure. As in the *Phaedrus*, a discussion of the merits of two kinds of devotion (of the lover and the non-lover in the model, of the homosexual and the heterosexual lover in the adaptation) is followed and superseded by a deeper and more revealing disquisition on the true, divine nature of Love, which holds central position in the overall plan of the work. Plutarch is moreover at pains to indicate his relationship with the *Phaedrus* at the very outset, in the introductory conversation between Autobulus and Flavianus. He does so rather slyly, with a species of *recusatio*.

ΦΛΑΟΥ. ἄφελε τοῦ λόγου τὸ νῦν ἔχον ἐποποιῶν τε λειμῶνας καὶ σκιὰς καὶ ἅμα κιττοῦ τε καὶ σμιλάκων διαδρομὰς καὶ ὅσ᾽ ἄλλα τοιούτων τόπων ἐπιλαβόμενοι γλίχονται τὸν Πλάτωνος Ἰλισσὸν καὶ τὸν ἄγνον ἐκεῖνον καὶ τὴν ἠρέμα προσάντη πόαν πεφυκυῖαν προθυμότερον ἢ κάλλιον ἐπιγραφέσθαι.
ΑΥΤ. τί δὲ δεῖται τοιούτων, ὦ ἄριστε Φλαουιανέ, προοιμίων ἡ διήγησις;

'Remove from your account for the time being,' says Flavianus, 'the poets' meadows and shady spots, and the gadding of ivy and smilax, and all the other ways in which, when they seize on this kind of location, they attempt (with more zeal than success) to borrow the lustre of Plato's Ilissus and his celebrated *agnus castus* and gently grassy slope.'

'My dear Flavianus,' replies Autobulus, 'why should my account need that kind of preface?'

The discourse does indeed eschew the *locus amoenus*, but the very denial signals a Phaedran presence, and the signal is amply justified by what follows. The greatest debtor is Plutarch, in his discussion of Love's divinity in 756 A–766 D: especially in 758 D–759 D, where he summarizes the doctrine of inspiration, quoting 245 A (758 F) and echoing the image of the charioteer (759 D);[42] then also in 764 B–766 B, where he summarizes and reworks the central ideas of the soul's quest for beauty and its return from embodiment to the gods and the bright beyond. This latter passage, too long to be quoted here, is a fascinating example of how Plutarch can reprocess Platonic material in an admirably supple and elegant manner, not only combining details from separate *loci* and dialogues but also adding new forms of amplification of his own invention. We begin by noting how the whole series of echoes of the wording of the *Phaedrus*, in 764 E ff.,[43] is prefaced with a comparison—of Eros with the Sun—drawn not from the *Phaedrus* but from the *Republic* (764 B–D). 765c then demonstrates Plutarch's readiness to adopt a Platonic image, but radically to change its application:

οὐ σεισμόν, ὥς τις εἶπε, κινούσης ἐπὶ σπέρμα καὶ ὄλισθον ἀτόμων ὑπὸ λειότητος καὶ γαργαλισμοῦ θλιβομένων, διάχυσιν δὲ θαυμαστὴν καὶ γόνιμον ὥσπερ ἐν φυτῷ βλαστάνοντι καὶ τρεφομένῳ καὶ πόρους ἀνοίγουσαν εὐπειθείας καὶ φιλοφροσύνης, . . .

This warmth does not, as a certain individual has maintained, set up a churning and cause the production of seed, as the atoms glide and are rubbed off in the smooth and tickling contact; rather, it produces an extraordinary fertile diffusion, as of the sap in a plant that sprouts and grows, which opens up the channels of acquiescence and affection.

---

[42] There is also an echo of *Tim.* 86 E–87 A here.
[43] Especially 241 A, 248 B, 249 C, 250 C ff., 253 E–254 B.

This is the image of the growing wing from *Phaedrus* 251 B–D, transferred from animal to vegetable, and exploited for an incidental side-swipe at Epicurus at the same time. Finally we find in 765 E that Plutarch is also willing and able to add evocative images of his own:

ἀνάκλασις δή που τὸ περὶ τὴν ἶρίν ἐστι τῆς ὄψεως πάθος ὅταν ἡσυχῇ νοτερῷ λείῳ δὲ καὶ μέτριον πάχος ἔχοντι προσπεσοῦσα νέφει τοῦ ἡλίου ψαύσῃ κατ᾽ ἀνάκλισιν, καὶ τὴν περὶ ἐκεῖνον αὐγὴν ὁρῶσα καὶ τὸ φῶς δόξαν ἡμῖν ἐνεργάσηται τοῦ φαντάσματος ὡς ἐν τῷ νέφει ὄντος. ταὐτὸ δὴ τὸ ἐρωτικὸν μηχάνημα καὶ σόφισμα περὶ τὰς εὐφυεῖς καὶ φιλοκάλους ψυχάς· ἀνάκλασιν ποιεῖ τῆς μνήμης ἀπὸ τῶν ἐνταῦθα φαινομένων καὶ προσαγορευομένων καλῶν εἰς τὸ θεῖον καὶ ἐράσμιον καὶ μακάριον ὡς ἀληθῶς ἐκεῖνο καὶ θαυμάσιον καλόν.

What our eyes experience when we see a rainbow is of course the phenomenon of refraction, which occurs when sight falls on a slightly damp but smooth and fairly thick cloud and comes into contact with the sun, by refraction. Because we thus see the light of the sun's rays we fall prey to the belief that the thing seen is actually in the cloud. This is just like the cunning way that Love works on souls that are noble and love beauty. He refracts their memories from the phenomena of this world, which we call beautiful, to that other marvellous Beauty, which is divine and lovable and truly blessed.

Plutarch here builds on Plato's 'flow of beauty' in *Phdr.* 255B–D, and produces an image that is eminently Platonic in feel, with its sparkle and its emphasis on the lover's vision of the transcendent in the material; but it is his own creation.

Phaedran echoes are not however confined to these two high points in Plutarch's discourse. They occur with considerable regularity through the whole dialogue. I can only summarize. In 749 F–750 C the wrangling of Pisias and Anthemion over the conduct of Bacchon's rich window draws (like *Amores* 38 ff.) on the description of the conduct of the lover in *Phdr.* 240 A and 241 CD. In 751 A–D the use of Sappho and Anacreon as points of reference recalls *Phdr.* 235 C (Socrates' citation of Sappho and Anacreon as probable sources of his own ideas about love; cf. *Amores* 46). 751 DE paraphrases *Phdr.* 250 E in attacking homosexual passion as something dark and ugly. 751 F echoes the image of the soul's wing, in the choice of the word πτεροφυήσας to describe the growth of the lover's strength and conceit. 762 D speaks of a man appearing to grow φαιδρότερον under the in-

fluence of love. 763 F brings a brief allusion to the notion of the
lover's ascent, followed by a quotation of the Phaedran phrase
μηδ' ἂν κελεύω εἴπῃς (*Phdr.* 235 D). Cicadas are used in an
explanatory image in 767 D (*Phdr.* 230 C and 258 E–259 D). And
finally, at the very end of the dialogue, 771 D repeats the proverb οὐ πόλεμόν γε ἀγγέλλεις from *Phdr.* 242 B.

Plutarch's *recusatio* at the beginning of the *Amatorius*, turns
out to be a rejection only of slavish and unimaginative use of
the *Phaedrus*; it is certainly not a rejection of the works itself as a
proper object of imitation. The whole dialogue is structured on
Phaedran lines, its central doctrines are from the *Phaedrus* and
are given in Phaedran language, and a host of other details of
conception and expression have been included too, creatively
adapted and blended with a wide range of other Platonic and
non-Platonic material.

My last example of the influence of the *Phaedrus* on a *logos ero-
tikos* is *Dialexeis* 18–21 of Maximus of Tyre, collectively entitled
What Was Socrates' Art of Love?: a relatively late example of the
form, drawing on the whole accumulated tradition.[44] Here, as
in a number of other cases in Maximus' œuvre, discussion of the
general topic at issue is tied to the specific example of Socrates.[45] The four constituent *Dialexeis* make a connected sequence, leading us from anecdotal opening to enlightening
conclusion. Maximus begins with a series of stories intended to
establish the distinction between virtuous and vicious love:
Actaeon of Corinth, Periander and his boyfriend, Harmodius
and Aristogeiton, and the Holy Band of Epaminondas (18. 1–3,
a set clearly indebted above all to *Symposium* 178 E and 182 C,
with some assistance perhaps ultimately derived from Aristotle
Politics 1311ª39 ff.). Maximus then comes to the point. Socrates, to judge from the way he flaunts his feelings in the dialogues, was a great lover too, and what is worse, gives every
indication of having been a hedonistic lover into the bargain. Is
this the scandal it might appear, or is there some respectable
explanation for his behaviour (18. 4–5)? The remainder of *Dialexis* 18 and the remaining three of the sequence construct a
case for the defence, a justification for Socrates's self-confessed

---

[44] Besides Plutarch's essay, perhaps also the *On Socrates and his Art of Love* of Favorinus: Barigazzi (1966), 161–9.
[45] Compare 8 and 9, on *diamones*.

ἐρωτική. As a first step it is argued that Socrates was not the only great figure thus to parade his erotic sentiments: indeed, the whole of Greek literature from Homer on is full of little else (18. 6–9).[46] Secondly, in *Dialexis* 19, the point is made that Socrates may have had benevolent, altruistic motives for his seemingly shocking behaviour; and that altruistic, self-denying love is as well-known a phenomenon as its hedonistic counterpart. The third component, *Dialexis* 20, adds little to the development of the argument, being mainly concerned to underline and to illustrate the contrast between good and bad love. It is left to *Dialexis* 21, the last in the sequence, to bring the enquiry to a decisive conclusion. Maximus goes back on his tracks to make an important revision. So far he has been speaking of 'good' and 'bad' love—but in fact, 'bad love' is not love at all. Eros is a god and it is only good love that deserves to be called by his name; 'bad love' is mere desire. True love is a rational state and a stage on the road to virtue. But that is not all. Love is also the good soul's reaction to embodied reflections of transcendent beauty, reminding it of the extra-celestial home it once knew. And it was with this understanding of Love's nature that Socrates was working all along. Those erotic feelings he flaunted, to such scandalous appearance, are properly to be understood as signs of virtue.

The Phaedran culmination to this sequence is again obvious. Maximus in *Dialexis* 21. 7–8 reworks the myth of the *Phaedrus* as Plutarch had done at the high point of the *Amatorius*. His reworking is both more perfunctory than Plutarch's and more distant from the model, but the Phaedran presence does still extend to at least some details of expression beside the central concepts. Most notably, there is his description of the penetration of our world by an outflow of beauty in 21. 8 BC:

οὕτω καὶ τὸ κάλλος τὸ ἄρρητον καὶ ἀθάνατον ἔρχεται μὲν πρῶτον δι' οὐρανοῦ καὶ τῶν ἐν αὐτῷ σωμάτων, καὶ εἰσπεσὸν ἐκεῖ, ἀκραιφνὲς μένει καὶ ἀμιγὲς καὶ ὁλόκληρον· ἐπειδὰν δὲ ὑπερκύψῃ τοῦ οὐρανοῦ εἰς τὸν δεῦρο τόπον, ἀμβλύνεται καὶ ἀμαυροῦται· καὶ μόλις ἂν αὐτοῦ γνωρίσαι τὴν ἐπιρροὴν ναύτης θαλάττιος, συνήθης τῷ ποταμῷ, διὰ μνήμης ἔχων τὴν ἐκείνου φύσιν, ὁρῶν αὐτὴν ἀμυδρὰν ἐν γῇ πλανωμένην καὶ ἀνακεκραμένην ἀλλοτρίᾳ φύσει· ὁ δέ, ἐπειδὰν ἐντύχῃ, καὶ γνωρίσῃ καὶ ἴχνος αὐγῶν φανὲν

---

[46] A similar exercise in special pleading to Ovid, *Trist.* 2. 1. 361 ff.

ὥσπερ ὁ 'Οδυσσεὺς ἀποθρώσκοντα καπνόν, σκιρτᾷ καὶ φλογοῦται καὶ
φαιδρύνεται καὶ ἐρᾷ.[47]

So ineffable and immortal beauty spreads first through the heavens,
and as it enters that realm remains pure and uncontaminated and
whole. But when it dips beneath the heavens to our realm down
below, it is blunted and weakened. A sailor at sea, who knows this
river and has some recollection of its nature, can scarcely recognize it
when he sees it spread dimly about the earth and mingled with
foreign matter. But when he does encounter it and recognizes the
appearance of so much as a trace of its radiance, like Odysseus catching sight of the smoke rising from Ithaca, he leaps, and blazes up and
brightens, and falls in love.

This is an interpretative paraphrase of the doctrine of the
Phaedrus rather than a close reworking, but the original phrasing is nevertheless echoed in at least two places: in the clause
ἐπειδὰν δὲ ὑπερκύψῃ τοῦ οὐρανοῦ εἰς τὸν δεῦρο τόπον; and in the
pair of verbs σκιρτᾷ . . . καὶ φαιδρύνεται.[48]

But Maximus' concluding exposition does not exhaust his
debts, any more than Plutarch's were confined to the central
discussion of the *Amatorius* or those of the *Amores* to the speech of
Callicratidas. As was the case with the *Amatorius*, the whole
structure of his four-part exposition follows Phaedran precedent. A series of partly illuminating but incomplete answers to
the initial question about Socrates is overtaken and concluded
with a finally satisfactory answer of an altogether different
order of profundity—just as Socrates' second speech in the
Phaedrus overtakes both his first speech and the speech of
Lysias.[49] What is more, Maximus also follows the *Phaedrus* in his
use of the story of Stesichorus' *Palinode* to introduce the final
retractatio in *Dialexis* 21 (21. 1 A–C).[50]

Yet more material from the *Phaedrus* appears at the beginning

[47] Reading ναύτης θαλάττιος with the Ms, rather than the Teubner ⟨πλὴν⟩ ναύτης
θαλάττιος, and hesitantly accepting αὐγῶν for αὐτῶν. The river pictured here is the Nile:
see Hdt. 2. 5. 2; Aristides 35. 9–10.

[48] The same pair of verbs occurs in a similarly Phaedran context in Clement, *Strom.*
5. 13. 83. 1. We should perhaps think of a common source in an earlier reworking of this
section of the *Phdr.* (as also in the parallel case of Maximus, 11 (2 A, 5 A, 6 AB), and Clement, *Protr.* 6. 68. 1–3).

[49] This structure is admittedly not unique to the *Phdr.*; one sees it also in *Symp.* and
Gorg.

[50] Cf. *Phdr.* 243 AB. For other echoes of this passage, see Lucian, *Apol.* 1; *Pro imag.* 15;
and perhaps, as suggested above, Chariton, 8. 1. 3.

of the sequence, in *Dialexis* 18, as Maximus establishes his initial portrait of Socrates the lover: in a near-quotation of 234 D in 18. 4 B; in references to 230 B and 257 A in 18. 4 FG; in a further reference to 234 D in 18. 5 G ff.; in an allusion to 236 D in 18. 6 F; and in a paraphrase of 235 C in 18. 7 B. Of particular interest here is the use of *Phdr.* 235 C in 18. 7 B. This is the passage (already mentioned in connection with both the *Amores* and the *Amatorius*) where Socrates attributes his ideas on love to the inspiration of Sappho and Anacreon. In the other two cases, I suggested that the Platonic precedent had prompted further use of those two poets in the imitations. Whether or not the claim seemed plausible there, it bears repetition here. For, soon after he has paraphrased Plato's own allusion to the two poets in 18. 7 B, Maximus moves on to his argument that Socrates' erotic impulses had impeccable parallels (18. 8–9); and here Sappho and Anacreon are two of his three star-witnesses. What is more, Anacreon and his erotic career are again invoked by way of illustration in both *Dialexis* 20 and *Dialexis* 21. All this goes well beyond the very brief allusion to the two in the *Phaedrus*, but that brief allusion is surely its ultimate inspiration.[51]

This survey of second-century *logoi erotikoi* has inevitably been somewhat one-sided. A proper account of any of them individually would highlight the influence of many other sources apart from just the *Phaedrus*. Collectively, though, they show that the *Phaedrus* did enjoy a particularly privileged place in this species of writing, as a point of reference which any work on love with stylistic and intellectual pretensions was bound to acknowledge. To the novelist it provided a source of erotic imagery to set beside the offerings of the poets, a model of appropriately sweet and sparkling style, and a means of establishing his *paideia*. To the composer of dialogue and *dialexis* it constituted a still more fundamental pattern, not merely of diction and of isolated concepts, but of structure and of overall sequence of thought as well.

[51] It is interesting to note that the passage of the *Phaedrus* from which ps.-Lucian, Plutarch, and Maximus all take their cue is distinctly ironic in tone (cf. Rowe (1986) on *Phdr.* 235 C 3–4); but the irony is lost on authors who respect Sappho and Anacreon as much as they do Plato and cannot contemplate the possibility that Plato may not have felt the same way. For comparable examples of irony being lost in the process of imitation, see nn. 8, 55–6.

4. PASSING THE WORD

Since late antiquity the *Phaedrus* has been found most impressive and memorable as a text about love, beauty, and the soul.[52] Its other major topic, modes of discourse and communication, though it holds the stage for a good two-fifths of the dialogue, has by comparison been little studied. This neglect is however not quite so marked in the second century and before. Although it is true that the relevant pages of the *Phaedrus* have left fewer traces than those so far considered—certainly nothing on the scale of the three *Erotikoi* or of Dio's two *Orations*—there is still enough of interest to merit attention.

As before, a background to literary exploitation can be sought in the curricula of the schools. As a treatise on rhetoric and dialectic, the *Phaedrus* was of obvious interest both to philosophers and to rhetors; all the more so as, unlike its companion-piece the *Gorgias*, it explicitly allowed for the possibility of a genuine science of rhetoric and offered prescriptions for its realization. Thus, among the philosophers, we find 271 D ff. cited by Alcinous in *Didaskalikos* 6 in his definition of rhetoric; 237 B (on the need to define terms) at the beginning of Albinus' *Isagoge*; and no fewer than seven passages, all bearing on points of rhetorical and dialectical technique, quoted by Galen in his *De placitis Hippocratis et Platonis*.[53] Among the rhetors, both Nicolaus in his *Progymnasmata* and the anonymous author of the *Techne* in volume I of Spengel's *Rhetores Graeci* cite *Phdr.* 267 D for the proper function of an epilogue; pseudo-Hermogenes gives the same passage, along with 266 D, for both prologue and epilogue; and Nicolaus, again, cites 270 B for the division of an encomium by somatic, psychic, and external excellences.[54]

We have already seen how Cicero felt it appropriate to echo the setting of the *Phaedrus* at the beginnings of two of his rhetorical essays, the *De oratore* and the *Brutus*, evoking it directly in the former and obliquely in the latter, and thus setting himself

---

[52] Cf. Rowe (1986), 7.

[53] *De plac.* 5. 721 Kühn (262 AB); 5. 729 (261 E–262 C); 5. 730 (263 A–D); 5. 754 (265 C–E); 5. 755 (271 C–272 B); 5. 756 (273 DE).

[54] Ps.-Hermogenes *Meth.* 12 (ii. 436. 9 ff. Spengel); Nicolaus *Progymn.* prol. (iii. 451. 3 f. Spengel); 8 (iii. 479. 20 ff. Spengel); Anon. *Techne* (i. 454. 1 ff. Spengel = *Cornuti Artis Rhetoricae Epitome*, 207, p. 41 Graeven).

in line with the best traditions of reflective writing on the art of speech. In the same spirit, he echoes its conclusion—the somewhat ambiguous reference to Isocrates in 278 E ff.—at the end of the *De oratore* too, when he makes Catulus and Crassus dwell briefly on the promise of the young Hortensius.[55] Rather more aggressive, however, is the use made of the *Phaedrus* in Aelius Aristides' *Against Plato; In Defence of Oratory* (*Oration* 2). This declamation too has already claimed our attention for the way in which it seeks to appropriate the Phaedran doctrine of beneficial madness and to turn it against Plato's condemnation of rhetoric in the *Gorgias*. Setting Plato against Plato in this way, and thus discrediting him for inconsistency, is in fact the oration's principal strategy, and one to which the *Phaedrus* has an obvious utility. Particularly useful were Plato's words at 269 D—words which, at least at face-value, directly assert the claim of rhetoric to be a τέχνη which the *Gorgias* so stridently denies. Aristides duly refers to the passage in declaring his programme in 2. 137, and quotes it at greater length in his triumphant peroration in 2. 459. More trivially, but with equal smugness, he co-opts Phaedrus' challenge to Socrates in 236 B to help phrase one of his own many challenging apostrophes to Plato in 2. 156.

Such cheeky and self-assertive reuse of the *Phaedrus* in support of his own values and pieties as a sophist is indeed characteristic of more of Aristides' orations than just the second. Very much the same is done in *Against Plato: In Defence of the Four* (*Oration* 3), where the apparently favourable assessment of Pericles in the *Phaedrus* is used to discredit his treatment in the *Gorgias*, as part of the larger argument to exonerate all the four great Athenian statesmen from Plato's attack.[56] The obvious passage, 269 E–270 A, is appealed to no fewer than five times, and there is a whole series of more-or-less pointed echoes of other elements of the dialogue too.[57] Thirdly, and finally, we may note *On a Remark Made in Passing* (*Oration* 28), in which the *Phaedrus*, interpreted as Plato's eulogy of his own literary powers,

[55] Again, as in the case of Sappho and Anacreon (n. 51), the irony of the Platonic model seems to be lost in Cicero's imitation (cf. Rowe (1986), on 278 E 5 ff.).

[56] Yet another irony is lost here (cf. n. 51): Rowe (1986), on 269 E 1–270 A 8.

[57] 3. 34; 59; 204; 567; 573. See also 3.192 (263 D); 306 (268 E); 315 (236 B); 583 (274 C ff.); 588 (265 C + 277 E); 618–19 (238 D); 680 (248 D).

is called in to defend Aristides' own sophistic tendency towards self-praise.[58] In all this Aristides plays a neat double-game. By so conspicuously criticizing and correcting Plato, and drawing amused attention to traits which a more respectful reader might have ignored, he aims to appropriate some of the great man's standing for himself. At the same time, by working frequent and knowledgeable allusions to his work into the texture of his declamations, he lays claim to the true *paideia* of which acquaintance with Plato is a necessary condition.

But the value of rhetoric and of its practitioners is not the only topic of the second half of the *Phaedrus*. Its concern is more general than that, with all forms of verbal communication, written and spoken; and its main aim is to hold up a kind of didactic communication, dialectical conversation, as the ideal. This educational aspect of the dialogue has also left its traces.

Three times in his *Dialexeis*, Maximus of Tyre uses the image of the farmer, sowing seed and tending the resulting growth: in 5. 8 EF, of the growth and flowering of virtue in the human soul; in 19. 4 F, of the virtuous and altruistic lover; and in 25. 4 B–5 C, of the speaker of truly beautiful *logoi*. Here are the first and the last of those three passages.

ὦ Ζεῦ καὶ ᾿Αθηνᾶ καὶ ῎Απολλον, ἐθῶν ἀνθρωπίνων ἐπίσκοποι, φιλοσόφων ὑμῖν μαθητῶν δεῖ, οἳ τὴν ὑμετέραν τέχνην ἐρρωμέναις ψυχαῖς ὑποδεξάμενοι ἄμητον βίου καλὸν καὶ εὐδαίμονα ἐκκαρπώσονται· ἀλλὰ ἐστὶν σπάνιον μὲν τὸ τῆς γεωργίας ταύτης χρῆμα, μόλις δὲ καὶ ὀψὲ παραγινόμενον.

O Zeus, Athena, and Apollo, you who watch over human ways, you need philosophical pupils, who will receive your art with vigorous minds and reap a fine and happy harvest in their lives. But this kind of husbandry is a rare phenomenon, appearing seldom and tardily.

"ποῖον οὖν ἐστιν τὸ ἐν λόγοις καλόν;" φαίη ἄν τις. μήπω μέ, ὦ τάν, ἔρῃ· ὄψει γὰρ αὐτό, ἐπειδὰν ἰδεῖν δυνηθῇς ... καὶ γὰρ τῶν ἐκ γῆς φυομένων παντοδαπὸς μὲν θεατὴς ὁδοιπόρος, ὁ δὲ γεωργός, ὑγιής· ὁ μὲν ἄνθος ἐπαινεῖ φυτῷ, ὁ δὲ μέγεθος, ἢ σκιάν, ὁ δὲ χρόαν· τῷ δὲ γεωργῷ ὁ καρπὸς τὸν ἔπαινον μετὰ τῆς χρείας ἔχει ... λέγε, τίνας εἶδες καρποὺς ἐν τῷ λόγῳ; τίνας ἔλαβες;

'What then is beauty of discourse?', someone will say. Do not ask yet, my good sir. You will see it when you are able ... In the case of plants growing from the earth, any passer-by can look on them in

---

some way or another, but only the farmer can judge them soundly. One man praises the plant's flower, another its size, or its shade or its colour. But for the farmer it is its fruit, its usefulness, that merits his praise . . . Tell me, what fruit have you seen in this discourse of yours? What have you gathered?

The model for both of these passages (and for 19. 4 F) is *Phaedrus* 276 A–277 A, especially 276 B 1–8 and 276 E 4–277 A 4, where Socrates uses the contrast between serious farming and the preparation of 'gardens of Adonis' as an image for that between truly fruitful dialectic and the cultivated *paidia* of philosophical writing. The actual wording of the imitations is not close—no closer than the co-optation of the image makes inevitable—but the combination of the borrowed image with an evident similarity of context guarantees that we are indeed dealing with a case of conscious and deliberate *mimesis*.

The other second-century authors on whom this passage from the *Phaedrus* exerted its influence are the Christians Irenaeus and Clement; in this detail too, as in others already surveyed, Christian apologetic takes its stylistic cues from contemporary pagan philosophical writing. Irenaeus' evocation, at the beginning of his *Contra omnes haereticos*, is very brief, and may not even count as a conscious borrowing. He speaks simply of sowing seeds which will, he hopes, bear fruit in the minds of his readers.[59] Given such well-known scriptural uses of the image as the parable of the Sower,[60] it may be that he did not think of it as Platonic at all. Clement, however, is another matter. We have seen before, in considering the use made of the myth, how thoroughly he had absorbed the concepts, the images, and the vocabulary of that part of the *Phaedrus*. The same holds also for the dialogue's treatment of writing and teaching, which comes through time and again in the preface to the *Stromateis*, as Clement sets out and defends his purposes in composing his treatise.

The first echo comes very early on, in 1.1.1.2:

καλὸν δ' οἶμαι καὶ παῖδας ἀγαθοὺς τοῖς ἔπειτα καταλείπειν. οἱ μέν γε παῖδες σωμάτων, ψυχῆς δὲ ἔγγονοι οἱ λόγοι.

---

[59] *Contra omnes haereticos*, 1, prol. 3.
[60] Mark 4: 3–9; Matthew 13: 4–9 and 18–23; Luke 8: 4–15.

It is a fine thing, I think, to leave good children to posterity. Children are offspring of the body, books are offspring of the soul.' (cf. *Phdr.* 278 A).

But it is only a little later, with 1. 1. 11. 1 and 1. 1. 14. 1–4, that Clement gets properly into his stride. 1. 1. 11. 1 is a tissue of reminiscences from 274 E, 276 A, and 276 D, with a dash of Thucydides 1. 22. 4 thrown in for good measure:

ἤδη δὲ οὐ γραφὴ εἰς ἐπίδειξιν τετεχνασμένη ἤδε ἡ πραγματεία, ἀλλά μοι ὑπομνήματα εἰς γῆρας θησαυρίζεται, λήθης φάρμακον, εἴδωλον ἀτεχνῶς καὶ σκιαγραφία τῶν ἐναργῶν καὶ ἐμψύχων ἐκείνων, ὧν κατηξιώθην ἐπακοῦσαι, λόγων τε καὶ ἀνδρῶν μακαρίων καὶ τῷ ὄντι ἀξιολόγων.

This treatise is no script worked up for public display, but a set of reminders stored up for my old age, a medicine for forgetfulness, no more than an image and a silhouette of those lucid and living words and men, blessed and truly remarkable, whom I was judged worthy to hear.

1. 1. 14. 1–4 picks up the same passages and adds several more (?244 A ff.; ?247 A; 275 C; 276 D 4):

ἡ μὲν οὖν τῶνδέ μοι τῶν ὑπομνημάτων γραφὴ ἀσθενὴς μὲν εὖ οἶδ' ὅτι παραβαλλομένη πρὸς τὸ πνεῦμα ἐκεῖνο τὸ κεχαριτωμένον, οὗ κατηξιώθημεν ὑπακοῦσαι, εἰκὼν δ' ἂν εἴη ἀναμιμνήσκουσα τοῦ ἀρχετύπου τὸν θύρσῳ πεπληγότα ... ταῦτα δὲ ἀναζωπυρῶν ὑπομνήμασι τὰ μὲν ἑκὼν παραπέμπομαι ἐκλέγων ἐπιστημόνως, φοβούμενος γράφειν ἃ καὶ λέγειν ἐφυλαξάμην, οὐ τί που φθονῶν (οὐ γὰρ θέμις), δεδιὼς δὲ ἄρα περὶ τῶν ἐντυγχανόντων, μή πη ἑτέρως σφαλεῖεν καὶ παιδὶ μάχαιραν, ᾗ φασιν οἱ παροιμιαζόμενοι, ὀρέγοντες εὑρεθῶμεν. "οὐ γὰρ ἔστι τὰ γραφέντα μὴ ⟨οὐκ⟩ ἐκπεσεῖν" καίτοι ἀνέκδοτα ὑπό γ' ἐμοῦ μεμενηκότα, κυλιόμενα δὲ ἀεὶ μόνῃ μιᾷ χρώμενα τῇ ἐγγράφῳ φωνῇ πρὸς τὸν ἐπανερόμενον οὐδὲν πλέον παρὰ τὰ γεγραμμένα ἀποκρίνεται· δεῖται γὰρ ἐξ ἀνάγκης βοηθοῦ ἤτοι τοῦ συγγραψαμένου ἢ καὶ ἄλλου του εἰς τὸ αὐτὸ ἴχνος ἐμβεβηκότος.

These written memorials of mine, I am well aware, are feeble when compared to that inspiration bestowed by Grace, which I was judged worthy to hear; but they may serve as an image to remind him who has been touched by the thyrsus of their original ... But as I use my notes to kindle fresh flame in these truths, there are some things which on purpose I have removed and let pass, being afraid to write what I have been on my guard even against speaking. I do not do this because I begrudge them (that would be wrong), but because I am afraid for those who may read them, lest they should come to grief in some other way and I should be convicted of offering 'a knife to a

child', as the proverb has it. 'What has been written cannot help but
get out', although remaining unpublished by me. As it rolls on its way
it can only ever speak to those who question it with the one voice that
is written into it, and can return no answer other than its contents; it
must have help either from its author or from someone else who has
followed the same path.

As with the pilgrimage of the soul, so with the problems of
the responsible Christian teacher; images and phrases from the
Phaedrus seem to spring automatically to the tip of Clement's
pen as he seeks to express his thoughts in a language and a style
that will find favour with the cultivated literary palates of the
pepaideumenoi for whom he writes.

This survey began with a discourse by Dio of Prusa, composed and delivered on or shortly before the turn of the first and
second centuries.[61] It comes to an end with Clement of Alexandria, whose career extended some fifteen years into the third. In
between it has emerged how rich a point of reference the *Phaedrus* provided for second-century culture, rhetorical, philosophical, and literary—rich both in terms of the number of different
authors who imitated or recalled it, and in terms of the number
of different elements of the dialogue to which they resorted. It
has naturally been impossible to deal with all detectable cases
of imitation and borrowing: some do not fit the necessarily
approximate and selective framework I have built my discussion round; many involve brief quotations or borrowings of
phrases of a relatively superficial, decorative kind, which are
easier to list than to discuss. Something of this gap will, I hope,
be made good by the catalogue which follows in the Appendix.

APPENDIX

The following list is heavily indebted to other people's indexes: prin-
cipally to L. Spengel's to the Teubner *Rhetores Graeci* (Leipzig, 1853–
66) from which the rhetores are regularly cited in this list; C. A.
Behr's to his translation of Aristides (Leiden, 1981–6); M. D.
Macleod's to the OCT of Lucian (1972–87); O. Stählin's and U.
Treu's to the GCS Clement (Leipzig, rev. edn., 1972–80); C. L.
Kayser's to the Teubner Philostratus (Leipzig, 1870–1); and W. C.

---

[61] For the dating of Dio 1, C. P. Jones (1978), 116–119 and 138.

Helmbold's and E. N. O'Neil's *Plutarch's Quotations* (Baltimore, 1959).
Help has also come from the secondary apparatus of M. Schanz's edition of the *Phaedrus* (*Platonis Opera ... Omnia*, VI; Leipzig, 1882).

(1) 227 A–230 E

(i) *Setting the scene*: Hermogenes, *Id.* 2. 4 (ii. 358. 24 ff. Sp.); Harpocration, *ap.* Hermias 32. 1 ff. Couvreur; Ps.-Lucian, *Amores*, 31;
Demosth. 1; *Philopat.* 3; Lucian, *Dom.* 4; *Anach.* 16; *Navig.* 35. Achilles
Tatius, 1. 2. 3; Dio, 1. 52 ff.; 36. 1–8; Plutarch, *De genio* 575 D; *Amat.*
749 A; Justin, *Tryph.* 3; Clement, *Strom.* 2. 20. 111. 3; Athenaeus, 1.
25 B; Philostratus, *VS* 2. 587; 619; *Vit. Ap.* 6. 3; *Imag.* 23; *Her.* 3–5;
Maximus, 18. 4 F.

(ii) *Myths and Monsters*: Galen, *Plac.* V. 356 Kühn; Lucian, *Fug.* 10;
Prom. Es 5; Plutarch, *Amat.* 756 B; *Adv. Col.* 1119 B; Maximus, 33. 6 B;
Clement, *Protr.* 6. 67. 1; Athenaeus, V. 220 F; Philostratus. *Her.* 3. 5;
16. 5; *Gymn.* 38 (25) (= p. 152. 3 Jüthner).

(2) 230 E–234 C: *Speech of Lysias*

Philostratus, *Ep.* 44.

(3) 234 C–237 A: *Reaction to Lysias*

Theon, *Progymn.* (ii. 70. 15 ff. Sp.); Hermogenes, *Id.* 2. 10 (ii. 403.
21 ff.); Aristides, 2. 156; 3. 315; Ps.-Lucian, *Amores*, 46; Lucian, *Vit.
Auct.* 16; Plutarch, *Rect. Rat.* 40 E; 54 A; *Amat.* 764 A; 751 A–D; Maximus, 18. 4 B; 5 C; 7 B; 38. 4 G; Philostratus, *VS* 2. 597.

(4) 237 A–241 D: *First Speech of Socrates*

Albinus, *Isagoge* 1; Hermogenes, *Id.* 2. 4 (ii. 363. 16 ff.; 364. 10 ff.);
Menander Rhetor, iii. 334. 5 ff.; 335. 9 ff. Aristides, 3. 618–19; Ps.-
Lucian, *Amores* 38 ff; Lucian, *Dom.* 4; *Prom.* 13; *Philops.* 39; *Apol.* 1;
Anach. 16; Dio 36. 18–19. Plutarch, *Quaest. Conv.* 712 A; 746 D; *Gen. An.*
1026 D; *Amat.* 749 F; 752 C; *Ad. Am.* 51 D; *Conj. Pr.* 139 F; *Sto. Rep.*
1050 C. Maximus, 11. 2 C; 22. 3 F. Clement, *Protr.* 6. 68. 2; 7. 76. 6;
Paed. 2. 10. 93. 2; *Strom.* 5. 14. 93. 1; Athenaeus, 6. 254 D; 270 F.

(5) 241 D–243 E: *Interlude and Palinode*

Ps.-Hermogenes, *Meth.* 6 (ii. 430. 10 ff.); Aristides, 2. 52; Lucian, *Pro
Imag.* 15; *Apol.* 1; Chariton, 8. 1. 3; Dio, 18. 4; Plutarch, *Sept. Sap.*

151 D; *Amat.* 771 D; *Quaest. Conv.* 627 F; 706 D; 711 D; 748 C; *De Esu Carn.* 998 A; Maximus, 8. 3 C; 6 a; 21. 1 A; 40. 6 F; Philostratus, *Vit. Ap.* 6. 11.

(6) 243 E–257 B: *Second Speech of Socrates*

(i) *Madness* (243 E–245 C): Hermogenes, *Id.* 1. 6 (ii. 291. 15 ff.); Aristides, 2. 34; 35; 42; 46; 49; 52; 58; 164; Ps.-Lucian, *Amores*, 37; *Demosth.* 5; Dio, 1. 56–8; 36. 33–5; Plutarch, *Amat.* 758 D ff.; *Virt. Mor.* 452 B.

(ii) *Immortality of soul* (245 C–246 A): Hermogenes, *Id.* 1. 6 (ii. 294. 20 ff.); Alcinous, 5; 25; Harpocration, *ap.* Hermias 102. 10 ff. Couvreur; Plutarch, *Quaest, Conv.* 731 D; *De Esu Carn.* 996 B; *Gen. An.* 1013 C; 1016 A; Clement, *Paed.* 2. 9. 82. 1; *Eclog. Proph.* 22. 1; Numenius, fr. 47 des Places.

(iii) *Souls in the cosmos* (246 A–249 D): Ps.-Hermogenes, *Heur.* 4. 11 (ii. 255. 22 ff.); Hermogenes, *Id.* 1. 6 (ii. 290. 23 ff.); Anon., *Peri Schematon*, 52 (iii. 144. 14 ff.); Menander Rhetor, iii. 337. 7 ff; Alcinous, 4; 5; 25; 26; 33; Aristides, 3. 680; 28. 114; 142; 42. 4; Ps.-Lucian, *Amores*, 37; Lucian, *Pisc.* 22; *Bis accus.* 33; *Rhet. Prae.* 26; *Prom.* 18; *Sacrif.* 8; 10; Dio 36. 39 ff; Plutarch *Quaest, Plat.* 1004 C; 1008 C; *An seni* 786 D; *Quaest. Conv.* 679 E; 718 F; 740 B; 745 E; *Non Posse* 1986 F; 1102 E; 1105 D; *Prim. Frig.* 954 F; *De genio* 591 C ff.; *De facie* 943 D; *Def. Or.* 422 B; *Amat.* 762 A; 765 A; 766 B; 766 E; *Comm. in Hes.* fr. 10 (= 31 Sandb.); Ps.-Plutarch, *De fato*, 568 C; 570 AB; Maximus, 1. 5 E; 4. 4 C; 10. 3 B; 10. 9 C; 11. 10 DE; 20. 5 A; 26. 7 B; 41. 3 A; 41. 5; Athenagoras, *Leg.* 23; Ps.-Justin, *Cohort.* 31; Tatian, *Or.* 20; Basilides, *ap.* Hippolytus *Ref.* 7. 22; Valentinus, *ap.* Irenaeus *Contra Haer.* 1. 4. 5; 1. 5. 4; Clement, *Protr.* 6. 68. 3; 10. 106. 3; 12. 121. 1; *Paed.* 3. 2. 14. 1; 3. 11. 53. 1–2; *Strom.* 1. 1. 4. 3; 1. 15. 67. 4; 3. 3. 13. 1–2; 3. 13. 93. 3; 5. 1. 14. 2; 5. 3. 16. 1–3; 5. 4. 19. 2; 5. 4. 24. 2; 5. 4. 30. 5; 5. 8. 53. 1; 5. 13. 83. 1; 7. 2. 5. 6; 7. 2. 7. 2; 7. 3. 20. 8; 7. 7. 40. 1; 7. 7. 46. 8; 7. 7. 49. 4; Philostratus, *Vit. Ap.* 2. 22; 8. 7 (4); *Ep.* 56; Numenius, fr. 12 des Places.

(iv) *The soul of the lover* (249 D–257 B): Alcinous, 23; Ps.-Lucian, *Amores*, 48; Xenophon of Ephesus, 1. 3. 2; 1. 9. 6–8; Achilles Tatius, 1. 4. 4; 1. 9. 4; 2. 36. 2–3; 5. 13. 4; Longus, 1. 22. 4; 2. 7. 1; Dio, 36. 26. Plutarch, *Amat.* 751 DE; 762 E; 765 B; 766 E; *Quaest. Conv.* 654 DE; 745 E; *Exil.* 607 DE; *Aqu. Ign.* 958 E; *Quaest. Plat.* 1008 C; *Princ. Inerud.* 781 F; *San. Tu.* 125 B; *Virt. Mor.* 445 C; *Vit. Alc.* 193 D; *Vit. Pelop.* 287 DE; *Vit. Ant.* 932 B. Maximus, 18. 3; 19. 2–3; 20. 4; 20. 8 D; 21. 7 DE; Justin, *Trypho* 2. 219 D; Clement, *Protr.* 10. 89. 3; *Paed.* 2. 10. 86. 2–3; 2. 10. 89. 2; *Strom.* 1. 28. 176. 2; 5. 11. 73. 2; 5. 13. 83. 1; 5. 14. 138. 3; 5. 14. 95. 3; *Quis dives* 42. 6; Athenaeus, 3. 92 f; 15. 669 B.

(7) 257 B–279 B: *Rhetoric, dialectic, speaking, and writing*

Hermogenes, *Id.* 1. 12 (ii. 331. 8); 2. 4 (ii. 357. 9 ff.); Ps.-Hermogenes, *Meth.* 12 (ii. 436. 9 ff.); Anon., *Techne* (i. 454. 1 ff.); Nicolaus, *Progymn.* prol. (iii. 451. 3 f.); 8 (iii. 479. 20 ff.); Alcinous, 5; 6; Galen, *Plac.* 5. 721; 729; 730; 754; 755; 756 Kühn; *In Hippoc. de Nat. Hom.* 15. 12 Kühn; Aristides, 2. 42; 44; 137; 459; 3. 34; 59; 192; 204; 306; 567; 573; 583; 588; 26. 109; 28. 143–4; 32. 26; Ps.-Lucian, *Amores*, 31; Longus, 1. 25–6; Plutarch, *Amat.* 758 D; *Quaest. Plat.* 1001 A; *Adv. Col.* 1126 BC; *Vit. Peri.* 154 C; 156 A; 161 C; Maximus, 1. 2A; 2. 2 A; 5. 8 EF; 10. 4 D; 19. 4 F; 25. 4 B ff.; 27. 9 B; 38. 61; Irenaeus, *Contra Haer.* 1, prol. 3; Clement, *Strom.* 1. 1. 1. 2; 1. 1. 11. 1; 1. 1. 9. 1–2(?); 1. 1. 14. 1–4; 1. 15. 68. 3; 2. 20. 104. 3; Aelian, *Nat. An.* 5. 13; Philostratus, *Vit. Ap.* 7. 11; *VS* 2. 594; *Ep.* 73.

(8) 279 BC: *The final prayer*

Menander Rhetor, iii. 334. 5 ff.; 343. 3 f; Maximus, 5. 8 C; Clement, *Strom.* 2. 5. 22. 1; 5. 14. 97. 2.

VII

Psyche and her Mysterious Husband

E. J. KENNEY

John J. Winkler has argued that the title conventionally given to Apuleius, *Metamorphoses*, 4. 28–6. 24 'is fundamentally abusive to the narrative technique of the tale',[1] which is (in part at all events) a detective story in which the identity of Psyche's husband is not revealed explicitly until she takes the lamp to him. It is true that a reader skilled in deciphering literary riddles and conversant with Apuleius' poetic models ought to have little difficulty in putting a name to the cruel, wild, winged being described by the oracle, before whom Jove, the gods, and the Underworld itself all quail (4. 33. 1–2).[2] Nevertheless, as Winkler notes, 'Even the reader who comes to the tale knowing [or, it may be added, speedily foresees] the outcome must bracket that knowledge as he watches characters who do not know the outcome grapple with the problem'[3]—the situation, one may note in passing, in which Menander's audiences were placed. However, even the fully switched-on reader that I believe we are entitled to postulate for this rich

I am grateful to Dr Paula James for allowing me to see her paper 'Cupid at work and at play' in advance of its publication in the *Proceedings of the Groningen Colloquium on the Novel*. In particular I must note that her argument opened my eyes to the implications of Cupid's confession at 5. 24. 4 (see below, p. 185). Dr R. L. Hunter and Dr R. G. Mayer read a draft of the chapter, and I am indebted to both for helpful comments. Useful suggestions have been contributed by the audiences to whom the piece was read at Oxford, Loyola College in Maryland, and Ann Arbor; these are acknowledged in the notes as appropriate. Dr M. B. Trapp kindly furnished me with an advance copy of his paper (above, ch. VI) to which I am in particular obliged for the citation from Maximus of Tyre at n. 59.

[1] Winkler (1985), 89. Cf. James (1987), 145–6, 'Psyche becomes Psyche only when Cupid sees her for the first time. Similarly the Love God is revealed as Cupid in the moment Psyche gazes upon him; mention of his title has been avoided until that crucial scene. It would seem that Cupid and Psyche are both identified in each other's eyes.'

[2] 'A reader with even a smattering of Plato would recognise that "monster" as Cupid' (Tatum (1979), 50). However, those for whom Apuleius was writing were evidently expected to be at least as familiar with the topics and clichés of Greek epigram and Latin love-elegy.

[3] Winkler (1985), 90.

and sophisticated novel has to grapple with the problem of Cupid's identity in a sense not acknowledged by Winkler. For there is not one Cupid in Apuleius' story, but two.

And equally not only two Cupids but two Venuses. The implications of this duality have been touched on by Carl Schlam in his important monograph,[4] but they will bear further consideration. I want here to examine in some detail how Apuleius develops and manipulates the idea in his narrative. In adapting this Platonic duality to the exigencies of his story-line he set himself some tricky technical problems. Presumably he did so because he thought that the idea contributed to, if indeed it was not of the essence of, the message of the tale—whatever exactly that was. As will emerge, he goes to considerable lengths to incorporate and exploit the theme. Does the thing come off?

'We all know' says Pausanias in the *Symposium*,

that without Eros there is no Aphrodite. If there were only one Aphrodite there would only be one Eros, but since there are two it follows that there are two Eroses. And of course there *are* two goddesses: the elder, who has no mother, is the daughter of Uranus, and we call her Uranian; the younger is the daughter of Zeus and Dione, and we call her Vulgar [Pandemos]. It follows that the Eros who cooperates with the second of them is properly called Vulgar, and the other Uranian.[5]

That Apuleius had read this passage is shown, if demonstration be required, by his paraphrase of it in the *Apology* (12), which is worth quoting *in extenso*:

mitto ... dicere alta illa et diuina Platonica, rarissimo cuique piorum ignara, ceterum omnibus profanis incognita: geminam esse Venerem deam, proprio quamque amore et diuersis amatoribus pollentis; earum alteram uulgariam, quae sit percita populari amore, non modo humanis animis uerum etiam pecuinis et ferinis ad libidinem imperitare ui immodica trucique perculsorum animalium serua corpora complexu uincientem; alteram uero caelitem Venerem, praeditam optimati amore, solis hominibus et eorum paucis curare, nullis ad turpitudinem stimulis uel illecebris sectatores suos percellentem; quippe amorem eius non amoenum et lasciuum sed contra incomtum

---

[4] See Schlam (1970), 485 on the contrast between the two Venuses as 'fundamental to the novel'; also Schlam (1976), 35–7.

[5] Plato, *Symp.* 180 D 2. Eros also had two genealogies (cf. below), a point not exploited by Apuleius.

et serium pulchritudine honestatis uirtutes amatoribus suis conciliare, et si quando decora corpora commendet, a contumelia eorum procul absterrere; neque enim quicquam aliud in corporum forma diligendum quam quod ammoneant diuinos animos eius pulchritudinis, quam prius ueram et sinceram inter deos uidere. quapropter, etsi pereleganter Afranius hoc scriptum relinquat, 'amabit sapiens, cupient ceteri' [fr. 221 R.[3]], tamen si uerum uelis, Aemiliane, uel si haec intellegere unquam potes, non tam amat sapiens quam recordatur.

I need not set out that high and holy Platonic doctrine, known to most of the pious, unknown to the profane: that Venus is a twin goddess, each Venus having her own love/Love and different sort of lover. One Venus is vulgar, stimulated by common love, dominating not only human minds but animals too by her unrestrained force, binding the enslaved bodies of the smitten being in a fierce embrace. The other is the heavenly Venus, endowed with the best sort of love/ Love, only concerned with men, and with but few of them, not urging on her adherents with impulses and enticements to baseness; her love/ Love is not pretty and sportive, but rather unadorned and serious, recommending virtue to his lovers by the beauty of goodness. If she should commend beautiful bodies, she deters the lover from insulting them: nothing is to be loved in bodily beauty but what may remind the immortal soul of that beauty which it formerly saw among the gods in its true and uncontaminated guise. Therefore, though Afranius so elegantly writes that 'the wise man will love, the rest will desire', if you want the truth, Aemilianus, or if you can ever understand these things, the wise man does not so much love as remember.

This, it will be seen, develops explicitly only the theme of the two Venuses;[6] and it is of course understandable that Apuleius did not feel called upon to echo Pausanias' corollary, that 'heavenly' love can never be heterosexual.[7] In *Cupid & Psyche*, however, he exploits both dualities very thoroughly.

How he does this can best be appreciated by following the story as he tells it, identifying each Venus and each Cupid as they successively are represented or—an important qualification—implied. For convenience' sake I shall call them respectively Venus I (Urania) and II (Vulgaris) and (avoiding the inescapable associations of the name Cupid) Amor I and Amor II. In each case II will be seen to represent what may be

---

[6] But *proprio quamque amore* hints at two Cupids; to print *Amore* would spoil the ambiguity. Modern conventions of capitalization are not always helpful; cf. n. 16. See, however, below, p. 191 on *Caelus* and *Aether*.

called the popular-literary *persona*, such as would have been familiar to Apuleius' readers from the poets, from works of art, and indeed from actual cult. That *persona* was itself multi-faceted, reflecting varying perceptions of the deity. One thinks, for instance, of Aphrodite as she is portrayed by Euripides in the *Hippolytus* as both a jealous and vindictive anthropo-morphic goddess (1–8) and a cosmic force (447–50). Socrates' version of Eros' parentage in the *Symposium* (203 A 8–204 C 6) Platonizes a basic ambivalence frequently in evidence in the literary sources:[8] again one thinks of Euripides, in the prologue to his *Stheneboea* (29–32, p. 44 von Arnim). Apuleius, following the lead given by Plato, exploited contradictions which in the literary tradition were either presented as paradoxes without any attempt to reconcile them (as e.g. in Homer) or discreetly glossed over (as e.g. in Virgil).[9]

His conduct of the plot of *Cupid & Psyche* pivots on what I might call a chiastic structure: that is, the action is motivated by the opposing forces of Venus II (exclusively) and Amor I (almost exclusively; we shall note the exception when we come to it). Venus makes her first entry (4. 29. 5) furiously angry at the slight which has been put upon her, the neglect of her wor-ship in favour of Psyche. This motive, *spretae iniuria formae*,[10] and the phrase with which she is introduced, are calculated to put the reader instantly in mind of Virgil's Juno;[11] and the con-text and the tone and tenor of her speech enforce the parallel. This is the first speech in the story, as Juno's is the first in the *Aeneid*, and Venus' indignation motivates the plot as Juno's

---

[7] *Symp.* 181 C 2–6.

[8] As is well documented in Fliedner's monograph. Cf. esp. Cato, fr. 71 Malc. *aliud est amor, ... longe aliud est cupido. accessit ilico alter, ubi alter recessit; alter bonus, alter malus;* Afran. fr. 221 R.[3] *amabit sapiens, cupient ceteri* (cited by Apul. *Apol.* 12, on which see above); Non. p. 681. 13–14 L. *cupido ... inconsideratae est necessitatis, amor iudicii,* etc. (Fliedner (1974), 30–67). Apuleius himself, though as I argue here, the distinction between *personae* is crucial to his treatment of the story, does not make a consistent use of the names Cupido and Amor to differentiate them (cf. Fliedner (1974), 68–81). The idea of the duality or ambivalence of love can also be seen as related to the ancient and enduring conception of love as 'bittersweet'; cf. Lieberg (1962), 142–3.

[9] As Dr S. J. Harrison has pointed out, in the seducer of Juturna we can see, as it were, Jupiter II peeping through Jupiter I. On Virgil see further below, p. 198.

[10] It is worth noting that the plot of Xenophon's *Ephesiaka* is motivated by neglect of Eros (1. 2. 1). Another distant echo of the Callimachean Acontius?

[11] 4. 29. 5 *incendit animos ... capite quassanti* ∼ *Aen.* 1. 50 *talia flammato secum dea corde uolutans,* 7. 292 *tum quassans caput haec effundit pectore dicta.*

does that of the epic. 'The reader who has followed Apuleius attentively thus far may be prompted to anticipate the vast dimensions of Psyche's future suffering.'[12] This then is all Venus II. However, Venus I makes a fleeting appearance in her opening words: 'en rerum naturae prisca parens, en elementorum origo initialis, en orbis totius alma Venus...'. The Lucretian-Uranian impression of these words is, however, qualified in an interesting way by the thrice-repeated *en*. This word is never used by Lucretius; but it is the word with which both the speeches of Juno's agent Allecto begin,[13] and it is also used by Ovid's Latona, another goddess slighted by a mortal woman, in an outburst similar in tone to Juno's and in which Juno's name appears:

> en ego, uestra parens, uobis animosa creatis
> et nisi Iunoni nulli cessura dearum,
> an dea sim dubitor perque omnia saecula cultis
> arceor, o nati, nisi uos succurritis aris. (*Met.* 6. 206–9)

That Ovid's Juno as well as Virgil's was present to Apuleius' mind is strongly suggested by Venus' tone in a later episode when she refers to Psyche's pregnancy (6. 9. 4).[14]

Venus II then summons her son to her assistance. The models for this passage are the scenes in Apollonius and Virgil in which Eros / Cupid is asked to make Medea / Dido fall in love with Jason / Aeneas respectively.[15] This is emphatically Amor II that Apuleius presents, the wayward child of Hellenistic epigram and Roman elegy, equipped with all the familiar stereotyped attributes—wings, bow and arrows, torches, wound imagery and all the rest of it. His part in the interview, however, is purely passive and silent: to receive his orders, which are to make Psyche fall in love with the lowest outcaste wretch on

---

[12] Horsfall (1982), 41; cf. Price (1650), 234 'Virgilius (ex quo hunc locum delineasse Apulejus videtur)...'. It is a cardinal defect in Winkler's argument that he fails completely to take into account the effect of literary allusions of this kind.

[13] Virg. *Aen.* 7. 452, 545.

[14] Cf. Ov. *Met.* 2. 471–3, 3. 268–70; and Tatum (1979), p. 49 n. 40. Again, when Isis appears to Lucius (11. 5. 1) she announces herself in words clearly designed to recall Venus' exordium: 'en adsum tuis commota, Luci, precibus, rerum naturae parens, elementorum omnium domina, saeculorum progenies initialis...'; thus confirming one of the identities under which she is addressed by Lucius (11. 2. 1), that of *caelestis Venus*. Cf. below, p. 189.

[15] 4. 30. 4–31.3 ~ Ap. Rhod. 3. 111–66, Virg. *Aen.* 1. 657–9.

earth. He is dismissed with a kiss, and it is not until much later that we are told explicitly that he flatly disobeys his orders.

Venus now makes the first of her two state progresses, the first from earth to sea (4. 31. 4–7), the second from earth to heaven (6. 6). Apuleius' description of her marine cortège is heavily literary in inspiration, being obviously indebted to Homer, Moschus, and Virgil.[16] Nevertheless, this is essentially Venus I returning to her native element. The instant calming of the sea at her approach[17] is found in the epic models, but here it recalls the Lucretian Venus, for whom

> rident aequora ponti
> placatumque nitet diffuso lumine caelum. (DRN 1. 8–9)

Apuleius had in fact already glanced at the genealogy of Venus I in his description of the rumour that a new Venus had appeared in the guise of Psyche, *nouo caelestium stillarum germine*, 'from a new fertilization by drops from heaven' (4. 28. 4). This can only be a delicate allusion to the indelicate myth hinted at by Plato but expounded in full and gory detail by Hesiod: that Cronus, having castrated his father Uranus, threw his genitals into the sea, whence was born Aphrodite.[18] Having got Venus into the sea, Apuleius apparently makes no attempt to provide her with a plausible setting. When she next re-enters the story, she is discovered in the depths, *profundum gremium*, of Ocean, *lauantem natantemque*, disporting herself in the briny (5. 28. 2–3). Are we to imagine a submarine grotto such as those inhabited by Thetis or Cyrene? Apuleius may simply not have bothered about the matter; but he may have covered himself by a linguistic ambiguity. As well as its obvious sense 'the lowest depths', *profundum gremium* can also be read as meaning 'a

---

[16] Hom. *Il.* 13. 27–31, 18. 37–49; Mosch. *Eur.* 115–24; Virg. *Aen.* 5. 816–26. The sheer literariness of Apuleius (not by any means properly appreciated by his commentators) may be illustrated by the phrase *ille serico tegmine flagrantiae solis obsistit inimici* (4. 31. 7). *Inimici* here has at least three references: (i) the obvious one to the danger of sun-tan, not cultivated by ladies in antiquity, least of all by Venus; (ii) to the natural opposition between the elements personified by the two deities; (iii) to the Sun's role as informer in Venus' *affaire* with Mars (Hom. *Od.* 8. 302, Ov. *AA* 2. 573–4, *Met.* 4. 171–4, 190–2). Whether edd. should print *Solis* is a moot point; cf. above, n. 6.

[17] Reading *profundum* at 4.31. 4 with Koehler.

[18] Hes. *Th.* 176–200; cf. Apul. *Met.* 2. 8. 6 *illa caelo deiecta, mari edita, fluctibus educata ... Venus*, 10. 31. 2 (of an actress personating Venus) *corpus candidum, quod caelo demeat, amictus caerulus, quod mari remeat.*

remote bay'. If *TLL* is correct, this sense of *gremium* is otherwise confined to Pomponius Mela, and Ennodius, but in so inventive a writer and one so given to exploiting the ambiguities of language, that does not disqualify the suggestion.[19] I make the point in passing as a reminder that his interpreters have sometimes been too prone to ascribe to carelessness or incompetence what a more attentive reading may be justified in crediting to playfulness.

Exeunt then Amor II and (as she has now once more become) Venus I. Psyche's parents, alarmed by her lack of suitors, consult the oracle of Apollo at Miletus, who replies. with an arch authorial apology, in Latin elegiacs:

> montis in excelsi scopulo, rex, siste puellam
>   ornatam mundo funerei thalami.
> nec speres generum mortali stirpe creatum
>   sed saeuum atque ferum uipereumque malum,
> quod pinnis uolitans super aethera cuncta fatigat
>   flammaque et ferro singula debilitat,
> quod tremit ipse Iouis quo numina terrificantur
>   fluminaque horrescunt et Stygiae tenebrae. (4. 33. 1–2)

> On mountain peak, o king, expose the maid
> For funeral wedlock dismally arrayed.
> No human son-in-law (hope not) is thine,
> But something cruel and fierce and serpentine,
> That plagues the world as, borne aloft on wings,
> With fire and steel it persecutes all things;
> That Jove himself, he whom the gods revere,
> That Styx's darkling stream regards with fear.

In this immortal winged figure, serpentine and savage, who ranges the whole world with steel and flame, sparing nothing and nobody, and feared by the gods above and below the earth, we see blended both Amor I and Amor II. What Cupid is about meanwhile and whether it is Amor I or Amor II who is at work does not become apparent until later. Psyche is exposed, Andromeda-like, on her rock, carried off by Zephyrus, and tended by unseen hands in a fairy-tale palace. A hint, if one is wanted, that everything will come out right in the end, is given

---

[19] As Professor Russell points out, κόλπος and *sinus* are similarly ambiguous. Apuleius is fond of bilingual word-play, in the Latin Alexandrian tradition.

in the reference at 5. 3. 1 to *diuina Prouidentia*. The full implications of this hint emerge gradually as the narrative unfolds. This foreseeing power is revealed, through his repeated warnings, as Amor I; just as, conversely, the cruel blind Fortune against which he warns Psyche (5. 9. 2)[20] is identified as Venus II. This, it may be noted in passing, is an interesting and significant variation on the usual role of Tyche in the Greek romances. As a rule Tyche and Aphrodite are opposed forces;[21] in Apuleius' story blind Fortune = Venus II contends with foreseeing Providence = Amor I = (eventually, in the embracing figure of Isis in the denouement of the novel) *uidens Fortuna* (11. 15. 3).

That is to anticipate. Enter now the mysterious husband: 'iamque aderat ignobilis[22] maritus et torum inscenderat et uxorem sibi Psychen fecerat et ante lucis exortum propere discesserat' (5. 4. 3). The restraint with which, here and elsewhere, their love-making is referred to contrasts sharply with the tone of the erotic episodes in the body of the novel, especially those between Lucius and Photis. Such sensuality as there is, is all on Psyche's side, as she uses her charms to persuade her husband against his better judgement to let her see her sisters.[23] These scenes, as Price noted, are reminiscent of the temptation of Vulcan by Venus in *Aeneid* 8.[24] In the light of Venus' behaviour later in the story one might say that Psyche is here understudying Venus II. The words in which her husband says to her 'have your own way' are revealing: 'animo tuo damnosa poscenti pareto' (5. 6. 3). *animus* = θυμός, the appetitive part of the soul; *anima* = ψυχή. This is Amor I taking the high Platonic ground.[25] The suggestion that Psyche is a slave to her

---

[20] *orba* = *oculis, uisu orba*; cf. *TLL* s.v. 927. 74–928. 3.

[21] But contrast Xen. *Eph.* 1. 10. 2, where Eros and Fate are implicitly identified.

[22] *ignobilis* = both 'unknown' and 'base', referring back to Venus' instructions *amore fraglantissimo teneatur hominis extremi* (4. 30. 3). Is Apuleius here, as suggested by James (1987), p. 145 n. 20, glancing at the Platonic parentage of Eros, born of Poros and Penia?

[23] 5. 6. 9–10, 13. 5–6. This may be compared with the story told by Alcibiades in the *Symposium* (217 A 2–219 D 2) of his abortive attempts to seduce Socrates by his adolescent charms: Alcibiades = Eros II encountering Socrates = Eros I. I owe this interesting suggestion to Prof. Russell.

[24] Price (1650), 256–7.

[25] Prof. Charles Witke raises the interesting question, whether Psyche can be dichotomized like Venus and Cupid into Psyche I and II. Mythological models are lacking in

passions has implications on both levels I and II: the literary *ser-uitium amoris* and the philosophical *topos* that men are enslaved by their vices.[26] The idea will recur in the sequel. Irony is also at work in her professions of love: 'amo enim et efflictim te quicumque es diligo aeque ut meum spiritum, nec ipsi Cupidini comparo' (5. 6. 7). *Spiritus = anima =* ψυχή: she loves him as she loves life / herself; but under the obvious surface-irony there is a more profound implication. In spite of her professions she does not understand the true nature and value of love. Her devotion is purely physical, to Amor II. Amor I has yet to be revealed to her, and when he is, it will be for the wrong reasons.[27]

That revelation comes prematurely, through the operations of her *curiositas* and *simplicitas*: the lust to know what she is not supposed to know, and the failure to understand what she is shown and told. She takes the lamp and sees her husband as he really is. The great description of the sleeping Cupid (as she now discovers him to be) incorporates the stock attributes of the Hellenistic-elegiac godling, with a marvellously sensuous emphasis on his wings. The effect, however, is to inspire wonder and awe. The spirit of the description is closer to that of Isis in her great epiphany (11. 3. 4–4. 3) than to the raptures of Lucius over the charms of Photis (2. 9. 6). There is a sense throughout of latent power and majesty, made explicit in the concluding sentence: 'ante lectuli pedes iacebat arcus et pharetra et sagittae, magni dei propitia tela' (5. 22. 7). The dangerous toys of a naughty unbiddable child, as we met them at his first

her case, and in the Platonic analysis the soul is tripartite. If two Psyches may indeed be distinguished, it is Psyche II, actuated by *curiositas* and *simplicitas*, who is most in evidence. Perhaps Psyche I is symbolized by her ideal beauty. It is hardly possible to detect consistent characterization in her personation of the tragic heroine at 4. 34. 3–6 or her pious observances at the shrines of Ceres and Juno (6. 1–4). Certainly Apuleius does not exploit the contrast, if he meant his readers to feel it, as he does with Venus and Cupid.

[26] For the specifically Platonic notion of domination by pleasure or desire cf. Plat. *Rep.* 329 C, *Phaedo* 69 A, and Powell on Cic. *De sen.* 41, 47.

[27] Her unawareness is further underlined by the last words of her blandishments, *tuae Psychae dulcis anima* (5. 6. 9). Under the surface irony—ψυχή and *anima* being common lovers' endearments—there is reflected her ignorance of the one thing that might save her, a true and perfect union with Love (Amor I). To achieve this she must keep faith; if she does, her child will be divine (i.e. begotten by Amor I?), if not, it will be mortal (i.e. begotten by Amor II?) (5. 11. 6). In this connection the words *uisa . . . detectae* [s.v.l.] *fidei colluuie* (5. 23. 6) are significant: her breach of faith is equated with demotion to the lower level of love, Plane II.

appearance and as we shall meet them again, are transformed
into the venerable attributes of a mighty god. The ambiguity of
the description—Amor I shining through, as it were, the external trappings of Amor II—is signalled in the first ironical
sentence: 'uidet omnium ferarum mitissimam dulcissimamque
bestiam, ipsum illum Cupidinem formonsum deum formonse
cubantem' (5. 22. 2). The import of the oracle is now made
plain: *this* is the real Amor (I), not the mythical monster (II).
The potent and worshipful reality of love is revealed in its true
splendour through the meretricious embellishments of popular
imagination and poetic romancing.

Psyche's reaction to this wonderful sight is naïve and ignorant; she is not yet ready for it. In her childish curiosity she starts
to handle Cupid's weapons. The wording strongly suggests that
this action occurs on the naïvely sensual plane of her love-
making: she sees them as the attributes of the only Cupid she
knows, Amor II. She accidentally pricks herself with one of the
arrows,[28] and 'sic ignara Psyche sponte in Amoris incidit
amorem' (5. 23. 3). One might have expected this to mean that
she is now really in love, i.e. with Amor I. However, her subsequent actions seem to speak the same purely sensual devotion
as before: 'tunc magis magisque cupidine fraglans Cupidinis
prona in eum efflictim inhians patulis ac petulantibus sauiis
[like Photis and, later, Venus; see below, p.192] festinanter
ingestis de somni mensura metuebat' etc. (5. 23. 3). It is not
easy to know precisely what to make of this; but unless Apuleius
is merely revelling in verbal exuberance for its own sake (something he does, I believe, less often than some critics make out),
the point would appear to be that Psyche, still unaware (*ignara*)
of her husband's true identity, is still worshipping him under
his false or factitious one: she is lavishing on Amor I the sort of
sensuality that belongs rightly to Amor II.

Cupid awakes when a drop of hot oil from the lamp falls on
him, and flies away, with Psyche clinging desperately to his leg
until she is too tired to hold on any longer and falls to the
ground. This curious scene, rendered more curious still by the
language employed by Apuleius to describe it, is generally

---

[28] This motif seems to have been suggested to Apuleius by the wounding of Venus in
Ovid: *Met*. 10. 525–8, cf. 636–7.

glossed by the commentators from Plato's *Phaedrus*: 'but when the soul, through inability to follow, fails to see, and through some mishap is filled with forgetfulness and evil and grows heavy, then growing heavy loses its wings and falls to earth, then . . .'.[29] The parallels are not exact—for one thing Psyche in the story has no wings, though she has in art — but the resemblances are too close not to be significant. The implication would seem to be the same as in the preceding scene, that she is not yet fit to associate with Love (Amor I), that she lacks true understanding and does not see clearly what she thinks she sees.[30] Cupid perches in a cypress tree, a literary touch in the style of Amor II,[31] and reproaches her. His speech is truly remarkable. It is the first explicit admission that he disobeyed Venus' orders, but that disclosure had to be made at some stage and somehow. What is surprising is the phrase in which he makes the admission: 'sed hoc feci leuiter, scio, et praeclarus ille sagittarius ipse me telo meo percussi' (5. 24. 4). This is a striking avowal, Amor I owning and deploring the acts of Amor II.[32] These then are not two gods, but one god with two natures, a higher and a lower. The irresponsible use of his weapons is one of the trademarks of Amor II, and Eros / Cupid in love is a paradox exploited by Hellenistic epigrammatists.[33] This explains how he was led to yield to Psyche's importunity against his better judgement, 'ui ac potestate Venerii susurrus inuitus succubuit' (5. 6. 10): that was Amor I failing to withstand the promptings of his lower self (II). In so failing, he was meeting Psyche on the plane of Venus II.

His reproaches continue 'teque coniugem meam feci, ut bestia scilicet tibi uiderer et ferro caput excideres meum quod istos amatores tui oculos gerit' (v. 24. 4). She has culpably misunderstood his nature, the true nature of love. Her sisters will come to a sticky end; her punishment is to lose him. With these

---

[29] Plat. *Phaedr.* 248 c. For the popularity of *Phdr.* during the second century AD see below, n. 59.

[30] Cf. perhaps Plat. *Phdr.* 248 A 5–6 βιαζομένων δὲ τῶν ἵππων τὰ μὲν εἶδεν, τὰ δ' οὔ; Ferrari (1987), 135, 'The wrong for which these [sc. the fallen] souls are accountable is just their ignorance—their failure of knowledge'.

[31] Bion, fr. 13 (10). 3, Longus 2. 6. 1.

[32] For a somewhat different interpretation see James (1987), 146–7.

[33] Anon. *AP* 12. 112 (*HE* 3710–11), Meleag. *AP* 5. 179 (4028–37), 12. 113 (4312–13), 13. 144 (4554–7).

words he leaves her, not to re-enter the plot until much later, and then, as we shall see, in the (passive) role of Amor II. However, the operation of his power, as Amor I, continues to be felt from off-stage. This is immediately apparent in the episode of Psyche's attempted suicide, the first of several such attempts.[34] The river which withholds its co-operation does so 'in honorem dei scilicet qui et ipsas aquas urere consueuit' (5. 25. 2).[35] Her subsequent meeting with Pan, though introduced with the word *forte*, is anything but fortuitous. Pan is in the know, *casus eius non inscius* (5. 25. 4); and the counselling session for which he has evidently been briefed is one for which his traditional pre-eminence in the love-life of Arcadia well qualifies him. What is particularly striking about his advice to rehabilitate herself with Cupid is the concluding phrase in which *both* Amores are embraced: 'luctum desine et pone maerorem precibusque potius Cupidinem deorum maximum percole et utpote adolescentem delicatum luxuriosumque blandis obsequiis promerere' (5. 25. 6). That implies both the complaisances of the elegiac lover and the pious observance of the votary. This off-stage influence of Cupid is evident throughout Psyche's wanderings and her ordeals. The uncharacteristic astuteness with which she contrives the deaths of her wicked sisters can only have been prompted by him; one remembers, not for the only time in the story, the Callimachean and Ovidian Acontius.[36] Cupid is behind the assistance given by the ants, the reed, the eagle, and one must suppose the tower.[37] Venus' reactions to Psyche's successful performance of her tasks indicate that she is fully aware of what is happening.[38]

All this time Cupid is keeping his bed, in his mother's chamber (presumably on Olympus), *uulnere lucernae dolens*, ill with the pain of the burn received from the drop of hot oil (5. 28. 1). In the context this looks like a metaphor for his being in love; any mention of wounds, fire, and pain in association with

[34] This is a recurrent motif in the Greek romances.

[35] An Ovidian motif: *Am.* 3. 6. 23–4 and the following catalogue of rivers in love. It has been prepared for by the last verse of the oracle: if even Styx fears him, *a fortiori* all other rivers must.

[36] Callim. fr. 67. 1–4 Pf., Ov. *Her.* 20. 25–8. That love inspires the lover to daring is an idea at least as old as Plato: *Symp.* 179 A 7–8.

[37] 6. 10. 5–6, 12, 15, 17. 3–19. 7.

[38] 6. 11. 2, 13. 3.

Cupid cries out so to be understood. This is not altogether easy to fit in to the allegory.[39] He had already fallen in love with Psyche (albeit *qua* Amor II) when he first saw her. When he resumes his active role in the story it is because his wound has healed (*cicatrice solidata reualescens*, 6. 21. 2), whereas on his final appearance on Olympus, to which we shall presently come, he is *amore nimio peresus et aegra facie* (6. 22. 1). Formally it might be expected that this second falling in love, if that is what it is, should be a counterpart to Psyche's pricking herself with the arrow, but it is not easy to make coherent allegorical sense of these developments. Moreover, the reproachful address to the lamp (5. 23. 5) seems to suggest that it acted with deliberate malice. If so, how does that square with the allegorical 'plot'? This may be one of the places where, however we account for them, we must be content to accept loose ends in Apuleius' conduct of the story.

Venus' state progress to the sea was as Venus I. When she leaves it to re-enter the plot it is very much as Venus II. She is discovered, as has been noted, *lauantem natantemque* (5. 28. 3). She learns from a garrulous tern[40] that in her absence and that of Cupid on his sick-bed, the love-life of the world has become a sordid mess: 'per hoc non uoluptas ulla non gratia non lepos, sed incompta et agrestia et horrida cuncta..., non nuptiae coniugales non amicitiae sociales non liberum caritates, sed enormis colluuies et squalentium foederum insuaue fastidium' (5. 28. 5). The theme of nature in travail through the absence of a deity was familiar especially from the myth of Ceres. The withdrawal of love, the fundamental creative force, was *ex hypothesi* catastrophic:

> excedat agedum rebus humanis Venus,
> quae supplet ac restituit exhaustum genus:
> orbis iacebit squalido turpis situ,
> uacuum sine ullis piscibus stabit mare,

---

[39] Cf. Schlam (1976), 33, on the 'anomalous' severity of the wound, which he believes 'reflects ... the traditional prominence on the monuments of the motif of Eros burned, *albeit with a torch*' (my emphasis). As Prof. Diskin Clay has suggested, it is possibly significant that the site of the wound is the shoulder, where the god's wings are attached.

[40] For the identification see Arnott (1964). This tale-bearing bird is Ovidian: *Met.* 2. 531–632.

alesque caelo derit et siluis fera,
solis et aer peruius uentis erit. (Seneca, *Phaedra* 469–73)

Let Venus be expelled from human life,
Who makes good and restores the exhausted race,
The world will lie inert, neglected, vile,
The sea will stagnate emptied of its fish,
The air will lack its birds, the woods their beasts,
And only winds will traverse heaven's paths.

This is the converse of what happens when love is present, as in
the Homeric Hymn to Aphrodite (1–6, 69–74) or the great
hymnic proem to the *De rerum natura* (1. 1–20). The emphasis of
the tern's report, however, is *moral*: the low, repellent, and
unsocial character of the resultant scene. There is love of a sort,
in the shape of base sensual couplings, *squalentia foedera*, but
there is no grace, no joy—the absence of *uoluptas* especially
recalls Lucretius. Marriage, friendship, family affections, have
all vanished. In a word, what is described is the disappearance
of civilization: *incompta et agrestia et horrida cuncta*—man has
regressed to savagery. In this picture Ovid too has had a hand:
in his sub-Lucretian excursus at *Ars amatoria* 2. 473–80 the
civilizing influence is ascribed to *uoluptas*.[41] It is, that is to say,
the absence of love in its higher guise—Venus I and Amor I—
that the tern is describing.

It is then all the more striking that the protagonists in the
ensuing scene are Venus II and (passively and by implication)
Amor II. Venus leaves the sea rather in the manner of a submarine missile breaking surface and confronts her ailing and, as
she accounts it, erring son in her *aureus thalamus* (5. 29. 1). The
situation and some of the language recall the complaints of
Aphrodite to Hera and Athene in Apollonius (3. 91 ff.), but the
tone of her abusive and threatening tirade is more like that of
Herodas' Metrotime.[42] The image of Cupid projected by her
words is once more that of the wild and wayward child of epigram and elegy. His weapons are not the *magni dei propitia tela*
revealed to Psyche, but 'gear' (*supellex*) of which she can strip
him at her pleasure (5. 29. 5, 30. 5). Her threats to discipline

---

[41] It will be revealed at the end of the story that the child of Cupid and Psyche is to
be called Voluptas.

[42] 'Fishwife' (Walsh (1970), 209) is not quite the *mot juste*.

him remind us that the figure of the chastened Cupid (Amor II) is familiar from epigram and art.[43] Venus continues to speak of him in this vein in the following scene, when she emerges from the interview, in which his part, as has been noted, has been entirely silent and passive,[44] to encounter Ceres and Juno. She asks for their assistance in the search for Psyche and appeals for their sympathy over the behaviour of her son (5. 31). Here too Apuleius has drawn on Apollonius, from the scene in which Hero puts in a plea for Eros (3. 106–10). 'The comfort they offer, said to be in deference to the power of Cupid, is filled with mocking irony: surely Venus must recognise her boy is growing up; how can she who fosters love throughout the world refuse to accept it in her own house? It is a scene of social comedy with the goddesses as upper class *matronae*'[45] and, one might add, tempering their ostensible sympathy with not a little purely feminine malice.

Venus returns to the sea in a huff, as unceremoniously as she had left it. The scene changes with the beginning of Book 6 (as it had done at the beginning of Book 5), now to Psyche's wanderings. These lead her in succession to shrines of Ceres and Juno, and to each goddess she addresses an elaborate prayer. Between the elevated tone of these invocations and the prosaic responses of the recipients there is a glaring discrepancy, analogous on the stylistic plane to that between Venus and Amor I and II. Psyche's language and style are echoed in Book 11 in Lucius' prayer to Isis and the goddess's reply. Just as Psyche lists the alternative locations where Juno may be found, so Lucius lists Isis' various divine identities, which include those of Ceres and of *caelestis Venus*; and Isis in her reply enumerates the names under which she is known to different peoples—which include Venus, Ceres, and Juno—in words which recall Venus' initial outburst in the Psyche story.[46] These adumbrations in Psyche's prayers of the higher mystical unity that is ultimately to be revealed in the figure of Isis—Plane I, so to call it—are

---

[43] Schlam (1976), 15–17.

[44] 'Cupid is strangely silent, as if to underplay the incongruity of his resumed Alexandrian role' (Walsh (1970), 209). He can hardly, however, be said to resume a role that for the most part is forced on him by the other characters. That Apuleius may not have wished to focus the incongruity too precisely may be allowed.

[45] Schlam (1976), 35.

[46] 11. 2. 1–2, 5. 1–4.

countered by the goddesses on Plane II: their responses are firmly grounded in mythological-literary 'reality'. Ceres' language signals a bathetic return to the level of the concluding episode of Book 5: Venus is *bona femina*, a relative and crony whom it will not do to offend. So too Juno: she must keep on the right side of her daughter-in-law (the Venus II genealogy) and of the law—this last being one of the recurrent references to contemporary Roman reality with which Apuleius likes from time to time to shatter the dramatic illusion.

Mention of the law raises a point which has exercised the commentators. Venus' claim to Psyche is based, not on her *hybris*, but on her alleged status as a runaway slave.[47] Apuleius nowhere explicitly justifies this notion, but allows it to emerge gradually and by implication as the story proceeds. The conceit of the soul as a runaway had been exploited by Callimachus and Meleager,[48] and the influence of Moschus' *Eros Drapetes* is clearly visible in Mercury's proclamation, of which more presently. Walsh speaks of 'another minor inconsistency resulting from a *mélange* of literary story and folk-tale',[49] but it is unnecessary to invoke folk-tale. This being very much Venus II who is directing proceedings, the point would rather seem to be that touched on earlier, that Psyche, deserted by Amor I because of her proved unworthiness of him, passes automatically under the dominion of Amor and Venus II; and that her designation as Venus' *ancilla* reflects the literary *seruitium amoris* and its philosophical counterpart, the image of men as the slaves of their passions.[50] It would have been crude and obvious to spell this out; as with the rest of the allegory, Apuleius prefers to let his readers make the connections for themselves.

However, Venus I makes one more appearance, and a spectacular one it is. Her ascent to Olympus (6. 6) is one of the most outstandingly pretty pieces of writing in the novel. Formally it may be seen as complementary to her earlier marine progress;

[47] 5. 31. 2 *Psychen illam fugitiuam uolaticam*, 6. 7. 3, 8. 2 *ancillam*; and Psyche's reference to Venus as her *domina*, 6. 5. 3.

[48] *AP* 12. 73 (*Epigr.* 41 Pf., *HE* 1057–62), 12. 80 (*HE* 4082–7); and cf. Lutatius Catulus' imitation, *aufugit mi animus . . .* (p. 43 Morel).

[49] Walsh (1970), 210. Another possible literary influence is the story of Io: Helm (1914), 194–5 = (1968), 211–12.

[50] Cf. *Apol.* 12, *trucique perculsorum animalium serua corpora complexu uincientem*, and above, n. 26.

thus the birdsong which now heralds her coming corresponds to the fanfares of the Tritons on that occasion. Literary models for an aerial progress were not to hand ready-made, and Apuleius draws on disparate sources. Venus' chariot is by Ovid out of Homer, recalling the car which Hera and Athene prepare for the attack on Ares and the chariot of the Sun in the story of Phaethon.[51] A car drawn by birds recalls Sappho's famous ode, though in that the motive-power is supplied by sparrows rather than doves, as here. Given the lecherous behaviour generally attributed to sparrows,[52] their demotion in favour of doves may possibly be a hint that this is Venus I rather than Venus II, for doves are a common symbol of conjugal devotion. The most striking similarity is with Lucretius:

> te dea te fugiunt uenti, te nubila caeli
> aduentumque tuum ...
> placatumque nitet diffuso lumine caelum ...
> aeriae primum uolucres te diua tuumque
> significant initum perculsae corde tua ui.
>
> (*DRN* 1. 6–7, 9, 12–13)

But we may also note that here too Isis is prefigured: '... ut canorae etiam auiculae prolectatae uerno uapore concentus suaues adsonarent, matrem siderum, parentem temporum orbisque totius dominam blando mulcentes adfamine' (11. 7. 4).

That this is indeed Venus I, Urania, Caelestis, that is paying this state call is demonstrated by the manner of her reception: 'cedunt nubes et Caelus[53] filiae panditur et summus Aether cum gaudio suscipit deam' (6. 6. 4). The reference to the story of her birth could hardly be clearer: *Caelus* = Οὐρανός, and *Aether* (who should have a capital letter) is Caelus' father. However, no sooner does she leave Olympus than a most extraordinary act of literary legerdemain is performed. Having exaggeratedly literal Homerism *nec rennuit Iouis caerulum supercilium* (6. 7. 2)—she takes Mercury back to earth with her, and

---

[51] Hom. *Il.* 5. 722–31, Ov. *Met.* 2. 105–10.

[52] Hinted at in the words *lasciuiunt passeres* (6. 6. 3). Other attested sources of motive-power are swans and Erotes: Bömer on Ov. *Met.* 10. 708–9.

[53] *caelum* MSS, but the neuter form blunts the point. The masculine is attested by Ennius; see *Ann.* 24 and Skutsch *ad loc.*

on their arrival addresses him as *frater Arcadi* 'Arcadian brother'
(6. 7. 3). This greeting presupposes her alternative parentage,
from Zeus and Dione. The instantaneous metamorphosis of
Venus I into Venus II is demurely signalled by Apuleius with
the two words *caelo demeat*. If proof be wanted that he knew
exactly what he was doing when he switched Venuses on the
reader in this way, it is here in the witty ambiguity of this
phrase: *caelo demeat* = both 'descends from Uranus', i.e. is
Venus I, and 'comes back to earth', i.e. ceases to be Venus I and
resumes her active role in the story as Venus II. Here too Ovid
had been before Apuleius, who may well have taken a leaf out
of his book. At *Met.* 4. 532 Neptune is alluded to by the poet as
Venus' *patruus*, i.e. brother of her father Jupiter; whereas in
addressing him the goddess invokes her other parentage: 'aliqua et mihi gratia ponto est, / si tamen in dio quondam con-
creta profundo / spuma fui Graiumque manet mihi nomen ab
illa' (536–8).[54] Far from showing himself indifferent to the contradiction (Bömer *ad loc.*), Ovid wittily exploits it by, in effect,
allowing the goddess to correct the more genteel version of her
nativity.

The completeness of this retransformation is emphasized in a
manner by no means flattering to the goddess in the proclamation made by Mercury on her behalf: 'si quis a fuga retrahere
uel occultam demonstrare poterit fugitiuam regis filiam,
Veneris ancillam, nomine Psychen, conueniat retro metas
Murtias Mercurium praedicatorem, accepturus indiciuae
nomine ab ipsa Venere septem sauia suauia et unum blandien-
tis adpulsu linguae longe mellitum' (6. 8. 2–3). This, as has
already been noted, is evidently suggested by Moschus' *Eros
Drapetes*, but what Moschus only implies in his description of
the kiss that is offered as reward,[55] is made lubriciously explicit
by Apuleius in words calculated to remind the reader of the
kisses bestowed on Lucius by Photis: '... iam patentis oris inha-
latu cinnameo et occursantis linguae inlisu nectareo prona
cupidine adlibescenti' (2. 10. 4). For the Roman reader the
point is underlined by the rendezvous, *retro metas Murtias*, a
name connected by popular etymology with Venus and a place

[54] I owe this reference to Dr R. B. Fowler.
[55] οὐ γυμνὸν τὸ φίλημα, τὺ δ' ὦ ξένε καὶ πλέον ἕξεις, 5.

in an area notoriously frequented by prostitutes.[56] This is the goddess who is now claiming Psyche (a human soul) as her *ancilla*.

Psyche, in despair, gives herself up, and Venus proceeds to put her through it, with the assistance of her henchwomen Consuetudo, Sollicitudo, and Tristities, personifications of the experiences and sufferings which were traditionally part and parcel of the life of the (literary) lover, projected by the poets as the devotee of Amor II. There follow her ordeals, in which, as has been said, she is sustained by the agents of Amor I, an unseen but felt off-stage presence. The last of them ends in disaster with the mysterious episode of the casket which proves to contain *infernus somnus ac uere Stygius* (6. 21. 1). Once more Psyche's *curiositas* is her undoing, and this, her last though this time unwitting, suicide-attempt is, it would appear, successful. A literary influence here may be the *subita dementia* which overcame Orpheus when the end of *his catabasis*-ordeal was already in sight.[57] But what exactly is this 'deathly sleep'? It can only be a metaphor for the spiritual death of the soul that is wholly given over to the lower kind of love, that is wholly under the domination of Venus II and Amor II. 'She that liveth in pleasure is dead while she liveth'; though St Paul lends a unique authority to the proposition he did not invent it.[58] From this situation only one power can avail to rescue it.

The soul is persuaded that beauty and value exist nowhere but here [in this world], unless it secures divine, chaste Love to be its physician, its saviour, its guide. Love, who has come to it through the medium of bodily forms, is its divine conductor to the truth from the realm of Hades here; Love conducts it to the Plain of Truth where Beauty, concentrated and pure and genuine, has her home. When we long to embrace and have intercourse with her after our separation, it is Love who graciously appears to lift us out of the depths and escort us upward, like a mystic guide beside us at our initiation.[59]

---

[56] Catull. 55. 4, *Priap.* 27. 1–2, Juv. 3. 65, SHA *Heliog.* 26. 3, cf. 32. 9.

[57] Virg. *G.* 4. 485–91.

[58] *1 Tim.* 5: 6; Sall. *Cat.* 2. 8, Lucr. 3. 1046, Sen. *Ep.* 77. 18.

[59] Plut, *Amat.* 764–5 tr. Helmbold; cf. Walsh (1981), 29–30. For the Plain of Truth see Plat. *Phdr.* 248 B. As is shown by Trapp (above, ch. VI), the *Phaedrus* was especially popular during the second century AD, and Apuleius' awareness of it would have been due at least as much to its diffusion and reception in contemporary literary, philosophical,

That passage from Plutarch's *Amatorius* offers, it seems to me, the most enlightening commentary on what Apuleius appears to be getting at in this episode of Psyche's deathly swoon and Cupid's sudden epiphany as *deus ex machina* (6. 21). But if this was indeed his intention, it was not altogether plain sailing to integrate it with the mechanics of the narrative. Cupid's wound, we learn, has now healed and he can no longer bear his separation from Psyche. 'With one bound our hero was free'; he leaves his room via the window (a comic-elegiac touch)[60] and flies to the rescue. This is evidently Amor I in charge again, as his masterful words on parting make clear: 'cetera egomet uidero', 'leave the rest to me.' But what are we supposed to make of his method of waking Psyche from her trance, *innoxio punctulo sagittae suae*? Presumably this wound is 'harmless' in contrast to those inflicted by his *alter ego*, Amor II? However, the real problem comes with what happens next. With no more transition than is supplied by a bare *interea*[61] he reappears in Olympus as Amor II in the form of an ailing and apprehensive child: 'interea Cupido amore nimio peresus et aegra facie matris suae repentinam sobrietatem pertimescens ad armillum redit'; and in this guise he makes his submission to Jupiter (6. 22. 1). We are back with the wayward godling and the chastised Eros. This metamorphosis is, if anything, even more abruptly contrived than that of Venus on her return from Olympus; and, as if to make sure that the reader does not miss it, Apuleius glosses it with the words *ad armillum redit*, 'reverted to type'. There is no way of putting a flattering construction on

and rhetorical culture as to close study of Plato's text. 'A vague knowledge of Eros in the *Phaedrus* was part of the standard learning of any rhetorician' (Hunter (1983), 109 n. 43). For a parallel to the passage of the *Amatorius* just quoted compare Maximus, 10. 9 c Hobein: 'When the soul leaves here it is as if it quitted the land of the Cimmerians for the bright aether. Free from the flesh, free from desires, free from accidents, it clearly sees and considers truth itself, mingling with the gods and their children above the topmost vault of heaven. It is an enlisted member in the host of heaven under the generalship of Zeus...'. On knowledge of Plato generally at this time see also De Lacy, in Bowersock (1974).

[60] Prop. 4. 7. 16, Ov. *AA* 2. 245–6, 3. 605, *Fast.* 6. 577–8; Trenkner (1958), 129–30, Trendall–Webster (1971), 134–5.

[61] A hint of the imminent transformation may possibly be felt in the ambiguous words *amator leuis in pinnas se dedit* (6. 21. 4), which can mean both 'her fickle lover flew away', with a backward glance at *feci leuiter* (5. 24. 5) and 'her lover flew nimbly away' (*leuis* predicative).

this phrase.[62] It can only be taken as meaning that the real Cupid is back and that all his behaviour in the meantime has been out of character. Strictly speaking this is true in the sense that, as we have seen, Amor II has been almost entirely passive (the important exception being of course his action in falling, or inducing his higher self to fall, in love with Psyche), and Amor I has controlled the action. By actually drawing attention to this and emphasizing that in the denouement of the story it is Amor II who is on stage, Apuleius seems to be going out of his way to invite his readers to note a fundamental inconsistency in his conduct of it. The alert and fully switched-on reader that we have felt entitled to postulate might surely expect that the upshot of the tale will be the reunion of the soul (Psyche) with Love on the Plain of Truth, that she will be joined with Amor I. Instead, we have a wedding with Amor II on a conventional literary Olympus. And what are we to make of Cupid's (Amor II's) submission to Jupiter in fear, not of Venus II, but of Venus I—for that ought to be the implication of her *repentina sobrietas*, if the words are pressed?[63]

The setting of the last scene of the story is one, as just noted, that on the face of it stoutly resists allegorizing interpretation. 'Nous sommes au dénouement d'une comédie bourgeoise', as Grimal puts it:[64] reconciliation all round, a legitimate marriage, feasting, singing, and dancing. It is perhaps possible to glimpse a hint here and there of the higher love, or at least the rejection of the lower. The words of Jupiter as he ratifies the marriage may be read as conveying a hint that this is, after all, Amor I who is being joined to Psyche. The goings-on of his

---

[62] It means literally 'returned to the wine-jar' (cf. Otto s.v. *anus* 4), an unflattering equivalent of the more urbane *ad ingenium redire* (Ter. *Ad.* 71, *Hec.* 113); cf. *Met.* 9. 29. 1 (of an adulterous wife) *exasperata ad armillum reuertit et ad familiares feminarum artes accenditur.*

[63] Venus had shrunk from invoking the aid of Sobrietas, describing her as *rustica squalensque femina* (5. 30. 4). This recalls the *squalentia foedera* of the tern's report, but Sobrietas' attributes are rather those of the virtuous Sabine women of old: cf. Ov. *Med. Fac.* 11–12, *Her.* 4. 102 (Phaedra) *si Venerem tollas, rustica silua tua est.* She would seem to belong with Mens Bona and Pudor as forces inimical to Amor and Venus II; cf. *Am.* 1. 2. 31–2.

[64] Grimal (1963), 135. The Greek romances generally end with a marriage or the reunion of a married couple; cf. Chariton, 8. 1. 4, 'I imagine that this last episode will be welcome to my readers. No more brigandage or slavery or law-cases or fighting or starvation or war or captures, but legitimate love and a regular marriage.'

unreformed self (Amor II), of which much is made in Jupiter's address to him in the preceding chapter (6. 22. 3–4), are pointedly contrasted with the limitations which marriage will impose on his conduct (6. 23. 3). His new role of husband united in regular matrimony, *nuptias . . . legitimas et iure ciuili congruas*, is in sharp contrast to his first appearance as home-wrecker (4. 30. 4). The conferment of immortality on Psyche and the promise that her union with Cupid will be eternal are phrased with appreciable solemnity (6. 23. 5); in the light of the Platonic-Plutarchan background all this can perhaps after all be read as assuring the expectant reader that Psyche has indeed finally made it to the Plain of Truth.

Some compromise was forced upon Apuleius by the exigencies of the plot of the novel as a whole. In these concluding chapters of *Cupid & Psyche* he had to manage a transition back to the main narrative. The story is told by the bandits' house-keeper, a drunken old woman, to their captive Charite, ostensibly to cheer her up. Thus the final emphasis on feasting and merriment is appropriate to its larger context. It is also neat and appropriate that the story should end, in the revelation of the divine child's name, with an accent on pleasure. The word *uoluptas* abounds in evocative ambiguity. Looking at the tale against the background of the novel as a whole we recall that the first chapter of Book I ends 'lector intende; laetaberis', and that the last words of Book II are 'gaudens obibam'. We recall also that Lucius, who overheard and has just repeated the tale, is in the resumed action of the novel to find himself, not for the first or last time, in danger of his life (6. 26), ultimately because of his own surrender to pleasure of the lower sort, *seruiles uoluptates*. The situation of Psyche must in some sense be a comment on his own. Finally, though Voluptas had some exiguous claims to divinity in her own right,[65] Apuleius must have relied on his readers to remember, having echoed the *De rerum natura* more than once in connection with her, that in the very first line of the poem Lucretius identified Venus herself as *hominum diuumque uoluptas*.[66] They might also have remembered that Lucretius took great care to dissociate that Venus from the purely sensual passion held up to scorn in the great diatribe of Book 4.[67]

[65] See Pease on Cic. *ND* 2. 61.
[66] Kenney (1977), 13 and n. 26, Schlam (1976), 38–40.
[67] Kenney (1981), 20–1.

Apuleius' *Metamorphoses* is neither formally nor thematically *sui generis*. Its basic plot and themes are essentially similar to those of the surviving Greek romances and the *Satyricon*: lovers separated and reunited. In the romances the lovers are united in the fullest sense, however much time they may have spent in each other's company meanwhile, only after their love has been put to the proof by suffering. In the *Metamorphoses* Lucius achieves his perfect union in the shape of Isiac initiation only after a long period of physical and spiritual separation, from his human shape and from understanding of the true nature of love. A lower and a higher love, two antithetical and incompatible Venuses, contend for the mastery over him. Finally he rejects the *seruiles uoluptates* represented by Photis for the goddess whose service is perfect freedom, Isis, who among other things is also *Venus Caelestis*.[68]

Into this story is inset the tale of Cupid and Psyche. There have been those, and there possibly still are, who deny it any special relevance to the main plot. This position seems to me very hard to sustain. I find it to be self-evident that whatever Apuleius was getting at in *Cupid & Psyche* is in some way related to whatever he is getting at in the book as a whole. It has been duly noted that he 'has here adopted the Alexandrian technique exploited by Callimachus in his *Hecale* and taken over by Catullus in his sixty-fourth poem; *Cupid and Psyche* is a story within a story, and designed to illuminate the larger whole'.[69] To this it need only be added that Apuleius shows himself so much and so continuously the conscious heir of the Alexandrian literary tradition, both as known to him directly and as mediated through his Latin models,[70] that it is inconceivable that he was not fully aware of the purpose and application of the 'insetting' technique. In adopting it he intended it to carry its full literary weight.

Does it work as he uses it? His conduct of the story of the love of Cupid and Psyche, the soul with Love, on the two planes which I have tried to distinguish in my analysis, posed certain technical problems. Apuleius had a message, but his first *stated* priority was to entertain: 'lector intende: laetaberis'. He was

<hr/>

[68] 11. 15. 5, 2. 1.
[69] Walsh (1970), 190.
[70] On 'two-tier' allusion in Latin poets see Hinds (1987), p. 151 n. 16 and Index s.v. 'allusion'.

just as keenly aware as Lucretius and Horace had been of the
need for a judicious proportion of *utile* and *dulce*. Allegory is not
easy to manage well: to be effective it must neither dominate
the narrative nor be submerged in it.[71] This rule, as I account
it, Apuleius respects, and does so with great adroitness. If the
message is in some respects elusive and there appear to be loose
ends in the treatment, that cannot be unhesitatingly ascribed in
all cases to negligence rather than to conscious artistic choice or
instinct—though there are no doubt moments when his innate
exuberance lets rip and he writes *securus cadat an recto stet fabula
talo*. He had clearly read his Virgil to some effect; and it may be
suggested that among the lessons that he learned from the
Aeneid was one in the artistic conduct of allegory. Thus the first
scene between Venus and Cupid is, as we have noted, indebted
to the *Aeneid* (1. 657–90), which in turn drew on the *Argonautica*
(3. 111–66). In Apollonius Eros is very much the Hellenistic
naughty boy, Amor II.[72] In Virgil the *situation* is Apollonian,
but the *character* of Cupid, addressed by his mother as *meae uires,
mea magna potentia*, is rather that of the all-powerful cosmic
force, Amor I. Using a technique that he applies with great
effect elsewhere (the headless corpse of Priam on the seashore is
the most striking example), Virgil superimposes one Cupid on
the other.[73] The hint would seem not to have been lost on
Apuleius.

[71] Cf. Hough (1966), 124, on the point of exact balance between 'naïve allegory' and
'realism': 'Neither theme nor image is dominant, we experience them together and feel
that they are inseparable. This happens in the work of Shakespeare. Our sense of the
centrality of Shakespeare comes largely from the perfect balance between image—the
concretely realized individuality of his characters, and theme—the power of typifying
moral and metaphysical qualities. And this balance is also found in lesser writers'—
including, I would suggest, Virgil (see below).

[72] His other, cosmic, identity is hinted at in the ball with which his mother bribes
him (3. 132–41); see Hunter *ad loc*. However, this is not, as in Virgil, a blending of identities so much as a learned footnote, a knowing nudge to the reader.

[73] Cf. Fliedner (1974), 63, noting that the love-god is successively and chiastically
styled *Cupido* (658), *Amor* (663), *Amor* (689), and *Cupido* (695).

VIII
Aristides and the Prose Hymn

D. A. RUSSELL

1

Ten of Aristides' extant speeches (*Orations* 37–46 Keil) are
usually designated 'hymns'.[1] They are: *Athena*,[2] *The Sons of
Asclepius*, *The Well of Asclepius*, *Heracles*, *Dionysus*,[3] *Asclepius*,
Zeus,[4] *The Aegean Sea*, *Sarapis*,[5] and *Poseidon*. They certainly
form a very striking display of high sophistic culture, combining rhetorical splendour with a sense of pride in places and
monuments and a concern for religion and theology which we
should believe to be rooted in deeply felt sentiment. No one
who reads the *Hieroi Logoi*[6] can fail to think Aristides a man of
genuine religious temper.

Some of these speeches (37–41 K, together with the fragmen-
tary *Water of Pergamum* (53 K)) were among those known by
the time of the rhetor Menander[7] as Μαντευτοί, 'speeches com-
manded by prophecy'. In these, Aristides acknowledges the
authority of a dream whose instructions he fulfils by making the
speech; this is explicit in *Athena* (37. 1, 29), *Sons of Asclepius* (38.
1. 24), *Dionysus* (41. 1), and *Heracles* (40. 1, 22). Is this experience or literary convention? In *Hieroi Logoi* 4. 25, Aristides tells
us that Athena and Dionysus were subjects prescribed by
dreams, and that he wrote down in his dream-diary as much as
he could remember of the wonderful things he dreamed he was
saying. On the other hand, it is perhaps prudent to recall the

---

[1] Text: Keil (1898). Trans.: Behr (1981), with notes; (Latin), W. Canter (1566), last
printed in S. Jebb's edn. (Oxford, 1722–30). See also: Behr (1968), Boulanger (1923),
Gigli (1975), Klock (1986), Lenz (1964), Mesk (1927), Norden (1898).

[2] Jöhrens (1981) for text and comm.

[3] Uerschels (1962) for text and comm.

[4] Amann (1931) for trans. and comm, with excellent intro. on the genre as a whole.

[5] Höfler (1935) for edn. with comm.

[6] Behr (1968), Nicosia (1984), Schröder (1986); Dodds (1965), 39–45, with refs to
earlier work.

[7] iii. 344. 1 Sp.: χαριέστατον δὲ καὶ τὸ τοιοῦτον μέρος παρέσχηται ἐν τοῖς Μαντευτοῖς
Ἀριστείδης. οὗτος γὰρ τὸν Ἀσκληπιὸν (42 Keil) καὶ τὴν Ὑγίειαν [not extant]
συγγέγραφεν.

advice of Menander[8] that one should 'make up dreams and
pretend to have heard voices'. Such a fiction was plausible
because the belief was current; and in Aristides' heated mind
vision and reality, inspiration and the pride of his skill were no
doubt indissoluble.

The dating of the speeches has been the subject of much controversy. The only two for which firm evidence exists, in the
subscriptiones of some manuscripts, are *Athena* and *Heracles*. Of
these, *Athena*, whether or not it is the dream-speech alluded to
in the *Hieroi Logoi* is dated to 153, and *Heracles* to 166. The information seems reliable. It is also widely held, and also widely
denied,[9] that *Sarapis* is the earliest, written in 142, when Aristides was 25 and had lately visited Egypt and so acquired first-
hand knowledge of the cult. The evidence of this is that the
hymn begins, as we shall see, with an important programmatic
statement about the nature of the prose hymn. This is in itself
not a convincing argument: there is no reason why pro-
grammes should be written first, and the analogy of poetical
programmatic pieces—in Horace or Juvenal, for example—
does not support the case. Others[10] think that *Zeus* is the earliest of these speeches, on the ground that it seems to observe
rhetorical prescripions particularly closely. This is equally
unconvincing. The topics of the hymns are very conventional,[11]
and the prescriptions of Menander at least are to some extent
dependent on Aristides himself. The truth is that only firm data
about Aristides' movements in the early part of his career could
resolve the issue, and we do not possess such data. It is more important, I think, to recognize the marked differences in style
within this group of compositions. They fall roughly into two
classes, or rather can be arranged in a stylistic spectrum, with
very clear differences between the extremes. At one end of the
spectrum, the dominant features are 'hymnic' elements derived
from the language of cult or from Plato—especially *Symposium*,
Timaeus, and *Phaedrus* (237 A, 244 A). We have short cola,
simple non-periodic structures, asyndeton, anaphora, and
other Gorgianic figures like isocolon, and a distinctly grandiose

---

[8] iii. 390. 4 Sp.: χρὴ δὲ καὶ ὀνείρατα πλάττειν καὶ ἀκοήν τινα προσποιεῖσθαι ἀκηκοέναι.
[9] Mesk (1927), 664; Behr (1968), 53; (1981), 419; against, Amann (1931), 35.
[10] e.g. Amann (1931), loc. cit.
[11] Amann (1931), 1–14.

choice of vocabulary. At the other end, there is much more
periodic structure and a closer resemblance to the epideictic
style used for regular encomia of men or places. To the first
class belong *Athena*, *Zeus*, *Sarapis*, and *Dionysus*. To the second
belong *Poseidon* and *The Aegean Sea*. *Heracles*, *Asclepius*, and *The
Well of Asclepius* have features of both, but perhaps come closer
to the second group. For my own part, I find it difficult to see
much difference in sentiment between the two sets, though
Amann[12] feels sure that *Zeus*, *Asclepius*, and *Sarapis* are much
better than the others, 'less pedantic and artificial', because
they reflect Aristides' personal devotion to Zeus and the two
healing gods. I fear this may be a circular argument. We know
of the devotion, and so we find it in the speeches. In any case,
there is no reason to think that any chronological inferences
should be drawn from classifications like this, We know that
Aristides composed verse hymns contemporaneously with his
prose hymns.[13] What is to prevent him also using diverse rhetorical techniques as the fancy moved him, sometimes tending to
the Platonic part of his repertoire, sometimes more to the Isoc-
ratean? In what follows, I shall illustrate both main types: the
'hymnic' mainly from *Sarapis* and *Dionysus*, the 'epideictic' from
The Aegean Sea.

2

I turn first to the great programmatic statement of *Sarapis* (45.
1–14).[14]

It begins with ironical envy of the poets: how happy and
trouble-free they are! This is a classical topic, elegantly developed by Isocrates (*Evagoras*, 8–11).[15] It is also the theme of
two well-known second-century texts, one of which Aristides

---

[12] Amann (1931), 19 ff.

[13] Boulanger (1923), 300–3; Mesk (1927), 668–72.

[14] Part trans. in Russell and Winterbottom (1972), 558–60. Discussion in Mesk
(1927) and Gigli (1975).

[15] Isocrates makes the essential points that poets can represent god in human situ-
ations, and can use foreign, metaphorical, or coined words; their metre and rhythm can
charm in the absence of good sense, as can be seen if you take it away. The prose enco-
miast has harder rules to follow.

must have known: the passage in Dio's *Olympicus* (*Or.* 12. 62–
72) in which the sculptor Phidias is made to appear similarly
envious of the poets' ease and their infinite and malleable
material, so different from the scarce and obdurate stone in
which he is forced to work. The other text is datable to 165/6,
and so must be later than *Sarapis*; it is in Lucian's *Quomodo historia conscribenda sit* (8),[16] where Lucian contrasts the factual responsibility of history with the poets' licence for fable.
Naturally enough, Aristides looks at the matter as a rhetor. He
begins by criticizing poets' subjects (ὑποθέσεις) for being not
only 'neither true nor plausible' but 'without coherence either'
(οὐδ' ἐχούσας σύστασιν). The terminology is that used to criticize declamation subjects (ὑποθέσεις) as ἀσύστατοι, 'not holding
together', though the doctrine is not quite the same as that of
Hermogenes[17] for whom the 'implausible' is simply a variety of
the 'incoherent'. He goes on also in a purely rhetorical vein.
Poets use thoughts (νοήματα) and arguments (ἐνθυμήματα)
which are not intelligible without their context. So far from
appreciating them when we hear them in their place, our
understanding and acceptance come afterwards, when the
whole mass is somehow grasped simultaneously (ὁμοῦ δὲ πάντων
λεχθέντων συνέντες ἀπεδεξάμεθα). Then indeed we feel pleased
with ourselves for being so intelligent. Poets, then, do not have
to make their words immediately intelligible. Nor do they have
to reproduce the entire sequence of events from beginning to
end, but can freely dismiss themes after a brief mention, introduce events without preparing them, or abridge in the middle.
They can dispense with beginning or middle or end. They have
despotic power over their thoughts.

Secondly (ἔπειτα, 2), they have licence to suspend gods ἀπὸ
μηχανῆς, make them travel or drink with humans, and (like
Athena in the *Odyssey* (19. 34)) carry a lamp to light their
human friends on their way. All this refers to drama and epic;
but Aristides soon comes closer to his own enterprise, and turns
to the lyric poets' hymns and paeans. In these, he says, a couple
of strophes or periods is enough to complete the whole job. An
invocation, a single narrative, a claim to wisdom, and the work

---

[16] Homeyer (1965), 185–8, for notes on this passage.

[17] 32–3 Rabe: τὸ ἀπίθανον—'Socrates keeps a brothel' or 'Aristides commits a
crime'—is the fifth of eight species of ἀσύστατα: Russell (1983), 43–4.

is done. He illustrates the point mainly from Pindar, whom he knew well.[18] The rhetor Menander makes a similar point, perhaps derived from Aristides, when he contrasts the poets' licence to use a single part of a subject to make a whole poem with the demand for exhaustiveness made on the orator.[19]

And yet, Aristides continues, we respect the poets so much that we voluntarily surrender to them a monopoly of hymn-writing, as though they were in truth the spokesmen of the gods that they claim to be. This is then seen to be a paradox. We do not use in relation to the gods the very instrument, λόγος,[20] whose business it is to propound aright (ὑποθέσθαι) what is appropriate, to organize it with due consideration, and to execute it with all the exactness to which the human mind can attain. We use it instead for every other purpose: to praise festivals, to relate actions and wars, to create myths, and to plead in the courts. Even in religious contexts, prose is the vehicle of the regulations that enjoin rituals and sacrifices. It is only hymns that we leave to the poets.

This is not altogether easy to interpret. The triple function of λόγος, as Keil says,[21] corresponds to the three main heads of rhetoric: invention (forming the ὑπόθεσις), disposition, and verbal expression. The prose genres are, it seems: epideictic, history, myth-writing, and forensic oratory. This is a somewhat idiosyncratic list, as it omits deliberative oratory and highlights two narrative genres, one factual and one fictional. μῦθοι can hardly be said to be a genre in the sense in which the others are; but I take it that Aristides is thinking primarily of Plato, and perhaps also of the fables and myths of orators of his own day. Menander (339) cites Plato for 'mythical' hymns, but (341–2) also allows much novel invention. Dio's and Fronto's writings contain myths that would meet Aristides' criteria.[22]

Surely, he continues, all men should honour the gods with

---

[18] See esp. 28. 55–8. Aristides is the source of about 40 fragments of Pindar, and most of these seem to be due to his own reading, though some naturally come from Plato.

[19] iii. 343. 20 Sp: τῷ μὲν ⟨γὰρ⟩ ποιητῇ ἐξαρκεῖ καὶ μέρος τι ἀπολαβόντι καὶ κατακοσμήσαντι τῇ ποιητικῇ κατασκευῇ πεπαῦσθαι, ὁ δὲ συγγραφεὺς πειράσεται διὰ πάντων ἐλθεῖν.

[20] This implies reading ᾧ δέ at 353. 20 K, with Keil.

[21] Note on 353. 20.

[22] Dio Prus. *Or.* 5, *Or.* 36; Fronto *De feriis Alsensibus* 3. 8 ff. (pp. 12–18 Haines).

whatever means they have. This is an old commonplace[23] used
in a context very like the present by Libanius in his hymn to
Artemis (1. 305 F): the poet honours a god by offering a hymn
in metre, the orator gives a hymn without metre. It would be
absurd, continues Aristides, to suggest that none but poets are
beloved of god, for if this were so priests would all be poets. Nor
can it be that metre is needed for prophecy, since oracles and
dream-messages usually come in prose: witness Delphi,
Dodona, Trophonius—and the dreams of Asclepius and of Sarapis. This is the first mention of Sarapis in the speech (354.
20 K); it seems quite casual, so that one cannot help wondering
whether this elaborate prologue was really written for this particular occasion.

We have now reached the end of Aristides' dismissal of the
poets' claim. He is next to make his positive statement on behalf
of the orator. This is based on two arguments: (*a*) the first is
that prose is 'by nature' prior to poetry, which was a later technique, designed to add charm and grace to words. And what is
older ($\pi\rho\epsilon\sigma\beta\acute{\upsilon}\tau\epsilon\rho\upsilon\nu$), as even the poets agree, is better ($\ddot{\alpha}\mu\epsilon\iota\nu\upsilon\nu$,
354. 27 K). This looks like the contrary of what seems to have
been the standard ancient view,[24] that poetry was at one time
more widely used and understood, but has been replaced by the
more modest and intelligible medium of prose, not only for science and philosophy, but for oracles as well. For Aristides,
'words and discussions' come first. Their 'priority' is one of
value as well as of time; and the consequence is that non-
metrical hymns should be more, not less, acceptable to the gods
than verse. Here again is a position with which many would
disagree: the contrary view, namely that metre, song, and
rhythm are necessary for divine themes and prose inadequate,
is attributed to Cleanthes,[25] and of course accords with his own
brilliant use of the poetical form in his Hymn to Zeus. (*b*) Aristides' second argument is more difficult. It is that the poet's
$\mu\acute{\epsilon}\tau\rho\upsilon\nu$ ('metre') stands to true $\mu\acute{\epsilon}\tau\rho\upsilon\nu$ ('measure'), which the
orator must always observe, as the individual measures that

---

[23] e.g. Herodas 4. 12; Hor. *Odes* 2. 17, 3. 23; Juv. 12. 1 ff; Men. Rhet. iii. 437. 22–
5 Sp., with Russell–Wilson ad loc.

[24] The main texts (discussed in Norden (1898), 32–3) are: Aristot. *Rhet.* 3. 1. 9; Plut.
De Pythiae oraculis 24; Strabo 1. p. 18; Varro in Isidore, *Etymologiae*, 1. 38. 1–2.

[25] Phld., *De musica*, col. 28. 1 (p. 79 Kemke).

tradesmen use stand to the general principle of measure. Poets have unjustly appropriated to themselves the good standing (εὐφημία) of a notion of μέτρον which is not exclusively theirs. The orator's μέτρον does not merely measure lines of verse, but the whole discourse, which it pervades completely, starting 'right from the name' (ἄρχεταί γε εὐθὺς ἐκ τοῦ ὀνόματος, 355. 13 K). What does this mean? Keil[26] supposed it was 'the author's name', this being the very beginning of the text of the title. Daria Gigli[27] takes the 'name' to be the word μέτρον itself: the discourse begins 'in measure', '*come dice il nome stesso*'. Behr,[28] if I understand him right, thinks Aristides means that 'measure' starts with the 'measure' or due use of the individual word. This fits best with what follows. Aristides goes on to say that 'measure' forbids us to exaggerate or fall short of the proper value (ἀξίας) and obliges us to put the normal construction on each word. In other words, the characteristic hyperboles, metaphors, and metonymies of poetry are not allowed. The principle *also* forbids inserting unnecessary words for the sake of the metre, as poets often do. In 'periods', it demands 'self-sufficiency' (τὸ αὔταρκες), a very difficult thing to achieve. And finally its supervision ensures that the whole speech possesses 'due measure' (συμμετρία) and achieves its intended aim.

All this is sometimes taken—the case is well made by Gigli,[29] with much reference to Dionysius' *De compositione verborum*—as a statement of the pervasiveness of rhythm in *Kunstprosa*. It is of course true that Aristides has much concern for rhythm,[30] and a defence of prose hymns might well rest on this. But his defence is, I think, a different one. If we contrast the phrases:

$$τὸ\ ἔπος \ldots μετρεῖ\ μόνον\ εἰ\ πληροῖ\ τὸν\ τόνον\ (355.\ 10)$$

and:

$$καὶ\ τὸν\ σκοπὸν\ τὸν\ προταθέντα\ εἰ\ πεπλήρωκεν\ ἐπισκοπεῖ\ (355.\ 19),$$

we see that the poet's μέτρον deals with 'making up a line' and the orator's with 'making up a proposed aim'. The words

---

[26] Note on 355. 13 K.
[27] Gigli (1975), p. 243 n. 29.
[28] Behr (1981), p. 420 n. 22.
[29] Gigli (1975).
[30] Boulanger (1923), 430–5.

σκοπός and προτείνειν both suggest that what is meant is a
measure of sense rather than of rhythm. So the older view[31]
that Aristides is playing on the word μέτρον rather than making
a statement about the rhythmical form of prose seems justified.
Again (356. 2), we are told that one can attain μέτρον without
the poet's μέτρα, and fail to attain it with the poet's μέτρα. The
first half of this is true if μέτρον in prose is 'rhythm', but the
second half is not, since writing a perfect verse is necessarily
'attaining the μέτρον' in this sense, though not in any sense
which involves completeness and economy of meaning. No
doubt Aristides is vague and sophistical, and we should not
press him too far. But it does seem reasonable to conclude that
the crucial passage (355. 13–19) refers specifically to (*a*) correct
use of words, (*b*) economical use of words,[32] (*c*) self-contained
periods, and (*d*) complete fulfilment of the intended function.

It remains true of course that the poets have many advantages (13); orators, by contrast, have to remain 'in their
measure' and remember their position. They are like soldiers
who have to keep in rank. Nevertheless the vow must be kept,
'for we were saved', and it is not right to spend more time talking about μέτρον.

3

This transitional passage at least belongs to the specific occasion of *Sarapis*. There was a vow, now to be fulfilled. Aristides
has been rescued from a storm at sea—an experience which
occurred to him more than once on his many travels. It is
plausible, not certain, that the episode here in question was on
his return from Egypt to Asia in 142. But whenever it was, the
speech was delivered at Smyrna, where Sarapis was worshipped with splendour in a great annual festival. In the eloquent conclusion of his hymn (33), Aristides both celebrates the
city and expresses his own gratitude and devotion. It may serve
as a first specimen of his grander manner:

---

[31] Boulanger (1923), 306.

[32] Or, conceivably, the avoidance of artificially lengthened or abbreviated forms; for
this *topos* in discussions of poetic licence, see Dio Prus. *Or.* 12. 67 τὰ μὲν μηκύνων τὰ δὲ
συναιρῶν.

O ruler of the fairest city
of all those on which thou lookest down[33]
the city which gives thy annual festival;
O universal light of all mankind,
who didst appear to me in splendour but the other day,
when, as the sea surged and rose high all around me,
and nothing could be seen
save impending and almost present doom,
thou didst raise thy hand
and disclose the hidden heavens
and grant us sight of land and anchorage,
so far beyond all hope
that when we trod the ground we could not believe it.
All thanks to thee for this, O thou much honoured;
do not desert me now
but make me truly safe;
accept with graciousness the hymn now made,
as a thank-offering for the past
and a supplication and invocation for the future,
that it may be happier and better than the present.

4

Reduced to its bare bones, the *Sarapis* prologue is essentially that suggested by Menander for his *Sminthiakos* (437. 6–27 Sp.). The basic point is that the gods accept the humblest sacrifice if it is the most the worshipper can give. It has been variously interpreted. For some it implies that Aristides really was an innovator in composing prose hymns. This cannot be right; praises of gods in prose were already a recognized genre, for which Quintilian[34] gives comprehensive rules:

In gods, we shall first venerate the majesty of their nature in general terms, and then the power of each individually and any inventions which have given useful service to mankind. Thus the power of Jupiter will be shown to consist in ruling all things, that of Mars in war, that of Neptune in his control of the sea. Similarly with inventions: Minerva has the arts, Mercury letters, Apollo medicine, Ceres

---

[33] Sarapis is here identified with the Sun, both being also Zeus: Nilsson (1950), 490–1.

[34] Quint. 3. 7. 7–8.

corn, and Bacchus wine. Next come any actions that antiquity attributes to them; while honour is also added to gods by parentage (e.g. if one is a child of Jupiter), by age (as with those born of Chaos), and finally by their offspring (as Apollo and Diana lend honour to Latona).

If such rules were commonplace in the first century, Aristides is indeed doing nothing new in this sense. It is true that our main Greek authority, Menander, is much later and himself sees Aristides as a classic model (344. 2); but there is an earlier Greek text which is also relevant. This is a piece attributed to Alexander Numeniu,[35] the author of which is generally thought to be a man known to have composed a consolation to Hadrian on the death of Antinoos in 130—a great rhetorical and poetical opportunity.[36] Alexander recommends various arguments which we can see (for example) in *Zeus, Sarapis,* and *Dionysus.* In particular, he advises the orator to use both the φιλόσοφος λόγος that god is 'unborn and undying' and Plato's special view that the lesser gods were produced from the 'first god' and received the universal λόγος from him.[37] He may also, but in second place, use the common opinions of men, who have many different concepts of and names for the gods they worship. And thirdly, he can adduce the fact that gods worshipped under different names can be seen to be one, like Apollo and Helios or Hecate, Artemis, and Selene. (Thus, in the closing prayer of *Sarapis,* the god is also Helios, as he is Zeus in Alexandrian cult.) Universal worship is the highest praise; if a god is recognized by some nations only, these must be shown to be the wisest and best. Finally, the orator should enumerate the god's power and deeds. Over what τέχναι does he or she preside? What has he or she done among men or among gods? What animals are sacred in the cult? With what other gods does he or she consort? All these themes are in Aristides. As they appear in Alexander, they form a well-worked-out and rather obvious adaptation of the encomium-scheme used for human subjects. To go further back, we have only to think of some very

---

[35] Spengel, *Rhetores Graeci,* iii. 4–6; also in Walz, *Rhetores Graeci* ix. 331–9.

[36] Suda 3, 481, 22 Adler. For the literary importance of Antinoos' life and death, see above p. 82ff.

[37] Amann (1931), 6 ff, gives parallels in Aristid. and Menander's *Sminthiakos* for this sort of thing: see Menander iii. 438 Sp. and Russell–Wilson (1981), 354, 357.

influential passages of Plato's *Symposium* and *Phaedrus*. In *Symp.*
177 B, alluded to in *Heracles* (1), Plato puts prose and poetry on
a level, exactly as Aristides does in the prologue of *The Aegean
Sea*,[38] Menander (333 Sp.) adduces Plato as the model for all
the types of hymns he enumerates.

A more subtle way of viewing Aristides' apparent claim to
novelty is advanced by Behr.[39] He believes that Aristides, in
this prologue, is expressing dissatisfaction with the hymn style
he has so far developed and thus anticipating innovations seem
in *Dionysus*. But this too seems implausible. The disadvantages
of which Aristides complains are the disadvantages of prose *vis-
à-vis* poetry. They are not overcome by stylistic innovation.
Moreover, there are not such clear distinctions of style between
Sarapis and *Dionysus* as this theory would require. The passage
from *Sarapis* I quoted above is as highly rhythmical and poetical as anything in the later speech.

There is however the prologue to *Dionysus*, another programmatic passage, to be taken into account. It is quite short:

> Let Asclepius[40] guide me, he who revealed the dream:
> let Dionysus himself guide me, to whom we are to dance,
> and Apollo the Muses' leader,
> father of the one and brother of the other, as the story goes.
> Perfect hymns and speeches concerning Dionysus
> let us leave to Orpheus and Musaeus
> and the ancient lawgivers,[41]
> ourselves, as a token (as it were) that we are not uninitiated.
> let us address the god with voice proportionate;
> lengths and shortnesses and all things in nature
> are dear to him.
> The dream's command concurs:
> we must be versatile in our speech.

There are several problems in this passage. First, what is
the initiation? Behr and Uerschels,[42] for example, take it as

---

[38] *Heracles* 1 (πολλοὶ γὰρ οἱ καταλογάδην ᾄδοντες τὰ σά, πολλὰ δὲ ποιηταὶ ... ὑμνήκασιν)
echoes Pl. *Symp.* 177 B: εἰ δὲ βούλει αὖ σκέψασθαι τοὺς χρηστοὺς σοφιστάς, Ἡρακλέους μὲν
καὶ ἄλλων ἐπαίνους καταλογάδην συγγράφειν. For *The Aegean Sea*, see below pp. 215–19.

[39] Behr (1968), 21.

[40] Keil is clearly right to delete the first αὐτὸς in this sentence (330, 14 n.).

[41] This refers to the discussion of the use and abuse of wine in Plato's *Laws* 1. 636 E–
650 B, and 2. 666 A.

[42] Uerschels (1962), ad loc.

metaphorical, the initiation into rhetoric. This is indeed a
common metaphor. But Dionysus had his mystery cult; and it is
hard to imagine that there is not also a hint of this. The speaker
will offer a 'token' (σύμβολον) a sign of belonging; he is a
worthy and recognized worshipper. More serious are the difficulties of 'voice proportionate' (συμμέτρῳ τῇ φωνῇ) and
'lengths and shortnesses' (μήκη καὶ βραχύτητες). According to
Uerschels, the voice is 'metrical' and the 'longs and shorts' are
vowel-quantities. Certainly the language admits this: both
Plato[43] and Dionysius[44] use μήκη καὶ βραχύτητες in just this
sense. Uerschels can also point out that 'all things in nature
(ὁτιοῦν ἐν τῇ φύσει) can be taken as underscoring the point
made in Sarapis that the language of prose is more 'natural'
than that of verse, so that its 'longs' and 'shorts' are specially
phenomena of 'nature'. I think this is too ingenious. Behr[45] is
surely right to return to an older view, and translate 'a suitable
address' and 'length and brevity'. Aristides means that *anything*
appropriate will please the god. The speech need not be long.
He is in fact apologizing for a short address—a 'full loving cup'
for the moment, as he says at the end. The model for the thought is
in Isocrates' insistence on συμμετρία, the appropriate scale for
any element in a speech.[46]

5

This is in fact the shortest of the hymns. It does however illustrate the tone and style of the genre very well, and accordingly
I offer a translation with some explanations and an analysis of
the rhetorical framework. Place and date are uncertain: Behr[47]
says Pergamum, 145–7; Uerschels[48] thought Smyrna, where
Dionysus was important and the cult-name *Briseus* (5) is
attested.[49]

[43] Pl. *Rep.* 400 B: οἶμαι δέ με ἀκηκοέναι οὐ σαφῶς ἐνόπλιόν τε τινα ὀνομάζοντος αὐτοῦ
ξύνθετον καὶ δάκτυλον καὶ ἡρῷόν γε, οὐκ οἶδ᾽ ὅπως διακοσμοῦντος καὶ ἴσον ἄνω καὶ κάτω
τιθέντος . . . μήκη δὲ καὶ βραχύτητας προσῆπτε.
[44] Dion. Hal. *De comp. verb.* 15: περὶ τὰ μήκη καὶ τὰς βραχύτητας.
[45] Behr (1981), 245.
[46] Isocr. *Panath.* 33: ἔξω . . . τῆς συμμετρίας τῆς συντεταγμένης τοῖς προοιμίοις.
[47] Behr (1981), 419.
[48] Uerschels (1962).
[49] Nilsson (1950), 341: Dionysus Briseus was associated with drama and music.

(i) *The first theme is the birth; the special circumstances make this a particularly important section, and it is clearly marked out, more so than in the other hymns.* (331. 1–7 K)

> Zeus lies with Semele;
> and when Semele was with child,
> Zeus, wishing to be both to Dionysus—
> both father and mother—
> sent Semele from earth to Olympus in fire
> and himself taking up his child
> stitched him into his thigh
> and carried him ten months
> dwelling at first in Nysa beyond Ethiopia;[50]
> and, when the time came,
> he summoned the Nymphs and undid the stitching;
> and so Dionysus was born,
> his father's child on both sides.

(ii) *Second comes the theme of the special honour given by Zeus in consequence of the miraculous birth* (331. 7–12 K). *Dionysus, we are told here, is 'unique'; but much the same could be said of Athena, and Aristides does say that in his hymn to that goddess* (Or. 37. 2).

> And so Zeus honoured him especially above all gods and men;[51]
> for neither he nor any other
> stood in both these relationships to any being.
> The God, therefore, so they say,[52] is both male and female,[53]
> because his father partook of both natures to bring him to birth.

(iii) *Zeus and Dionysus are the same.* (331. 13–14 K) *This is a syncretistic identification found in cult, but made by Aristides also about other gods* (Asclepius 4, Sarapis 21); *in all these passages, Aristides expresses the identification not as his own, but as the tradition of others.*

> I have heard some tell another tale about this,
> that Dionysus is Zeus himself.
> What greater thing could be said?

---

[50] Reading ὑπὲρ Αἰθιοπίαν or ὑπὲρ Αἰθίοπας for the manuscripts' Αἰθιοπίας, which is the wrong case for this sense of ὑπέρ. Cf. Hdt. 2. 146.

[51] Cf. Plato *Symp.* 180 A: οἱ θεοὶ διαφερόντως αὐτὸν ἐτίμησαν.

[52] Cf. the *Rhet.* attributed to Aristides (ii. 125 Spengel): one should say περὶ τῶν μυθικῶν οὐχ ὅτι ἐγένετο ἀλλ' ὅτι λέγεται γενέσθαι. This habit of claiming vague authority, and at the same time disowning personal belief, goes back at least to Plato: *Meno* 81 A, *Gorg.* 493 A, which seem to be alluded to also in the following section ('I have heard...').

[53] The topic of the bisexual god again recalls Plato, *Symp.* 190 B (of the moon).

(iv) *Opposite qualities are combined in Dionysus, as a corollary of his bisexual nature.* (331. 13–17 K)

> In his shape too he resembles his nature,
> for he is as it were in every way his own twin;
> he is counted among the boys and among the girls;
> and, as a male,
> he is both beardless and Briseus,
> warlike and peaceful.[54]

(v) *The next topic, association with other gods and humans (cf. Alexander Numeniu 339. 5 W) is developed at great length, and makes the framework of the hymn down to 333, 12 K. There are nine subdivisions: relations with Pan (331. 17–19), Hera (331. 19–332. 3), the Sileni (332. 3–10), the Bacchae (332. 10–16), Aphrodite (332. 16–18), Ares, Athena, and Hephaestus (332. 18–20), the Eleusinian goddesses (332. 20–333. 4), the Nymphs (333. 4–8) and finally Eros, who is wholly dependent on Dionysus (333. 9–12). These subdivisions are very unequal in length and treatment, and Aristides is anxious to avoid monotony or predictability.*

> They make Pan his dancing votary,
> Pan the most complete of gods,
> as Pindar says and the Egyptian priests know.[55]

> They say too that he alone of the gods
> reconciled Hera to her son,
> bringing Hephaestus unwillingly to heaven
> and setting him upon an ass.[56]
> That there is a riddle in the tale is plain,
> plain too is whither the riddle tends;[57]
> it shows that the power of the god is great and invincible,
> and could give wings not only to horses[58] but to an ass
> —as the Spartan poet said of him
> that he milked lions.[59]

---

[54] This combination of qualities is again part of the traditional picture of Dionysus: e.g. Eur. *Ba.* 861, Hor. *Odes,* 2. 19. 27.

[55] Pan is 'complete' because he is 'all', τὸ πᾶν: cf. Cornutus 27 (p. 49. 4 Lang): τοῦτον εἶναι καὶ τὸν Πᾶνα, ἐπειδὴ τῷ παντὶ ὁ αὐτός ἐστι. The reference to Pindar is fr. 114 Turyn = 99 Snell. The Egyptian priests are perhaps those of Hdt. 2. 145, who believed Pan to be the oldest of gods.

[56] Aristides omits the detail that Dionysus made Hephaestus drunk in order to bring him home.

[57] οἷ τελευτᾷ: cf. Pl. *Symp.* 181 E.

[58] The implication is that he is more powerful than Poseidon, father of the winged horse Pegasus.

[59] Alcman fr. 56 Page.

Nothing shall be bound so firmly
by disease, by anger, or by any misfortune,
that Dionysus cannot set it free.
Former enemies shall be fellow drinkers,
old men shall be young again
and sport at the god's bidding.[60]

Witness to this are the Sileni who dance around him;[61]
witness to the ease of his power
are wand for spear,
fawnskin for lionskin,
and cup for hollow shield,
as though for Dionysus it was the same to fight as to drink,
and there is not much interval between his battle and his triumph.

They say he subdued Indians and Tyrrhenians;[62]
I think this riddle means, by Tyrrhenians, the West,
and by the others the eastern regions of the earth;
for Dionysus rules it all.

The Bacchanals who go before him
in place of cavalry and archers
and the attendant gear of which I spoke just now[63]
give assurance also
that armies of women as well as men
were part of Dionysus' order;
it is not so much making men into women
as putting women in men's place
that makes the Dionysiac spirit.
So great, so versatile, so universal in harmony is he![64]

---

[60] These actions are 'liberating' and Aristides passes into a description of the 'liberating' effects of Dionysus 'Lyaeus' as the wine-god. He specifies disease, anger and misfortune: cf. Plato, *Laws*, 672 D: φάρμακον ... αἰδοῦς μὲν ψυχῆς κτήσεως ἕνεκα δεδόσθαι, σώματος δὲ ὑγιείας τε καὶ ἰσχύος. Wine rejuvenates—as in Eur. *Ba.* 188 ff., and again in *Laws* 666 B: ἢν τοῖς ἀνθρώποις ἐπίκουρον τῆς τοῦ γήρως αὐστηρότητος ἐδωρήσατο τὸν οἶνον φάρμακον, ὥστε ἀνηβᾶν ἡμᾶς.

[61] The old Sileni are an instance of his power to rejuvenate.

[62] Presumably referring to Dionysus' outwitting and destroying the Tyrrhenian pirates who kidnapped him (*H. Hom. Dion.*, Ovid *Met.* 3. 582–691, etc.). In Philostr. *Imag.* 1. 19, there is a naval battle between a Tyrrhenian ship and the sacred ship of Dionysus and the Maenads; so also Lucian *Dial. Mar.* 5. 1 makes a dolphin (i.e. a former Tyrrhenian pirate) say that Dionysus ἡμᾶς καταναυμαχήσας καὶ μετέβαλε, δέον χειρώσασθαι μόνον ὥσπερ τοὺς ἄλλους ὑπηγάγετο.

[63] i.e. the wand, fawnskin, and cup.

[64] παναρμονίους: the word comes from Pl. *Phdr.* 277 E: ποικίλη μὲν ποικίλους ψυχῇ καὶ παναρμονίους διδοὺς λόγους, ἁπλοῦς δὲ ἁπλῇ. Dionysus can play all tunes and affect all souls.

We see this also in another way:
he works with Aphrodite
to open theatres[65]
and be the leader of banquets and revels;
fiery too is he
when he joins Athena and Hephaestus,[66]
The Heralds and the Eumolpidae[67]
set him beside the goddesses of Eleusis,
as overseer of crops and food for man.

And here I must add
that he alone of divine apparitions
stalked abroad in the Median danger;
so humane he is to all, though it is to the Greeks that he inclines.[68]

And mingling with the Nymphs
he has danced, and still dances, [69] many and various dances among
    men,
seizing them in their inner being, more firmly than Eurycles[70]
and makes a man a dancer
'though he were unmusical before';[71]
he leaps and plays and wants to sing
even from his couch or chair.[72]

This god can do all things.
The marvellous tyrant of mankind,[73] Eros,
drew from Dionysus' springs,
and visits the whole earth

[65] Dionysus and Aphrodite are the divinities who are Aristophanes' patrons in Pl. *Symp.* 177 E. In 'open theatres' Aristides makes a brief reference to the aspect of Dionysus' worship that would be most familiar to his hearers—his association with the guilds of performers, οἱ περὶ τὸν Διόνυσον τεχνῖται.

[66] In calling Dionysus ἔμπυρος, Aristides links him with the divinities who are patrons of ἔμπυροι τέχναι, arts involving the use of fire.

[67] i.e. the hereditary priestly families responsible for the Eleusinian cult.

[68] See Hdt. 8. 65, Plu. *Them.* 15. The story is meant to show Dionysus' uniqueness, his φιλανθρωπία (cf. *Athena*, 10, *Asclepius*, 18, etc.) and his philhellenism. Aristid. uses it very similarly in *Panath.* 320: ὁ μὲν Ἴακχος ἐξεφοίτησεν καὶ μετέσχεν τῶν δρωμένων καὶ νέφη παρὰ ταῖν θεαῖν εἰς τὴν ναυμαχίαν ἐγκατέσκηψεν καὶ θεοὶ καὶ ἥρωες οἱ κοινοὶ τῶν Ἑλλήνων σύμμαχοι συνηγωνίσαντο.

[69] ἐχόρευσεν τε καὶ χορεύει: a favourite figure with Aristid., cf. *Athena*, 13, διεῖλέν τε καὶ διαιρεῖ.

[70] Eurycles, the 'ventriloquist' daemon that speaks from the belly from other people, was known from Ar., *Wasps* 1018 ff, Pl. *Sophist*, 252 c, and perhaps other classical sources.

[71] κἂν ἄμουσος ᾖ τὸ πρίν: from Eur. *Stheneboea*, but probably best known from Plato's quotation, *Symp.* 196 E. It is a very hackneyed phrase.

[72] i.e. even a sick man gets up to dance.

[73] Cf. Eur. *Hipp.* 538.

under Dionysus' guidance;
without him,[74] he has no place, no action, and no bed.

(vi) *Dionysus' activity is universal and unremitting.* (333. 12–17)

He oversees the limits of night and day,
the one by being torchbearer and guide of sight himself,
the other by entrusting it to others;[75]
Yet even then he is not idle,
but passes his time always in movement and activity.
He is both the oldest of gods and the youngest[76]
and a lover of every passing hour and happening.

(vii) *Final greeting and conclusion.* (333. 17–19)

Hail to Iacchus, under all his many names;[77]
the cup of friendship is for the moment full.

6

To set against this 'hymnic' and 'poetical' piece, I take the
speech of thanks to *The Aegean Sea*, also short, also of uncertain
occasion. Boulanger[78] took it as an early work, between 142
and 146, before Aristides was ill; he was at Delos in 144, and
Delos seems a likely setting. Behr, on the other hand, associates
it with the crossing of the Aegean made in 155, when Aristides
was to deliver his *Panathenaicus* in Athens. It certainly has much
in common with the *Panathenaicus*.

(i) *Prologue: literary antecedents, occasion, plan of speech.* (347. 8–17)

But[79] no one has yet properly sung the praises of the sea, neither poet
nor prosewriter. Homer tells us of the 'violet sea', the 'wine-dark sea',

---

[74] τούτου χωρίς: a typical trait of hymns—without the god, nothing can be done:
Aesch. *Ag.* 1448: τί γὰρ βροτοῖς ἄνευ Διὸς τελεῖται; In general, see Norden (1913), pp.
157 n. 3, 159 n. 1.

[75] ἡμέραν (333. 13) and νύκτα (333. 14) are rightly deleted as wrong glosses. Dionysus is a god of the night—he has torchlight festivals, and the mysteries are nocturnal.
But his worship goes on night and day: Eur. *Ba.* 187, 237, 424, 1008.

[76] In Pl. *Symp.* 195 B Eros is young, ibid. 178 Eros is old; Dionysus combines both.

[77] Cf. Men. Rhet. iii. 445. 25 Sp. μέλλων δὲ πληροῦν τὴν ὑπόθεσιν χρήσῃ ἀνακλητικοῖς
ὀνόμασι τοῦ θεοῦ. Ov. *Met.* 4. 16 'plurima … nomina, Liber, habes'.

[78] Boulanger (1923), 161; Behr (1968), 87.

[79] πέλαγος δέ …: for δέ in the first sentence (perhaps just a literary device, not necessarily implying a missing prelude) cf. *Or.* 39. 1. Xen. (*Conv., Oecon., Apol., Lac. Resp.*)
begins on some occasions with connections which seem to imply something just said.

and the 'purple brine'.[80] Others say similar things: but in general the poets speak ill of the sea. They call it 'brackish' or 'roaring',[81] or something like that. I shall leave for the moment what can be said in praise of the sea as a whole, the greatness and quality of its usefulness to mankind and the purposes for which God made it. Instead, I shall simply pay my debt to the Aegean and sing its praises, beginning with the excellence of its situation, just as, in the case of a city, one would begin by praising its situation.[82]

(ii) *The central position of the Aegean; its ideal climate.* (347. 18–348. 17)

It is set in the very centre of the inhabited world and of the sea. To the north it leaves the Hellespont, the Propontis, and the Euxine; to the south, the rest of the sea. It separates Asia from Europe at the point where the two first part company after the Hellespont. On both its shores it has nations of great fame and civilization, Ionia and Aeolis on one side, Hellas on the other. It is the only sea that can properly be said to be within the confines of Hellas, if one thinks of a single Hellenic race on both continents. If banks of rivers earn fame for their trees and meadows, it is indeed right that the shores of the Aegean should be famous, adorned as they are by such nations, and with Hellenes as their very neighbours—though it is the moderateness of the climate, consistently tolerable in all seasons, that is the special feature of the Aegean and the settled quality of these countries.[83] This can be proved by both sides in the argument: those who say that Attica lies under the fairest part of the heavens and those who say the same of Ionia inevitably agree that the best conditions anyway exist in this region. As the Aegean extends along both shores, it owns whichever of them one thinks the better; and if it were necessary, as in other disputes, to make mutual concessions and come to a compromise, then the Aegean is the answer. It is the Aegean that enjoys the finest climate.

(iii) *Advantages of nature: variety and ease of passage.* (348. 18–349. 28) (*This section seems to merge* (349. 10 ff.) *into the topic of divine favour; which Aristides combines with all the points he makes in the last part of the speech.*)

---

[80] *Il.* 11. 298, 23. 316, 16. 391; Eur. *Tr.* 1.

[81] Ar. *Clouds* 284, Bacch. 17. 76.

[82] On 'situation' or 'position' (θέσις) as an *encomium*-topic, see Men. Rhet. iii. 346–7 Sp. and 383 Sp. with Russell–Wilson (1981), 250, 288–9.

[83] The claims of Ionia and Attica to a perfect climate go back to classical literature: Hdt. 1. 142 and Hippocr. *Air Waters Places*, 12 are for Ionia, Pl. *Tim.* 24 c and Xen. *Poroi*, 1 praise: the climate of Attica.

Such then is its position, such the region of the world in which it lies. Its nature too is a cause of wonder. Its size makes it among the most famous of seas and most extensive, if you look at it every way from one end to the other. It would take an untold number of days to circumnavigate the Aegean. Yet it is no bare expanse, it does not lead the eye into infinite distance and cause depression and despair. There are many seas in the Aegean and many bays, and the sea looks different in different places. You can break your journey in the middle of the sea and find land, cities, and countryside, like so many sea-girt continents. You can plan your voyage for yourself; you can turn back before crossing the whole sea, having accomplished your purpose just the same. This is not at all like Homer's sea;[84] there is no need to cross an empty waste before landing on some inhabited spot, so that the loneliness of it all makes the journey pleasing to no god. No; here

> the Nereids' dances
> spiral their fairest tread[85]

because this is the most populous and flourishing part of the sea. You can sail as far as you like, and go on foot wherever you prefer not to sail round, but cross to the other coast and take to the sea from there.[86] This is the only sea which is as populous as land; it has cities in it at intervals, just as cities on the mainland are separated by intervening stretches of country. The sudden moods of the sea and the distances of the journey make the Aegean terrifying, but the rests on the way make it friendly. No sea is quicker stirred, but no sea saves life so readily. In this it is truer than any other to its divine nature; for the divine should be terrible in its strength but saving in its gentleness.

(iv) *The beauty of the sounds and sights of the Aegean and its islands.*
(349. 23–351. 5)

Its sound too, as it laps against its gifts and its children, is sweeter than that of any other sea. It is a sound such as the poets say Pans and Satyrs make in the mountains and trees as they enjoy the summer season. This is because it has as its citizens and inhabitants the most musical of the gods, Apollo and Artemis, whom Zeus the father of all brought into being here, because it is the most beautiful place in the world, to be perfect in music. He brought Leto past two or three other islands[87] to Delos, in the very centre of the Aegean, giving her Athena

---

[84] Cf. *Od.* 3. 270, 12. 351.

[85] Eur. *Tr.* 2–3.

[86] I follow Canter's 'atque ad aliud progrediens litus inde solvere'.

[87] *Panath.* 13, ἐπιβᾶσα τῶν νήσων εἰς Δῆλον καταίρει. It is not clear whether Aristides means by 'three other islands' the stages listed by Call. *Hymn* 4. 153 ff—Echinades, Corcyra, Cos—because he seems rather to be thinking of the Aegean itself.

to guide her on her way. The musical genius of the sea is plain to all, from the very fact that in the beginning it gave rise, as it were, to another choir of many islands which pattern the deep, bending towards one another and offering to sailors and passengers a vision more holy than any circle of dithyrambic dancers,[88] giving us also both comfort in danger and delight if the voyage goes as it should. Every island is both outside the circle and within it. They are like the fleet of boats going out to fish that toss on the water in the summer, before the west wind sets in. As you proceed, the view ahead and astern, and on both quarters, always ends in an island, so that at first you are at a loss to know which way to steer. These islands are what lifeboats are to sailors caught in a storm. They seem to come to meet you, stretching out a hand and calling you to them.[89] Such are the ingenuities of the Aegean—a mingling of land and sea, like the confusion of colours and rings on dappled deer or spotted leopards. And the whole sea here shines brilliantly; neither the flowery meadows of the mainlands nor anything else one might think of approach this beauty and diversity. And naturally so: all the beauties of the mainland are here, in these lands in the midst of the sea, but the mainlands do not have its beauty themselves. The islands adorn the Aegean as the stars adorn the sky. A man with no need to go to sea might well choose to do so simply to travel across the Aegean; it is so much the most beautiful of seas and of all things on earth. So beauty is the hallmark of the Aegean. It begins, in effect, where the islands begin, after you have crossed the open sea.

(v) *It is not only beautiful, but useful.* (35. 5–15)

Only the Aegean can never be called 'unharvested'.[90] It is not bare or unfruitful, but marvellously fertile in wine and corn and all the seasons bring, rich too in fish and game, as Homer says the sea of the happy should be,[91] providing all needs, all pleasures, and all spectacles, full of harbours, full of shrines, full of flutes and paeans, springs, and rivers, nurse of Dionysus,[92] and beloved of the Heavenly Twins and of the Nymphs. It gives a happy life to all who dwell and

---

[88] Cf. *Panath.* 11 of the Cyclades and Sporades χοροῦ σχῆμα σώζουσαι.

[89] Cf. *Panath.* 10 of Attica: πρώτη τοῖς ἐκ τοῦ πελάγους ὡσπερεὶ χεῖρα προτείνουσα εἰς ὑποδοχήν...

[90] e.g. *Il.* 1. 316, 327.

[91] In *Od.* 19. 109 ff. Odysseus relates the blessings that come from a good king: they include a sea abounding in fish.

[92] Behr (1981), 419, refers to Apoll. *Bibl.* 3. 5. 1 for the story that Dionysus took refuge with Thetis from his persecutor Lycurgus, and to Pausan. 3. 24. 3, where a local legend has Semele and Dionysus locked in a chest by Cadmus and thrown into the sea. But the reference remains obscure.

traffic on it, bringing profit and salvation to all on whom it sheds its favour.

(vi) *It is beautiful from end to end.* (351. 15–21)

As in beautiful bodies beginnings and ends are seemly, so in this sea and this alone both beginning and end give pleasure. It begins with the first row of islands to the south, and it ends at the Hellespont, which it flows round to form the glorious Chersonese. So, as the saying goes, its beauty runs 'from head to foot'. As to its inlets and bays, none can tell their number or their beauty.

(vii) *It carries men back and forth for festivals and to view the splendours of Greece.* (351. 23–352. 3)

All fear the Aegean, yet all long to cross it a second time, for people make this crossing for the pleasantest of reasons. The festivals, the mysteries, the beauties of Hellas fill this sea with ships. This sea brings together lovers of beauty and men of worth, provides spectacles of the greatest delight, and serves the most splendid gods in ways most beautiful.

(viii) *Closing prayer.* (352. 4–5)

Aegean, beloved saviour, let this be the song my music has sung for you. Take pleasure in it, I pray, and keep me and my fellow travellers for ever safe.

Let us leave Aristides here, on Delos or wherever he is. Though the thoughts of this piece are for the most part commonplace, and the rhetorical skeleton shows through so starkly, we sense also his pleasure in the sea and the islands, and can savour his picture of the fishing boats setting out. He never saw the Aegean, as we can see it in this century, from the air; but his picture of the gleaming waters and the dances and chains of islands almost makes one think he anticipated that vision also.

BIBLIOGRAPHY

(This list excludes most editions of ancient authors, though some special commentaries are included.)

ADLER, A. (1922), 'Kyknos (4)', *RE* xi 2: 244–2.

AMANN, J. (1931), *Die Zeusrede des Ailios Aristides* (Tübinger Beiträge, 12; Stuttgart).

AMELING, W. (1983), *Herodes Atticus* (2 vols.; Hildesheim, Zurich, and New York).

ANDERSON, G. (1976a), *Lucian: Theme and Variation in the Second Sophistic* (Leiden).

—— (1976b), 'Some Alleged Relationships in Lucian's Opuscula', *AJP* 97: 262–75.

—— (1977a), 'Lucian and the Authorship of *De saltatione*'. *GRBS* 18: 275–86.

—— (1977b), 'Patterns in Lucian's Prolaliae', *Philologus*, 121: 313–15.

—— (1982), 'Lucian: A Sophist's Sophist', *YCS* 27: 61–92.

—— (1984), *Ancient Fiction: The Novel in the Graeco-Roman World* (London and Sydney).

—— 1986), *Philostratus: Biography and Belles-letters in the Third Century A.D.* (London and Dover, N.H.).

—— (forthcoming) 'The *Pepaideumenos* in Action', *ANRW* II. xxxiii 1.

ARMAYOR, O. K. (1978), 'Did Herodotus Ever Go to Egypt?', *JARCE* 15: 59–73.

ARNIM, H. VON (1898), *Leben und Werke des Dion von Prusa* (Berlin).

—— (1913), *Supplementum Euripideum* (Kleine Texte, 112; Bonn).

ARNOTT, W. G. (1964), "Notes on *gauia* and *mergus* in Latin Authors', *CQ* 14: 249–62.

BALDWIN, B. (1973), *Studies in Lucian* (Toronto).

—— (1975), 'The Epigrams of Lucian', *Phoenix*, 29: 311–35.

BARDON, H. (1956), *La Littérature latine inconnue*, ii. *L'Epoque impériale* (Paris).

BARIGAZZI, A. (ed.) (1966), *Favorino di Arelate: Opere* (Florence).

BAR-KOCHVA, B. (1973), 'On the Sources and Chronology of Antiochus I's Battle against the Galatians'. *PCPS* 19: 1–8.

BARNES, T. D. (1971) *Tertullian: A Historical and Literary Study* (Oxford; second edn. 1985).

BEAN, G. E. (1965), *Inscriptions of Side* (Ankara).

BEHR, C. A. (1968), *Aristides and the Sacred Tales* (Amsterdam).

BEHR, C. A. (1981), *Aelius Aristides: The Complete Works*, ii. *Orations* xvii–liii (Leiden).

BENOÎT, F. (1952), 'L'Ogmios de Lucien et Hercule Psychopompe', in G. Moro (ed.), *Beiträge zur älteren europäischen Kulturgeschichte: Festschrift für Rudolf Egger*, i (Klagenfurt), 144–58.

BERNAND, A. and E. (1960), *Les Inscriptions du colosse de Memnon* (Paris).

BERNAYS, U. (1905), *Studien zu Dionysius Periegetes* (Heidelberg).

BIEBER, M. (1911), 'Die Medaillons am Konstantinsbogen', *Römische Mitteilungen*, 26: 214–37.

BLÜMNER, H. (1866), *De locis Luciani artem spectantibus* (diss. Berlin).

—— (1867), *Archäologische Studien zu Lukian* (Breslau).

BOMPAIRE, J. (1958), *Lucien écrivain: Imitation et création* (Bibliothèque des écoles françaises d'Athènes et de Rome, 190; Paris).

BOULANGER, A. (1923) *Aelius Aristide* (Bibliothèque des écoles françaises d'Athènes et de Rome, 126; Paris).

BOWERSOCK, G. W. (1969), *Greek Sophists in the Roman Empire* (Oxford).

—— (ed.) (1974), *Approaches to the Second Sophistic: Papers Presented at the 105th Annual Meeting of the American Philological Association* (University Park, Pennsylvania).

—— (1985), 'The Literature of the Empire: 2. Poetry', in *CHCL* i (Cambridge), 649–54.

BOWIE, E. L. (1970), 'Greeks and Their Past in the Second Sophistic', *Past and Present*, 46: 3–41; revised in M. I. Finley (ed.), *Studies in Ancient Society*. (London and Boston, 1974), 166–209.

—— (1982), 'The Importance of Sophists', *YCS* 27: 29–59.

—— (forthcoming), 'Poetry and Poets in Asia and Achaea', in S. Walker and A. Cameron (eds.), *The Greek Renaissance in the Roman Empire* (Paper from the 10th British Museum Classical Colloquium; *BICS*, suppl. 55, London).

—— (forthcoming), 'Greek Sophists and Greek Poetry in the Second Sophistic', *ANRW* ii. xxxiii/1 209–58.

BOYANCÉ, P. (1952), 'La Religion astrale de Platon à Cicéron', *REG* 65: 312–50.

—— (1963), 'Sur l'exégèse hellénistique du Phèdre' in *Miscellanea di studi Alessandrini in memoria di A. Rostagni* (Turin), 45–53.

BRANDSTÄTTER, C. (1894), *De notionum πολιτικός et σοφιστής usu rhetorico* (Leipziger Studien zur klassischen Philologie, 15).

BRANHAM, R. B. (1985), 'Introducing a Sophist: Lucian's Prologues', *TAPA* 115: 237–43.

BROWN, T. S. (1949), *Onesicritus; A Study in Hellenistic Historiography* (Berkeley and Los Angeles).

BRUNN, H. (1859), *Geschichte der griechischen Künstler* (Stuttgart).

BRUNT, P. A. (1979), 'Cicero and Historiography', in *Miscellanea di studi classici in onore di Eugenio Manni*, i (Rome), 311–40.

BUCHHEIT, V. (1962), *Studien zum* corpus Priapeorum (*Zetemata*, 28; Munich).

BURCK, E. (1934), *Die Erzählungskunst des T. Livius* (Berlin).

BUTTERWORTH, G. (1916), 'Clement of Alexandria's *Protrepticus* and the *Phaedrus* of Plato', *CQ* 10: 198–205.

CAMERON, ALAN (1982), 'Strato and Rufinus', *CQ* 32: 162–73.

CARNEY, T. F. (1960), 'Plutarch's Style in the *Marius*', *JHS* 80: 24–31.

CASTER, M. (1937), *Lucien et la pensée religieuse de son temps* (Paris).

CHAMPLIN, E. (1980), *Fronto and Antonine Rome* (Cambridge, Mass., and London).

CHRISTIAN, J. (1984), 'Dédale géographe: Regard et voyages aériens en Grèce', *LALIES* 3: 147–64.

CLARKE, W. M. (1976), 'The Manuscript of Strato's *Musa Puerilis*', *GRBS* 4: 382–4.

—— (1984), 'Observations on the Date of Straton of Sardis', *CP* 79: 214–20.

CLAUSEN, W. V. (ed.) (1956), *A. Persi Flacci Saturarum Liber: Accedit vita* (Oxford).

COLEMAN, K. M. (ed.) (1988), *Statius:* Silvae, *Book iv* (Oxford).

COLONNA, A. (1957), 'Dionysii Periegetae Vita Chisiana', *Bollettino del Comitato per la preparazione di edizioni nazionale dei classici,* 5: 9–12.

CORNELL, T. J. (1986), 'The Formation of the Historical Tradition of Early Rome', in I. S. Moxon, J. D. Smart, and A. J. Woodman (edd.), *Past Perspectives: Studies in Greek and Roman Historical Writing* (Cambridge) 67–86.

COUNILLON, P. (1981), 'Un autre acrostiche dans la périégèse de Denys', *REG* 94: 514–22.

CURTIUS, E. R. (1953), *European Literature and the Latin Middle Ages,* trans. W. Trask (London).

DANIÉLOU, J. (1973), *A History of Early Christian Doctrine before the Council of Nicaea,* ii. *Gospel Message and Hellenistic Culture,* trans. J. A. Baker (London).

DAVIS, K. S. (1973), *FDR: The Beckoning of Destiny, 1882–1928* (New York).

DESIDERI, P. (1978), *Dione di Prusa: Un intellettuale greco nell'impero roman* (Messina).

DILLON, J. (1971), 'Harpocration's *Commentary on Plato*: Fragments of a Middle Platonic Commentary', *California Studies in Classical Antiquity,* 4: 125–46.

DODDS, E. R. (1965), *Pagan and Christian in an Age of Anxiety* (Cambridge).

DOVER, K. J. (1981), *A Historical Commentary on Thucydides V*, with A. W. Gomme and A. Andrewes (Oxford).

EDWARDS, M. J. (1987), '*Locus Horridus* and *Locus Amoenus*', in M. Whitby, P. Hardie, and M. Whitby (edd.), *Homo Viator: Classical Essays for John Bramble* (Bristol), 267–76.

EFFE, B. (1977), *Dichtung und Lehre* (*Zetemata*, 69; Munich).

EGGER, R. (1943), 'Aus der Unterwelt der Festlandskelten', *Wiener Jahreshefte*, 35: 99–137; reprinted in Artur Betz and Gotbert Moro (edd.), *Römische Antike und frühes Christentum*, i (Klagenfurt, 1967), 272–311.

EISENHUT, W. (ed.) (1955), *Dictys Cretensis: Accedit papyrus Dictyis graeci ad Tebtunim inventa* (Leipzig).

ERIKSON, E. (1958), *Young Man Luther* (New York).

FAIRWEATHER, J. (1981), *Seneca the Elder* (Cambridge).

—— (1983), 'Traditional Narrative, Inference and Truth in the *Lives* of the Greek Poets, *PLLS* 4: 315–69.

FEHLING, D. (1971), *Die Quellenangaben bei Herodot* (Berlin).

FERRARI, G. R. F. (1987), *Listening to the Cicadas: A Study of Plato's Phaedrus* (Cambridge).

FINLEY, M. I. (1985), *Ancient History: Evidence and Models* (London).

FLIEDNER, H. (1974), *Amor and Cupido: Untersuchungen über den römischen Liebesgott* (Beitrage zur klassischen Philologie, 53; Meisenheim am Glan).

FOERSTER, R. (1886), *Lucian in der Renaissance* (Kiel).

FOGEL, R. W., and ELTON, G. R. (1983), *Which Road to the Past? Two Views of History* (New Haven).

FOLLET, S. (1968), 'Hadrien en Egypte et en Judée'. *Rev. Phil.* 42: 53–77.

FRASER, P. M. (1959), 'An Agonistic Dedication from Roman Egypt' *JEA* 45: 79–80.

FRÈRE, H., and IZAAC, H. J. (1943–4), *Stace:* Silves (Paris).

FRIEDLÄNDER, P. (1912), *Johannes von Gaza und Paulus Silentiarius: Kunstbeschreibungen justinianischen Zeit* (Leipzig).

GAMBERINI, F. (1983), *Stylistic Theory and Practice in the Younger Pliny* (Hildesheim).

GARNETT, R. (1895), 'On the Date of the Ἀποτελεσματικά of Manetho', *J. Phil.* 23: 238–40.

GARZYA, A. (1955–7), 'Paraphrasis Dionysii poematis de aucupio'. *Byzantion*, 25–7: 195–240.

—— (1957), 'Due Note: I', *GIF* 10: 156–60.

GEIGER, J. (1979), 'Munatius Rufus and Thrasea Paetus on Cato the Younger', *Athenaeum*, 57: 48–72.

—— (1985), *Cornelius Nepos and Ancient Political Biography* (*Historia* Einzelschriften, 47; Stuttgart).

GIGLI, D. (1975), 'Teori e prassi metrica negli inni a Sarapide e Dioniso', *Prometheus*, 1: 237–65.

GOMME, A. W. (1945), *A Historical Commentary on Thucydides I* (Oxford).

GOODYEAR, F. R. D. (1972), *The Annals of Tacitus*, i (Cambridge).

—— (1981), *The Annals of Tacitus*, ii (Cambridge).

GOW, A. S. F., and PAGE, D. L. (1965), *The Greek Anthology: Hellenistic Epigrams* (Cambridge).

—— (1968), *The Greek Anthology: The Garland of Philip* (Cambridge).

GRAINDOR, P. (1930), *Un milliardaire antique: Hérode Atticus et sa famille* (Cairo).

GRIMAL, P. (ed.) (1963), *Apulei Metamorphoses iv 28–vi 24* (*Le Conte d'Amour et Psyché*) (Paris).

HABICHT, C. (1969), *Die Inschriften des Asklepieions* (= *Altertümer von Pergamon, viii/3*: Berlin).

—— (1985), *Pausanias' Guide to Ancient Greece* (Berkeley, Los Angeles, and London).

HADOT, I. (1984), *Arts libéraux et philosophie dans la pensée antique* (Paris).

HAFNER, G. (1958), 'Herakles–Geras–Ogmios', *Jahrbuch des römisch-germanischen Zentralmuseums, Mainz*, 5: 131–53.

MAINES, C. R. (1955), *The Correspondence of M. Cornelius Fronto* (2 vols.; London and Cambridge, Mass.).

HALL, JENNIFER (1981), *Lucian's Satire* (New York).

HAMILTON, J. R. (1969), *Plutarch, Alexander: A Commentary* (Oxford).

HARDIE, A. (1983), *Statius and his Silvae* (Liverpool).

HEITSCH, E. (1961), *Die griechischen Dichterfragmente der römischen Kaiserzeit* i (Göttingen).

—— (1963), 'Ueberlieferungsgeschichtliche Untersuchungen zu Andromachos, Markellos von Side, und zu Carmen de viribus herbarum', *NGAW* 1963/2: 23–50.

—— (1964), *Die griechischen Dichterfragmente der römischen Kaiserzeit* ii (Göttingen).

HELDMANN, K. (1982), *Antike Theorien über Entwicklung und Verfall der Redekunst* (*Zetemata*, 77; Munich).

HELM, R. (1906), *Lucian und Menipp* (Leipzig–Berlin).

—— (1914), 'Das "Märchen" von Amor und Psyche', *Neue Jahrbücher für das klassische Altertum*, 33: 170–209 (= G. Binder and R. Merkelbach (edd.), *Amor und Psyche* (Wege der Forschung, 126; Darmstadt, 1968), 175–234.)

HELMBOLD, W. C., and O'NEIL, E. N. (1959), *Plutarch's Quotations*

(Philological Monographs of the American Philological Association, 19; Baltimore).

HENIGE, D. (1982), *Oral Historiography* (London, New York, and Lagos).

HENSE, O. (ed.) (1905), *C. Musonii Rufi Reliquiae* (Leipzig).

HINDS, S. (1987), *The Metamorphosis of Persephone: Ovid and the Self-Conscious Muse* (Cambridge).

HOFFA, W. (1912), 'Die Löwenjagd des Kaisers Hadrians', *Römische Mitteilungen*, 27: 97–100.

HÖFLER, A. (1935), *Der Sarapishymnos des Ailios Aristides*, (Tübingen Beiträge, 27; Stuttgart).

HOLFORD-STREVENS, L. (1988), *Aulus Gellius* (London).

HOMEYER, H. (1965), *Lukian: Wie man Geschichte schreiben soll* (Munich).

—— (1967), 'De malignitate Herodoti', *Klio*, 49: 181–7.

HORSFALL, N. M. (1982), 'Allecto and *Natura*: A Pattern of Allusion in Apuleius', *LCM* 7: 41.

HOUGH, G. (1966), *An Essay on Criticism* (London).

HUNTER, R. L. (1983), *A Study of* Daphnis and Chloe (Cambridge).

JACOB, C. (1981), 'L'Oeil et la mémoire: Sur la Périégèse de la terre habitée de Denys', in C. Jacob–F. Lestringant (edd.), *Arts et légendes d'espaces* (Paris), 23–97.

JAHN, O. (1868), 'Cyriacus von Ancona und Albrecht Dürer', in *Aus der Altertumswissenschaft: Populäre Aufsätze* (Bonn), 333–52.

JAMES, PAULA (1987), *Unity in Diversity: A Study of Apuleius' Metamorphoses* (Altertumswissenschaftliche Texte und Studien, 16; Hildesheim–Zurich–New York).

JÖHRENS, G. (1981), *Der Athenahymnus des Ailios Aristides mit einen Anhang zum Höhenkunst der Athena und Testimonia zur allegorischen Deutung der Athena* (Bonn).

JONES, C. P. (1971), *Plutarch and Rome* (Oxford).

—— (1974), 'The Reliability of Philostratus', in G. W. Bowersock (ed.) (1974), *Approaches to the Second Sophistic: Papers Presented at the 105th Annual Meeting of the American Philological Association* (University Park, Pennsylvania), 11–16.

—— (1978), *The Roman World of Dio Chrysostom* (Cambridge, Mass.).

—— (1986), *Culture and Society in Lucian* (Cambridge, Mass., and London).

JONES, R. M. (1926), 'Posidonius and the Flight of the Mind through the Universe'. *CP* 21: 97–113.

KENNEY, E. J. (1977), *Lucretius* (Greece and Rome New Surveys in Classics, 11; Oxford).

—— (1981), review of E. Ackermann, *Lukrez und der Mythos* (1979), *CR* 31: 19–21.

KERFERD, G. B. (1981), *The Sophistic Movement* (Cambridge).

KEYDELL, R. (1941), 'Die griechische Dichtung der Kaiserzeit, 1930–39', in *Bursians Jahrsbericht*, cclxxii A. Thierfelder (ed.) (Leipzig).

KLEINER, D. E. E. (1983), *The Monument of Philopappus* (*Archaeologica*, 30; Rome).

KLOCK, C. (1986), *Untersuchungen zu Stil und Rhythmus bei Gregor von Nyssa* (Beiträge zur klassischen Philologie, 173; Frankfurt-am-Main).

KLOTZ, A. (1909), 'Zu Dionysius Periegetes', *Rh. Mus.* 64: 476–7.

KOEPP, F. (1919), 'Ogmios: Bemerkungen zur gallischen Kunst', *Bonner Jahrbücher*, 125: 38–73.

KOESTERMANN, E. (1956), 'Die Feldzüge des Germanicus, 14–16 n. Chr.' *Historia*, 6: 429–79.

KONIARIS, G. (1983), 'On Maximus of Tyre: Zetemeta II', *Classical Antiquity*, 2: 212–50.

KUHNERT, E. (1909–15), 'Satyros und Silenos', in W. H. Roscher (ed.), *Ausführliches Lexikon der griechischen und römischen Mythologie*, iv (Leipzig), 444–531.

LAMBERT, R. (1984), *Beloved and God* (London).

LAURENS, P. (1965), 'Martial et l'épigramme grecque du 1ᵉʳ siècle après J.-C.', *REL* 43: 315–41.

LEBEK, W. (1973), 'Ein Hymnos auf Antinoos', *ZPE* 12: 101–37.

LEFKOWITZ, M. R. (1981), *The Lives of the Greek Poets* (London).

LENZ, F. W. (1964), *Aristeidesstudien* (Berlin).

LEO, F. (1910), *Die griechisch–römische Biographie nach ihrer literarischen Form* (Leipzig).

LE ROUX, FRANÇOISE (1960), 'Le Dieu celtique aux liens: De l'Ogmios de Lucien à l'Ogmios de Dürer', *Ogam*, 12: 209–34.

LESKY, A. (1966), *A History of Greek Literature*, trans. J. Willis and C. de Heer (London).

—— (1970), 'Ogmios bei Goethe', in Doris Ableitinger and Helmut Gugel (edd.), *Festschrift Karl Vretska* (Heidelberg), 116–20.

LEUE, C. (1884), 'Zeit und Heimat des Periegeten Dionysios', *Philologus*, 42: 175–8.

—— (1925), 'Noch einmal die Akrostichen in der Periegese des Dionysios', *Hermes*, 60: 367–80.

LIEBERG, G. (1962), *Puella divina: Die Gestalt der göttlichen Geliebten bei Catull im Zusammenhang der antiken Dichtung* (Amsterdam).

LIENHARDT, G. (1985), 'Self: Public, Private. Some African representations', in M. Carrithers, S. Collins, and S. Lukes (edd.), *Category of the Person* (Cambridge), 141–55.

LIVADARAS, N. A. (1964), 'Pour le rédaction de l'*Οἰκουμένης Περιήγησις* de Dénys le periégète', in A. Anastasiou, A. Kampylis, and A. Skiadas (edd.), *Χάρις Κωνσταντίνῳ Ι. Βουβέρη*, (Athens), 321–5.

LLOYD, A. B. (1975), *Herodotus, Book ii: Introduction* (Leiden).

MCCALL, M. H. (1969), *Ancient Rhetorical Theories of Simile and Comparison* (Cambridge, Mass.).

MCCARTHY, BARBARA P. (1934), 'Lucian and Menippus', *YCS* 4: 3–58.

MARTIN, J. (1946), 'Ogmios', *Würzburger Jahrbücher*, 1: 359–99.

MATZ, F. (1867), *De Philostratorum in describendis imaginibus fide* (diss. Bonn).

MAULL, I. (1955), 'Hadrians Jagddenkmal', *JOAI*, 42: 53–67.

MAXWELL-STUART, P. G. (1972), 'Strato and the Musa Puerilis'. *Hermes*, 100: 215–40.

MESK, J. (1927), 'Zu den prosa- und vershymnen des Aelius Aristides'. in *Raccolta di scritti in onore di F. Ramorino* (Milan), 660–72.

MILLAR, F. (1964), *A Study of Cassius Dio* (Oxford).

MITFORD, T. B. (1971), *The Inscriptions of Kourion* (Memoirs of the American Philosophical Society, 83; Philadelphia).

MOLES, J. L. (1978), 'The Career and Conversion of Dio Chrysostom', *JHS* 98: 79–100.

MOMIGLIANO, A. (1971), *The Development of Greek Biography* (Cambridge, Mass.).

—— (1978), 'Greek Historiography', *History and Theory*, 17: 1–28.

—— (1981), 'The Rhetoric of History and the History of Rhetoric: On Hayden White's Tropes', in E. S. Shaffer (ed.), *Comparative Criticism*, iii (Cambridge), 259–68.

—— (1985), 'Marcel Mauss and the Quest for the Person in Greek Biography and Autobiography', in M. Carrithers, S. Collins, and S. Lukes (edd.), *Category of the Person* (Cambridge), 83–92.

MRAS, K. (1949a), 'Die *προλαλιά* bei den griechischen Schriftstellern', *WS* 64: 71–81.

—— (1949b), *Apuleius' Florida im Rahmen ähnlicher Literatur* (Anzeiger der phil.–hist. Klasse der österreichischen Akademie der Wissenschaften, 12; Vienna).

MÜLLER, K. O. (1830), *Handbuch der Archäologie*. First edn. (Breslau; second edn. 1835; third edn. 1848).

NAUCK, A. (1889), 'Zu Dionysios Periegetes'. *Hermes*, 24: 325.

NEUGEBAUER, O., and VAN HOESEN, H. B. (1959), *Greek Horoscopes* (Memoirs of the American Philolosophical Society, 48; Philadelphia).

NICOSIA, S. (1984), *Elio Aristide: Discorsi Sacri* (Milan).

NILSSON, M. P. (1950). *Geschichte der griechischen Religion*, ii (Munich).

NORDEN, E. (1898), *Die antike Kunstprosa* (Leipzig; third edn. 1915, repr. Stuttgart, 1958).

OGILVIE, R. M. (1965), *A Commentary on Livy Books 1–5* (Oxford).

OLIVER, J. H. (1970), *Marcus Aurelius: Aspects of Civic and Cultural Policy in the East* (*Hesperia*, Suppl. 13; Athens–Princeton).

PAGE, D. L. (1955), *Sappho and Alcaeus* (Oxford).

—— (1978), *The Epigrams of Rufinus* (Cambridge).

—— (1981), *Further Greek Epigrams* (Cambridge).

PEEK, W. (1979), 'Zu den Gedichten des Marcellus von Side auf Regilla und das Triopion des Herodes Atticus', *ZPE* 33: 76–84.

PELLING, C. B. R. (1979), 'Plutarch's Method of Work in the Roman Lives', *JHS* 99: 74–96.

—— (1980), 'Plutarch's Adaptation of His Source-Material', *JHS* 100: 127–40.

—— (1986), 'Plutarch and Roman Politics', in I. S. Moxon, J. D. Smart, and A. J. Woodman (edd.), *Past Perspectives: Studies in Greek and Roman Historical Writing* (Cambridge), 159–87.

—— (1988), *Plutarch: Life of Antony* (Cambridge).

—— (1990), 'Childhood and Personality in Greek Biography', in C. B. R. Pelling (ed.), *Characterization and Individuality in Greek Literature* (Oxford), 213–44.

PERNICE, E. (1939), 'Die Quellen der Archäologie, griechisch-italische Kreis: Die literarischen Zeugnisse', in W. Otto (ed.), *Handbuch der Archäologie*, i (Munich), 239–328.

PÖHLMANN, E. (1970), *Denkmäler altgriechischer Musik* (Nuremberg).

PREGER, T. (ed.) (1981), *Inscriptiones graecae metricae ex scriptoribus praeter Anthologiam collectae* (Leipzig).

PRICE, J. (ed.) (1650), *L. Apuleii Madaurensis Metamorphoseos Libri XI, cum notis et amplissimo indice* (Gouda).

QUASTEN, J. (1968), *Patrologia*, second edn. (2 vols; Madrid).

RADERMACHER, L. (1916), 'Der Dichter Pankrates', *Berliner Philologische Wochenschrift*, 883–4.

RAWSON, ELIZABETH (1985), *Intellectual Life in the Late Roman Republic* (London).

REARDON, B. P. (1971), *Courants littéraires grecs des IIe et IIIe siècles après J.-C.* (Paris).

—— (1974), 'The Second Sophistic and the Novel' in G. W. Bowersock (ed.) (1974), *Approaches to the Second Sophistic: Papers Presented at the 105th Annual Meeting of the American Philological Association* (University Park, Philadelphia).

REINACH, A. (1913), 'Les "têtes coupées" et les trophées en Gaule', *Revue Celtique*, 34; 38–60; 253–86.

RICHTER, G. M. A. (1965), *The Portraits of the Greeks* (London).

ROBERT, L. (1938), *Études épigraphiques et philologiques* (Paris).

—— (1968), 'Les Épigrammes satiriques de Lucillius sur les athlètes: Parodie et réalités', in *L'Épigramme grec* (Entretiens Hardt, 14; Geneva), 181–295.

—— (1977), 'Deux poètes grecs à l'époque impériale', in *Stele* (Festschrift for Kontoleon; Athens), 1–20.

—— (1982), 'La Date de l'épigrammatiste Rufinus: Philologie et réalité', *CRAI*: 50–63.

ROBINSON, C. (1979), *Lucian and His Influence in Europe* (London).

ROSTAGNI, A. (ed.) (1944), *Suetonio de poetis e biografi minori* (Turin).

ROTHSTEIN, M. (1888), *Quaestiones Lucianeae* (Berlin).

ROWE, C. J. (ed.) (1986), *Plato: Phaedrus* (Warminster).

RUSSELL, D. A. (1963), 'Plutarch's *Coriolanus*', *JRS* 53: 21–8.

—— (1972), *Plutarch* (London).

—— (1983), *Greek Declamation* (Cambridge).

——and WINTERBOTTOM, M. (1972), *Ancient Literary Criticism* (Oxford).

SAKOLOWSKI, P. (1893), *De anthologia Palatina quaestiones* (diss. Leipzig).

SANDBACH, F. H. (1936), 'Atticism and the Second Sophistic Movement', in *Cambridge Ancient History*, xi (Cambridge), 678–90.

SCHACHTER, A. (1986), *Cults of Boeotia*, ii (*BICS*, Suppl. 38.2; London).

SCHLAM, C. (1970), 'Platonica in the Metamorphoses of Apuleius', *TAPA* 101: 477–87.

—— (1976), *Cupid and Psyche: Apuleius and the Monuments* (University Park, Pennsylvania).

SCHROEDER, H. O. (1986), *Publius Aelius Aristides: Heilige Berichte* (Heidelberg).

SHERWIN-WHITE, A. N. (1966), *The Letters of Pliny: A Historical and Social Commentary* (Oxford).

SIJPESTEIJN, P. (1969), 'A New Document concerning Hadrian's Visit to Egypt'. *Historia*, 18; 107–18.

SOLMSEN, F. (1975), *Intellectual Experiments of the Greek Enlightenment* (Princeton).

SOMMERBRODT, J. (1872), *Lucianea* (Leipzig).

STANTON, G. R. (1973), 'Sophists and Philosophers: Problems of Classification', *AJP* 94: 350–64.

STARK, K. B. (1852), *Archäologische Studien zu einer Revision von Müllers Handbuch der Archäologie* (Wetzlar).

STEINMETZ, P. (1982), *Untersuchungen zur römischen Literatur des zweiten Jahrhunderts nach Christi Geburt* (Wiesbaden).

STOCK, A. (1911), *De prolaliarum usu rhetorico* (diss. Königsberg).

STONE, LAWRENCE (1985), *The Past and the Present Revisited* (London and New York).

STRACHEY, LYTTON (1918), *Eminent Victorians* (London).

STROHMAIER, G. (1976), 'Uebersehenes zur Biographie Lukians', *Philologus*, 120: 117–22.

SZARMACH, M. (1985), *Maximos von Tyros: Eine literarische Monographie* (Toruń).

TATUM, J. (1979), *Apuleius and the Golden Ass* (Ithaca and London).

TAYLOR, A. J. P. (1965), *English History 1914–1945* (Oxford).

THEANDER, C. (1951), *Plutarch und die Geschichte* (Lund).

THIMME, A. (1888), 'Zwei Festvorlesungen des Lukianos', *Jahrbücher für klassische Philologie*, 34 (= *Neue Jahrbücher für Philologie und Pädagogik*, 58), 562–4.

TRAPP, M. B. (1986), *Studies in Maximus of Tyre* (D.Phil. thesis, Oxford).

TRENDALL, A. D., and WEBSTER, T. B. L. (1971), *Illustrations of Greek Drama* (London).

TRENKNER, SOPHIE (1958), *The Greek Novella in the Classical Period* (Cambridge).

UERSCHELS, W. (1962), *Der Dionysoshymnos des Ailios Aristides* (diss. Bonn).

WALBANKS, F. W. (1957), *A Historical Commentary on Polybius*, i (Oxford).

WALSH, P. G. (1970), *The Roman Novel* (Cambridge).

—— (1981), 'Apuleius and Plutarch', in H. J. Blumenthal and R. A. Markus (edd.), *Neoplatonism and Early Christian Thought: Essays in Honour of A. H. Armstrong* (London), 20–32.

WARDMAN, ALAN (1974), *Plutarch's Lives* (London).

WASZINK, J. H. (ed.) (1962), *Plato Latinus*, iv. *Timaeus a Calcidio translatus* (London and Leyden).

WELLMAN, M. (1934), 'Marcellus von Side als Arzt und die Koiranides des Hermes Trismegistos' (*Philologus* Suppl. 27/2; Leipzig).

WEST, DAVID, and WOODMAN, TONY (edd.) (1974), *Creative Imitation and Latin Literature* (Cambridge).

WEST, M. L. (1977), 'Balbilla did not save Memnon's soul', *ZPE* 25: 120.

—— (1978), 'Die griechischen Dichterinnen der Kaiserzeit', in H. G. Beck *et al.* (edd.), *Kyklos: Festschrift für R. Keydell* (Berlin).

—— (1982), *Greek Metre* (Oxford).

WEST, S. R. (1985), 'Herodotus' epigraphical interests', (*CQ* 35: 278–305.

WHITE, HAYDEN (1973), *Metahistory* (Baltimore).

—— (1978), *Tropics of Discourse* (Baltimore).

WIFSTRAND, A. (1933), *Von Kallimachos zu Nonnos* (Lund).

WILAMOWITZ-MÖLLENDORF U. VON (1928), 'Marcellus von Side', *Sitzungsberichte der preussischen Akademie der Wissenschaften, phil. hist. kl.*: 3–30 (= *Kleine Schriften* ii (Berlin, 1960), 192–228).

WILHELM, F. (1902), 'Zu Achilles Tatius', *RLM* 57: 55–75.

WILLIAMS, G. W. (1978), *Change and Decline: Roman Literature in the Early Empire* (Berkeley, Los Angeles, and London).

WILLIAMS, PHILIP (1979), *Hugh Gaitskell* (*London*).

WINKLER, J. J. (1985), *Auctor and Actor: A Narratological Reading of Apuleius's Golden Ass* (Berkeley, Los Angeles, and London).

WISEMAN, T. P. (1979), *Clio's Cosmetics* (Leicester).

—— (1981), 'Practice and Theory in Roman Historiography', *History*, 66: 375–93.

WOODMAN, A. J. (1979), 'Self-Imitation and the Substance of History', in David West and Tony Woodman (edd.), *Creative Imitation and Latin Literature* (Cambridge, 1979), 143–56.

—— (1988), *Rhetoric in Classical Historiography* (London, Sydney, and Portland, Oregon).

Index Locorum

This index is selective. It does not include passages referred to casually or those listed by M. B. Trapp on pages 170–3.

General Index

Please note that all Greek terms have been transliterated and may be listed either under the transliteration or under the English equivalent.